PREDICTING
DELINQUENCY
and CRIME

OTHER BOOKS BY THE AUTHORS

Sheldon and Eleanor Glueck

500 Criminal Careers, New York, Knopf, 1930.

One Thousand Juvenile Delinquents, Cambridge, Mass., Harvard University Press, 1934.

Five Hundred Delinquent Women, New York, Knopf, 1934.

Preventing Crime (editors), New York, McGraw-Hill, 1936.

Later Criminal Careers, New York, The Commonwealth Fund, 1937.

Juvenile Delinquents Grown Up, New York, The Commonwealth Fund, 1940.

Criminal Careers in Retrospect, New York, The Commonwealth Fund, 1943.

After-Conduct of Discharged Offenders, New York, Macmillan Co., 1945.

Unraveling Juvenile Delinquency, New York, The Commonwealth Fund, 1950; Cambridge, Mass., Harvard University Press. (Translated into Japanese; Spanish translation in preparation.)

Delinquents in the Making, New York, Harper, 1952. (Translated into Italian and French.)

Physique and Delinquency, New York, Harper, 1956. (Italian translation in preparation.)

By Sheldon Glueck

Mental Disorder and the Criminal Law, Boston, Little, Brown, 1925.

Probation and Criminal Justice (editor), New York, Macmillan, 1933.

Crime and Justice, Cambridge, Mass., Harvard University Press, 1936.

Cases and Materials on Criminal Law (with Livingston Hall), St. Paul, West Publishing Company, 1940; 1951; 1958.

War Criminals: Their Prosecution and Punishment, New York, Knopf, 1944. (Translated into Spanish.)

The Nuremberg Trial and Aggressive War, New York, Knopf, 1946. (Translated into Japanese.)

Crime and Correction: Selected Papers, Cambridge, Mass., Addison-Wesley Press, 1952.

The Welfare State and the National Welfare (editor), Cambridge, Mass., Addison-Wesley Press, 1952.

The Problem of Delinquency (editor), Boston, Houghton Mifflin, 1959.

By Eleanor T. Glueck

The Community Use of Schools, Baltimore, The Williams & Wilkins Co., 1927.

Extended Use of School Buildings, Bulletin No. 5, U. S. Government Printing Office, Washington, D. C., 1927.

Evaluative Research in Social Work, New York, Columbia University Press, 1936.

PREDICTING DELINQUENCY *and* CRIME

by

Sheldon and Eleanor GLUECK

Introduction by EARL WARREN
Chief Justice of the United States

HARVARD UNIVERSITY PRESS

Cambridge, Massachusetts · 1960

Second Printing

Publication of this book has been aided by a grant from the Ford Foundation

Library of Congress Catalog Card Number 59–6156

Printed in the United States of America

To
ROSCOE POUND
Architect and Prophet
of Jurisprudence

Preface

Since we published our first prediction tables[1] over a quarter of a century ago, the interest in devices for forecasting delinquent and criminal behavior has grown apace.[2] Largely in the United States, but increasingly also in foreign countries, it is recognized that effective instrumentalities for guiding the exercise of discretion in both sentencing and paroling are a *sine qua non* to a sound administration of criminal justice. More recently, also, it is realized that predictive techniques are the key to a realistic program of delinquency prevention.

Although some readers may feel that we should have postponed the publication of this volume until all the prediction tables presented herein have been validated (a task of many years), we have been impelled to its presentation not only by the increasing interest in our prognostic method and the constant flow of requests for information about the tables and their application, but also by a recently completed checking of our series of tables dealing with the prediction of behavior of juvenile offenders on probation, on probation with suspended sentence, in correctional schools, on parole, and during five-year and fifteen-year spans after the expiration of sentence (a research which took sixteen years to complete and which is summarized in Chapter IV). We have been encouraged also by the findings of a Progress Report issued in July, 1957, by the Research Department of the New York City Youth Board which has been, since 1952, applying one of our tables—the Social Prediction Table—designed to identify *potential* delinquents among young children at the time of school entrance (see Chapter X). In addition to this, other reports of the application of the tables by various investigators have appeared in the form of articles, to which reference is also made in Chapter X.

We wish to emphasize that this is not a Handbook of Prediction Tables. It is rather an attempt—and a pioneer one—to present an entire

[1] "Predictability in the Administration of Criminal Justice," 42 *Harvard Law Review* (1929), pp. 297–329; reprinted in 13 *Mental Hygiene* (1929), pp. 678 *et seq.*
[2] S. Glueck, "Two International Criminologic Congresses: A Panorama," 40 *Mental Hygiene* (1956), pp. 384–405; 599–630; A. G. Rose, *Five Hundred Borstal Boys*, Oxford, Blackwell, 1954; and Appendix A of the present work.

system of predictive devices covering the span of years from first court appearance until approximately age forty, and including predictive devices for the early identification of potential delinquents. The materials of this volume are therefore directed to those who want to consider the implications of such a network of prediction tables and to those students of delinquency and crime who are impelled to widen the borders of knowledge by experimenting with the application of the devices we have constructed to further ascertain their merits and their inadequacies. There remains much work to be done before such prediction tables will be entirely acceptable to judicial and administrative authorities, and to school administrators and clinicians concerned with the early detection of potential delinquents. But a beginning has to be made.

Thus far the response to the suggestion that prediction methods be employed in the administration of criminal justice has not been great, despite the growing interest in the general idea of predictability of human behavior under varying circumstances. Apart from the expectable conservatism of the agents of criminal justice, certain fundamental questions are being raised about the philosophy and technique of prediction. We discuss these issues in the last chapter. It is our hope that the thoughtful reader will at least agree that our predictive approach is a promising avenue of exploration for the understanding and treatment of criminalism and recidivism, and for the prevention of delinquency.

The tables here presented were built up over a period of thirty years and are a byproduct of our various follow-up and crime causation studies. We have not included a consideration of methods of prediction other than our own; or of various sophisticated mathematical problems involved in the construction of predictive devices.[3]

There remains the pleasant duty of acknowledging the encouragement and aid of various associates. We are, first and foremost, deeply indebted to Dean Erwin N. Griswold and Associate Dean David Cavers, of the Harvard Law School, for their enthusiastic support of our researches.

We wish next to express our appreciation to our Chief Field Investigator, George F. McGrath, for his supervision of the large task of gathering the field data required for the checking of a series of tables for the use of

---

[3] Excellent work along these lines has been done by Ohlin, Wilkins, and others. See L. E. Ohlin, *Selection for Parole*, New York, Russell Sage Foundation, 1951; and H. Mannheim and L. T. Wilkins, *Prediction Methods in Relation to Borstal Training*, London, H. M. Stationery Office, 1955.

juvenile courts—a feat of no mean proportion since the enquiry spanned sixteen years. Several members of our present and former staff participated in these investigations and we make our acknowledgment to them in Chapter IV in an accounting of the method of the project, but we wish here to thank Richard E. Thompson for assisting Mrs. Glueck in preparing summaries of the behavior of some of the offenders during peno-correctional treatment. To those members of our staff who have not been directly involved in the preparation of this volume, we express our gratitude for their devotion to our over-all research endeavors in the pursuit of which they each play a specialized role.

We are, as always, indebted to Rose W. Kneznek, Executive Secretary of the Bureau of Business Research of the Harvard Business School, not only for editorial suggestions and for assistance in abbreviating some of the original prediction tables, but for supervising the tabulation of the data appearing in Appendix C as well as for preparing this Appendix, and for assisting us in setting up the tables and exhibits and directing the typing of all the materials in Appendices B, C, and D. We are indebted, also, to Bertha W. Daniels of the Bureau for all the needed I.B.M. processing; and to Caroline M. Timmerman of the Bureau for her typing of all tables and exhibits.

We wish to express our great debt to Esther Ghostlaw of our staff, who has so patiently, cheerfully, and with such genuine interest typed and retyped the manuscript. And we want also to thank Richard Thompson for checking the footnotes and quotations.

We wish to express our appreciation to Dr. Hermann Mannheim and Leslie T. Wilkins, as well as to the Controller of Her Britannic Majesty's Stationery Office, for their gracious permission to reproduce, as Appendix A of the present volume, Chapter I of Mannheim and Wilkins' study, *Prediction Methods in Relation to Borstal Training*, which contains an excellent bibliography of prediction studies.

Finally, our obligation is great to the various philanthropic foundations that make it financially possible for us to carry on our researches.

Sheldon and Eleanor Glueck

Harvard Law School
Cambridge, Massachusetts
March 1958

Contents

Contents

xiii

APPENDIX A

APPENDIX B

Contents

Contents

APPENDIX C

Tables Concerning Agreement Between Predicted and Actual
Behavior of Juvenile Offenders during Peno-Correctional Treat-
ments on Which Prediction Validation Is Based from Onset of
Delinquency to Twenty-third Birthday, 256

Contents

APPENDIX D

From Prediction to Etiology: A Table Summarizing Significant
Differences Between Typical and Atypical Delinquents as
Derived from Social, Rorschach, and Psychiatric Prediction
Tables for Identifying Potential Delinquents, 263

Introduction

No subject needs greater attention in modern-day efforts to develop a sound administration of criminal justice than that of sentencing. Disparities in sentences alone have attracted nationwide attention and have even prompted the Congress of the United States to enact legislation establishing institutes and joint councils on sentencing to which judges and other individuals might come to discuss the problem. We have all observed instances of excessive sentences but, just as frequently, we have noted instances of commitments for periods far too short to enable institutional authorities to educate and train the individual to take his place in the community as a law-abiding, self-respecting citizen.

Most people will agree that such disparity in sentencing is a roadblock to the effective administration of criminal justice. But helpful suggestions in this field are rare, because of the absence of adequate, uniform records and because too few people have focused their continuing attention on it over a long period of time. Sheldon and Eleanor Glueck are rare exceptions. For decades, they have together devoted themselves to the study of human behavior and criminal lives in an effort to pinpoint the factors that will enable us to predict future behavior from past conduct. They believe a number of these factors are identifiable and that they significantly indicate the likelihood of an offender again engaging in delinquent conduct under certain circumstances.

This book, *Predicting Delinquency and Crime*, would establish a system for individualizing the sentence imposed upon a defendant by the use of a series of "prediction tables" which, based on defined traits and factors, would make possible the reasonable predictability of human behavior under given circumstances. In other words, it is aimed to provide a useful device for determining the kind of correctional and therapeutic action most suited to the particular defendant, as the representative of a relatively defined type.

To those who revolt at the suggestion of keeping uniform records or of using statistics in the evaluation of human possibilities, it can safely be said that the authors, in their modesty, would not claim these "prediction tables" afford the entire answer to our sentencing problem. They do assert with confidence that their use will help to point the way toward more enlightened sentencing procedures. All they ask for their tables is unbiased consideration. To this, the authors are at least entitled. Whether one agrees with their proposals, or in some other approach, is not a fair test of the value of this book. Its real value is in the fact that it springs from almost two lifetimes of research and careful writing in the field of this most baffling of human problems. It is a pioneering book, a forward-looking book for people of open minds, minds that are open to accept or reject the thesis solely on reason.

The more we know about human behavior, the better we will be able to discharge responsibilities of probation, sentencing, and parole selection. For this reason, no one can seriously question the importance of the problem which this book attempts to solve, and we all should be grateful for the really dedicated efforts of the authors, Sheldon and Eleanor Glueck.

EARL WARREN

PREDICTING DELINQUENCY
and CRIME

"I have had in mind an ultimate dependence upon science because it is finally for science to determine, so far as it can, the relative worth of our different social ends, and, as I have tried to hint, it is our estimate of the proportion between these, now often blind and unconscious, that leads us to insist upon and to enlarge the sphere of one principle and to allow another gradually to dwindle into atrophy."—Oliver Wendell Holmes, "Law in Science—Science in Law," in *Collected Legal Papers*, 1920, p. 242.

"NOTHING is more true of my profession than that the most eminent among them, for 100 years, have testified with complete confidence that something is impossible which, once it is introduced, is found to be very easy of administration. The history of legal procedure is the history of rejection of reasonable and civilised standards in the administration of law by most eminent judges and leading practitioners. . . The reason is a very simple one, and was given by one of the great lawyers of my country. He said in effect: 'Of course we oppose all reform; we grew up under the old system, and look at us as proof of its efficiency!' "—Mr. Justice Felix Frankfurter, quoted by Gerald Gardiner, in "The Machinery of Law Reform in England," 69 *Law Quarterly Review* (1953), pp. 54–55.

I

Why Predictive Devices

Introduction

A striking yet usually overlooked aspect of the history of penology and of code drafting is that all the reform devices of the present century—the juvenile court, probation, the indeterminate sentence, classification within institutions, parole, the youth and adult "authority" systems—depend for their efficiency on the *reasonable predictability of human behavior under given circumstances.* Yet all these forward-looking additions to the more traditional apparatus of criminal justice were adopted long before this indispensable basis for their success—predictability—was available, and this prerequisite is still largely ignored or minimized.

The authors believe that the concept of predictability is the most fruitful idea to have emerged in the history of criminology. Determination of the traits and factors most markedly differentiating children who remain non-delinquent from those who become delinquent, and delinquents or criminals who respond satisfactorily to one or another of the methods of peno-correctional treatment from those who recidivate, is a truly rational approach to the practical problems of criminal justice. Moreover, the integration of the differentiative traits and factors into syndromes constitutes the first significant break-through in the baffling quest for cause, cure, and prevention of delinquency and criminalism.

This is so because the inclusion in clinical, court, and parole board case histories of a confusing multiplicity of traits and factors without knowledge of their relative weight and significance for behavior, or vague speculation regarding some abstract unitary causal theory,[1] are both replaced, through the technique of prediction, by the focusing of attention on the influences *relevant* to behavior of one kind or another.

[1] See S. Glueck, "Theory and Fact in Criminology," 7 *British Journal of Delinquency* (1956), pp. 92–109.

Thus are causal influences made more meaningful.

This is true in respect to the traits and factors which, early in life, are demonstrated, by the predictive method, to constitute premonitory symptoms of delinquency. It is true, further, in connection with the sentencing practices of the courts, in respect to those traits and factors demonstrated to be most markedly related to success or failure under various forms of sentence: probation (with or without suspended sentence), or commitment to industrial schools, or to short-term institutions (e.g., jails and houses of correction), or to reformatories, or to various types of prison, or to parole; also in respect to the determination of the traits and factors which most accurately forecast success or failure during a reasonable period after completion of sentence.

There is no greater need in the entire field of justice as it concerns delinquents and criminals than a device for determining the kind of correctional and therapeutic endeavor most suited to the particular defendant as representative of a relevantly defined type. Improved penal codes, new prison structures, even competent and dedicated personnel, are not more important to the successful administration of criminal justice than is a system for adjusting the treatment of various offenders more appropriately to their specific traits and needs and thereby making sentences more effective in reducing recidivism. For if the law's coping with offenders is not to consist of the mechanical fitting of the punishment to suit the crime but is to develop more effective means of correcting the *criminal*, then a method of individualization that is more than "hunch" or guesswork has in our day become indispensable.

In 1929, Dean Roscoe Pound of the Harvard Law School, in the Foreword to an article by the authors that appeared in the *Harvard Law Review*[2] and later formed a chapter in *500 Criminal Careers*,[3] made some perceptive comments on the contrast between the nineteenth and the twentieth century's emphases in criminal jurisprudence. Pointing to the fact that in the past century, "the whole apparatus of criminal justice was shaped by the quest for means of ensuring an abstractly uniform, outwardly mechanical administration," he indicated that "inevitably there was a reaction from the futile, cast-iron, prescribed penal treatment characteristic of the last century."

[2] "Predictability in the Administration of Criminal Justice," 42 *Harvard Law Review* (1929), pp. 297–329; reprinted in 13 *Mental Hygiene* (1929), pp. 678 *et seq.*
[3] S. and E. T. Glueck, New York, Knopf, 1930, pp. 278–296.

Thus,

A movement for individualization on every side of the law took, in criminal justice, the form of a development of individualized penal treatment which was to make the penal treatment fit the criminal rather than the punishment fit the crime. But this movement for individualization and for preventive justice has itself brought about a reaction. On the one hand, it has seemed to threaten the general security. Men have come to fear that in our zeal to secure the individual life we may relax the hold of society upon the antisocial, impair the fear of the legal order as a deterrent upon antisocial conduct, and release habitual offenders prematurely to resume their warfare upon society. On the other hand, it has seemed to threaten the security of the individual life by committing too much to the discretion of administrative officers.[4]

The Meaning of "Individualization"

The basic problem in the sentencing aspect of criminal justice is, then, to retain administrative flexibility in order to avoid mechanical mass-treatment, but at the same time to supply the exerciser of discretion with a means of performing his functions intelligently, effectively, and fairly, instead of impressionistically or arbitrarily.

This problem is now being recognized as crucial both in the United States and among foreign thinkers in the field. The recently published *Guides for Sentencing*, prepared by a distinguished committee of judges under the auspices of the National Probation and Parole Association,[5] is one authoritative American recognition of the need to give some guidance to the intricate art of sentencing. Abroad, at the International Penal and Penitentiary Congress at The Hague, in 1950, it was the basic topic considered by the delegates in the following question: "Is a presentence examination of the offender advisable, so as to assist the judge in choosing the method of treatment *appropriate to the needs of the individual offender*?" And among the numerous contributors of papers from different parts of the world, there was unanimity in answering the question in the affirmative.[6] But, taking for granted the indispensability of an adequate presentence examination and report, the critical question remains as to how the judge is to determine the type of sentence "appropriate to the needs of the individual offender."[7]

---

[4] *Ibid.*, pp. 278–279.

[5] *Guides for Sentencing*, New York, National Probation and Parole Association, 1957.

[6] S. Glueck, "Presentence Examination of Offenders to Aid in Choosing a Method of Treatment," 41 *J. Crim. L. & Criminology* (1951), pp. 717–731.

[7] See S. Glueck, "The Sentencing Problem," 20 *Federal Probation* (1956), pp. 15–25.

The problem of how to "individualize the sentence" is unquestionably basic; yet it has either been ignored or discussed in hopeful but not very helpful generalities. It has been assumed that, given a probation officer's presentence investigation report, the judge (or the parole official in later passing judgment as to the time of release of a prisoner) will, by his "ripe experience," be able to decide which penal or correctional measure is suited to the particular case. But to individualize the sentence of a specific offender means, first, to differentiate him from other offenders in relevant aspects of personality, character, socioeconomic background, the motivations of his crime, and his special potentialities for reform or recidivism, and then to determine the punitive, corrective, educative, and medical measures best adapted to the solution of the particular offender's special problems in such a way that his chances of further commission of crime are reduced, if not eliminated.

If one pauses to reflect on all that this implies, it becomes clear that to speak about "individualization of justice" is one thing, and to accomplish it quite another. Of course, not all of the task of individualization is performed by the judge; the prosecutor, as well as the probation officer, makes recommendations. But the judge is called upon to make the fundamental choice which sets limits to what institutional and parole officials can do. And his choice, like that of the parole board which follows, involves the difficult art of prognosis—an informed decision if possible, a guess if something better is not possible—regarding the future conduct of the particular offender.

It is time that theoreticians in criminal law and practical penologists face the fact that the feasibility of a reliable technique of individualization is central to an effective administration of criminal justice. If, in fact, sound individualization cannot be accomplished with reasonable accuracy, then, irrespective of the probation officer's investigations and case histories, and despite the lofty aims of advanced correctional philosophy, the system will not work with adequate efficiency; and, judging by the high proportion of recidivism, it has in fact not worked too well.[8]

---

[8] In an intensive follow-up investigation of 510 "graduates" of the Reformatory at Concord, Massachusetts, some four-fifths of the ex-prisoners continued to commit crimes (and mostly felonies) during a five-year test period; *500 Criminal Careers*, p. 184. See, also, S. and E. T. Glueck, *Later Criminal Careers*, New York, The Commonwealth Fund, 1937; *Criminal Careers in Retrospect*, New York, The Commonwealth Fund, 1943; and *Five Hundred Delinquent Women*, New York, Knopf, 1934.

4

The Weakness of Existing Sentencing Practices

What is wrong with existing sentencing practices?

Some indication of their weakness is supplied by a number of studies which have tabulated sentences for similar offenses imposed by judges in courts of like jurisdiction over a period of years. Thus, one analysis was made of over 7,000 sentences imposed by six judges over a nine-year period in a county in New Jersey. Each of these judges dealt with such crimes as larceny, robbery, burglary, embezzlement, assault and battery, rape, and the like. Since there was no special assignment of cases to any particular judge, every judge received cases in which, considering them as a whole and over a long period of time, the felonies were committed under similar circumstances, and the offenders, as groups, did not vary in general personal makeup and social background. Yet the study disclosed that while Judge A imposed sentences of imprisonment in 36% of his cases and Judge B in 34% of his, Judges C, D, E, and F gave such sentences in 53, 58, 45, and 50%, respectively, of their cases. Thus an offender convicted of a serious crime had but three chances out of ten of going to prison under Judges A and B, and five out of ten if sentenced by Judges C, D, E, or F. Allowing the defendant to remain free in the community on probation, instead of sending him to prison, ranged, among the various judges, from 20 to 32%; suspension of sentence, from 16 to 34%. Other American studies have shown similar discrepancies in courts of different states.[9]

One of the authors once analyzed the sentences by judges in Massachusetts over a period of years, and found a refinement in the exercise of judicial discretion that it would be very difficult to justify.[10] In 194 successive admissions to prison in one year, no fewer than 53 separate types of sentence were imposed. The sentences varied so much that there was great difficulty in reducing them to a few categories. Not counting life imprisonment, they ranged from between two and a half years and three years at one extreme to between forty-two and a half and forty-five at the other. Even if the best available information regarding the characteristics and background of the offenders were laid before the judges as bases for the exercise of discretion—and this is not uniformly

[9] See F. J. Gaudet, "The Sentencing Behavior of the Judge," in *Encyclopedia of Criminology*, edited by V. C. Branham and S. B. Kutash, New York, Philosophical Library, 1949, pp. 449–461.

[10] See S. Glueck, *Crime and Justice*, Boston, Little, Brown, 1936, pp. 117–119.

the case—they could not possibly tell, in advance, that it would take X from two and a half to three years to reform; Y from two and a half to three and a half; A from forty to forty-five; B from forty-two to forty-five; or, if deterrence be stressed, that X's punishment should be half a year shorter or longer than Y's because they respectively need these different sentences to frighten them into not repeating their crimes or the public requires this fine distinction to deter it from violating the various laws. Such ultraprecision is on its face irrational. It satisfies neither the prisoner's nor the public's conception of justice; nor does it meet the demands of a realistic individualization of sentence.

Erraticism in sentencing is not limited to felonies; there is ample proof that it exists as well in the sentencing of misdemeanants. As far back as 1912, a Commission on the Inferior Courts of the County of Suffolk (Massachusetts) prepared a report showing wide discrepancies in dispositions, by totals and by individual offenses, in the various courts involved. The investigation concluded that "these courts . . . exercise within their several districts the same criminal jurisdiction . . . and although the social and economic conditions of their various districts do not differ essentially, there exists a radical and multiform variation and antagonism of practice in matters essential to the enforcement of law."[11] A study of the New York magistrates' courts showed like variations in sentence. In the 1914 report, the Chief Justice of those tribunals seems to have condoned this practice: "I have never attempted," he said, "although the power of assignment of magistrates to this court is vested in me, to lay down any iron-clad rules as to punishment, because individual cases exceptional in nature so often arise."[12] He overlooked the fact that, given enough cases, the "individual cases exceptional in nature" would turn up about as frequently before one judge as another.

It is not the lack of uniformity in itself that is important; but rather its basic *cause*. Commenting on the New Jersey study, the investigators fixed the judges' responsibility for the erratic results in these words:

> Given a sufficient number of cases, one could expect that two judges would give sentences whose average severity would be about equal (providing that the judges were influenced only by the circumstances of the crime and those of the prisoner). Conversely, given a sufficiently large number of cases, if one finds that the average severity of the sentences of two judges is appreciably

[11] Commission on the Inferior Courts of the County of Suffolk, 1912, p. 7.
[12] Annual Report, City Magistrates' Court, City of New York, 1915, p. 20.

different, one is justified in saying that the factors which determine this difference in the sentencing tendencies are to be found outside the circumstances of the crime and those of the prisoner and hence probably in the judge, since he is the other factor which is always present.[13]

The New Jersey study concluded that "the sentencing tendency of the judge seems to be fairly well determined before he sits on the bench. In other words, what determines whether a judge will be severe or lenient is to be found in the environment to which the judge has been subjected previous to his becoming an administrator of sentences."[14] With commendable candour, the Advisory Council of Judges of the National Probation and Parole Association calls attention to the all-too-human problem involved:

> Judges come to the bench with a wide variety of experience and background. These differences are reflected in the dispositions made in criminal cases:
> There are judges who regard sex offenses as the worst of all; there are judges who feel that the most heinous crimes are those committed with weapons.
> There are judges who favor the prosecution, and there are judges who tend to favor the defense.
> There are severe judges; there are lenient judges.
> There are judges who have surrendered their sentencing function to the probation department of the court; there are judges who have so little faith in the probation staff that they give its reports only the most perfunctory reading. And then there are judges who consider the probation report a valuable tool, who make use of its expert information, and who are aware of a variety of dispositions and treatment resources unknown to their predecessors.[15]

But even the most competent, experienced, and conscientious judge, who makes a serious effort not to allow his prejudices to obtrude, must, in the final analysis, resort to some sort of guess regarding the sentence. As one judge who gave much thought to the sentencing problem put it:

> The hunch system for the determination of the judicial sentence is one of the weakest points in the present administration of the criminal law. Something better must be devised. From all sides are heard criticisms of the existing method. Conscientious and thoughtful judges are the first to condemn it.

[13] F. J. Gaudet, G. S. Harris, and C. W. St. John, "Individual Differences in the Sentencing Tendencies of Judges," 23 *J. Crim. L. & Criminology* (1932–33), p. 813.
[14] *Ibid.*, p. 814.
[15] *Guides for Sentencing*, p. 6.

A defendant is tried in one part of a criminal court and is sentenced to two years in prison. He might have been tried in another part of the same court, in the same building, on the same day, and would have been given ten days or perhaps ten years.[16]

Erraticism in sentencing is an old story. In England, at the turn of the century, Sir Henry Hawkins, an experienced magistrate, criticized sentencing practices in these words:

> The want of even an approach to uniformity in criminal sentences is no doubt a very serious matter, and is due, not to any defect in the criminal law (much as I think that might be improved in many respects), but ... to the great diversity of opinion, and therefore of action, which not unnaturally exists among criminal judges. ...
>
> The result of this state of things is extremely unsatisfactory, and the most glaring irregularities, diversity and variety of sentences, are daily brought to our notice, the same offence committed under similar circumstances being visited by one Judge with a long term of penal servitude, by another with simple imprisonment, with nothing appreciable to account for the difference.
>
> In one or the other of these sentences discretion must have been erroneously exercised. ... Experience, however, has told us that the profoundest lawyers are not always the best administrators of the criminal law.[17]

Some legal philosophers have gone so far as to make a sort of virtue of erratic judicial practices. Thus Ehrlich, discussing "freedom of decision" on the Continent, cheerfully regards the personality of the judge as the desirable crux of the problem. The administration of justice, he says,

> has always contained a personal element. In all ages, social, political, and cultural movements have necessarily exerted an influence upon it; but

---

[16] The late Judge Joseph N. Ulman, of the Supreme Court of Baltimore, Maryland, quoted by H. E. Barnes and N. K. Teeters, *New Horizons in Criminology*, New York, Prentice-Hall, 1943, pp. 333–334.

[17] Richard Harris, (editor) *The Reminiscences of Sir Henry Hawkins Baron Brampton*, London, 1904, Vol. II, pp. 285–287. See, also, Sir S. Romilly, *Observations on the Criminal Law of England, as it Relates to Capital Punishments, and on the Mode in which it is Administered*, London, 1810, p. 17, in which the author says: "It has often happened, it necessarily must have happened, that the very same circumstance which is considered by one judge as matter of extenuation, is deemed by another a high aggravation of the crime. The former good character of the delinquent, his having come into a country in which he was a stranger to commit the offence, the frequency or the novelty of the crime, are all circumstances which have been upon some occasions considered by different judges in those opposite lights; and it is not merely the particular circumstances attending the crime, it is the crime itself, which different judges sometimes consider in quite different points of view."

whether any individual jurist yields more or less to such influences . . . depends of course less on any theory of legal method than on his own personal temperament. The point is that this fact should not be tolerated as something unavoidable, but should be gladly welcomed. For the one important desideratum is that his personality must be great enough to be properly entrusted with such functions. The principle of free decision is really not concerned with the substance of the law, but with the proper selection of judges; in other words, it is the problem of how to organize the judiciary so as to give plenty of scope to strong personalities. Everything depends upon that.[18]

So, also, Mr. Justice Cardozo has somewhere emphasized that "there is no guarantee of Justice except the personality of the Judge." But how these "strong personalities," once they are brought into the judicial service, are to function efficiently without being erratic or prejudiced in their sentencing judgments is a basic issue that cannot be avoided. No doubt, improvement in the selection and training of criminal court judges would be reflected in improvement in sentencing practices. But all judges exercising discretion in criminal justice should get as much assistance in that difficult art as is possible. Discretion there should certainly be; but the problem is to provide a technique whereby discretion shall be allowed ample creative scope and yet be subjected to rational external discipline, or self-discipline, designed to reduce erraticism.

Techniques for Improving Exercise of Judicial Discretion

There are several ways of approaching the problem, and they are not necessarily mutually exclusive. The familiar one is to permit sentence revision by some appellate body.[19] But such a twice-removed tribunal could not greatly improve on the quality of the original sentencing or at best could bring about only a superficial uniformity of sentence.[20] The fundamental problem—the fair and fruitful exercise of creative discretion at the sentencing stage—cannot be met by the appellate device.

Another method is to provide detailed legislative prescription of

[18] E. Ehrlich, "Judicial Freedom of Decision: Its Principles and Objects," trans. from his "Freie Rechtsfindung und Freie Rechtswissenschaft," Leipzig, 1903, by E. Bruncken, in *Science of Legal Method*, Modern Legal Philosophy Series, Vol. IX, Boston, 1917, p. 74.

[19] See S. E. Sobeloff, "Appellate Review of Criminal Sentences," 41 *Journal of American Bar Assn.* (1955), pp. 13–17.

[20] This is the distinct impression obtained from analysis of a large sample of the decisions of the English Court of Criminal Appeals. See, also, L. Hall, "Reduction of Criminal Sentences on Appeal," 37 *Columbia L. Rev.* (1937), pp. 521–556; 762–783.

criteria to which the judge will be bound in assessing the length and nature of the sentence. The difficulty here is that the legislature may surround the judge with so clumsy an apparatus of control of discretion as to permit but a poor counterfeit of scientific and just individualization. An illustration of a legislative device intended to cabin and confine judicial discretion is the Italian penal code project of the late Professor Enrico Ferri. In accordance with his policy of emphasizing the dangerousness of the offender and at the same time providing for necessary guarantees of the individual defendant's right to uniformity and objectivity of consideration at the sentencing stage, Ferri set down an elaborate schedule of "conditions of dangerousness" and "conditions of less dangerousness" to be prescribed in the code and to be applied by the judge as a basis for a complicated computation of the type and length of the individual convict's penal treatment. He listed no fewer than seventeen "circumstances of a greater dangerousness in the offender" (e.g., "dissoluteness or dishonesty of prior personal, family, or social life," "having acted through ignoble or trivial motives") and eight circumstances of "less dangerousness" (e.g., "honesty of prior personal, family, and social life," having "yielded to a special and transitory opportunity or to exceptional and excusable personal or family conditions"). Unlike the case of American judicial practice, however, Ferri's code set down provisions binding on the judge in assessing the various conditions of dangerousness and less dangerousness in terms of length of sentence. For example, "if there occurs only one circumstance of greater dangerousness, the judge shall apply the sanction in a measure not less than half between the minimum and maximum set forth for the offense committed by the accused," etc. Similarly, other fractions of the total indeterminate sentence are to be measured off by the judge, depending on the presence of two or more circumstances of more or of less dangerousness. In addition, the Ferri code provides a bewildering variety of punishments and other "sanctions."

Indeed, the Ferri system is so complicated and mechanical in conception and design that one has a picture of a judge checking up on whether, say, "circumstances of greater dangerousness" numbered 1, 3, 7, 10, 12, and 17 and "circumstances of less dangerousness" numbered 2, 4, 6, and 8 are applicable to the defendant, ascertaining which of the numerous sanctions or combinations thereof are pertinent and then using a computing machine to figure out just how much and what type of incarceration is called for in the sentencing of the particular defendant. In making such detailed provision to be automatically applied by means of a judicial arithmetic, the purpose of realistic individualized treatment is largely defeated.[21]

A less mechanical method is that set up in the Model Penal .Code drafted under the auspices of the American Law Institute.[22] This consists of criteria to be taken into account by the judge in assessing a sentence in the individual case. Judges tend, at present, to consider the type of criteria described in the Model Penal Code (e.g., that the convict has no prior record, or is a persistent offender, or a professional thief, or is dangerously abnormal mentally). However, spelling them out, even though there is no compulsion that they be followed or no indication of the weight to be assigned them in the sentence, ought to be helpful in reminding judges to consider, systematically, various matters deemed relevant to sentencing. Unlike the situation under the Ferri code, freedom of judicial discretion remains unhampered; but the listing of the considerations to be taken into account should, in the long run, bring about greater consistency of sentencing.

But the device of enumeration of criteria is not sufficient. The reason is that the judge has no way of knowing how closely related such criteria are to various types of postsentence behavior. Thus he has no way of assessing the weight to be given to one or another of the criteria.

An approach similar to the American Law Institute's has recently been made by the Advisory Council of Judges of the National Probation and Parole Association.[23] After wisely advising the judge that "moderation and objectivity should be his goals,"[24] the *Guides* provides some useful hints as to the kind of factors it would be helpful for the judge to take into account. Some of these are similar to, and may have been suggested by, the factors which have been proved in follow-up and predictive research to be relevant to expectable behavior. This is true, for example, of the following:

[21] A detailed analysis of the Ferri code will be found in S. Glueck, "Principles of a Rational Penal Code," 41 *Harvard Law Review* (1928), pp. 453–482; reprinted in S. Glueck, *Crime and Correction: Selected Papers*, Cambridge, Mass., Addison-Wesley Press, 1952, pp. 72–101.

[22] The American Law Institute, Model Penal Code, Tentative Draft No. 4, April 25, 1955, pp. 47–52. The Chief Reporter is Professor Herbert Wechsler; the sentencing provisions are largely the product of Professor Paul W. Tappan, Associate Reporter.

[23] *Guides for Sentencing*.

[24] *Ibid.*, p. 7.

The defendant whose first involvement in crime came late in life is more likely to succeed on probation than one who began at an early age and has continued in criminal behavior since then.[25]

Again,

The defendant whose parents, brothers, and sisters have respected society's demands of law and order, whose family life demonstrates mutual love and consideration, whose parents have given him reasonable and consistent discipline, and whose family members are eager to help him, is a better probation risk than one who does not have these advantages.[26]

Such hints are helpful, but not sufficient; since, as in the case of the Law Institute's criteria, on the basis of the single presentence report alone, the judge has no way of knowing the weight of the factors in relation to various types of expectable postsentence behavior.

The question presented, then, is whether there is available, for the purpose of a more efficient differentiation of treatment possibilities, an instrument which can aid the judge to make the most effective choice of sentencing alternatives. Since efficient individualization of justice promises to reduce recidivism, it is highly desirable. But cannot it be more surely brought about than by supplying the judge with a set of criteria or hints on sentencing which he should more or less take into account without knowing their relative weights in terms of expectable behavior?

Predictive Devices and Sentencing

It seems probable that the answer lies in the prediction table.[27] In several follow-up researches which have checked on the post-treatment careers of various classes of ex-prisoners, we have constructed a series

[25] *Ibid.*, p. 38. This age factor has been proved to be of great significance in various prediction tables growing out of follow-up studies. See pp. 82–83 hereof.

[26] This statement is reminiscent of the Glueck Social Prediction Table derived from *Unraveling Juvenile Delinquency*, New York, The Commonwealth Fund, 1950, pp. 260–262. It should be noted, however, that unlike the Social Prediction Table, the above statement does not indicate the relative weight to be accorded good discipline as opposed to poor or erratic; family cohesiveness as opposed to family disintegration; parental affection as opposed to various types of parental neglect. See p. 233 hereof.

[27] For an excellent history of prediction studies, see Appendix A of this volume, "Historical Survey of Prediction Studies in the Field of Criminology," which is Chapter I of *Prediction Methods in Relation to Borstal Training*, by Dr. Hermann Mannheim and Leslie T. Wilkins, London, H. M. Stationery Office, 1955. This is reproduced in the present volume through the kind permission of the authors and the Controller of Her Brittanic Majesty's Stationery Office, London.

of prognostic instruments that we present, systematically, in the following pages.

These tables, based as they are upon an analysis of *results*, should enable judges to individualize in terms of *objectified, systematized, and relevant experience*, instead of attempting to arrive at decisions from a mere reading of a presentence report covering much information, without knowing which parts of it are really relevant to subsequent behavior, or from checking on a list of unevaluated criteria presented in a code, or from taking certain hints into account. It will be shown, in the illustrations in Chapter VIII, that a judge having before him a battery of predictive tables embracing the entire range of available sentencing provisions could be greatly aided in assessing the individual case from the point of view of the probabilities of success or failure under one or another form of peno-correctional treatment and during substantial periods thereafter. In other words, by means of the prediction instruments the judge would have very pertinent organized data in the light of which to individualize, that is, to discriminate among several alternatives, and to choose the one most suited to the particular offender.

Prediction devices as aids to sentencing have to prove themselves in actual practice. A cautious way of doing this is for the judge, at first, to continue to make his sentencing decision in each case as he does at present; then to consult prediction tables and set down (or have his probation officer do so) the predictive indications.[28] After a few years, a thorough follow-up investigation can be made, to compare outcomes on the basis of the existing *ad hoc* method with outcomes as predicted by the tables.

Many years ago, Dean Roscoe Pound, opining that our first predictive instrumentalities (in *500 Criminal Careers*) came "at an opportune time," adverted to the significant potentialities of predictive devices in the perspective of history:

> When fifty years ago Massachusetts enacted the original probation law, the first stone of the edifice of preventive justice was well laid. In the present century for a time there was a rapid development which has set penal legislation and administration in a direction it must keep for a long time to come.

[28] Of course a condition precedent to successful use of prediction tables is that the utmost care be taken by the investigating officer to verify the predictive factors and to determine which subcategories of such factors are appropriate in the particular case under investigation.

But over-enthusiasm in the decades of progressivism, inadequate provision for administration of the new devices, the necessarily experimental character of some of them, leaving many things to be worked out by trial and error, and the strain put upon the whole machinery of criminal justice by post-war conditions in our large cities, have brought all the agencies of preventive criminal justice under suspicion. Study of the means of ensuring that the results of probation and kindred devices of individualized penal treatment may be made reasonably predictable is not merely in the right line of legal thought of today; it is needed to save for us one of the really epoch-making discoveries of American legal history. Let it once be made clear that probation laws may be administered with a reasonable assurance of distinguishing between the sheep and the goats, let it be shown that the illusory certainty of the old system may be replaced by a regime of reasonably predictable results as compared with one of merely predictable sentence, and the paths of a modern penal treatment will be made straight.[29]

By the cautious use of prediction tables to bring to bear in the individual case the organized precipitate of experience with other cases, the judge can approach that role of social physician which Aristotle, over two thousand years ago, had in mind when he said:

> The knowing what is just and what unjust, men think no great instance of wisdom, because it is not hard to understand those things of which the laws speak. They forget that these are not just acts except accidentally. To be just, they must be done and distributed in a certain manner. And this is a more difficult task than knowing what things are wholesome. For in this branch of knowledge it is an easy matter to know honey, wine, hellebore, cautery, or the use of the knife; but the knowing how one should administer these with a view to health, and to whom, and at what time, amounts in fact to being a physician.[30]

Predictive Devices and Parole

Thus far only the decisions to be made by the judge in the original imposition of sentence have been discussed. But the administrative agency that must decide when to release different types of prisoners into the community on parole must also exercise discretion. The parole system presents in our times another example of the ancient jurisprudential dilemma of discretion versus rule. Parole, like sentencing, requires the exercise of sound choice. Indispensable to the fundamental theory of parole is an extreme flexibility in the administration of a system designed to release a prisoner at a stage in his confinement when it will be most

[29] *500 Criminal Careers*, p. 279.
[30] *The Nichomachean Ethics*, Book V, VIII, 1137a.

advantageous to him and to society that he spend the remainder of his sentence under supervised freedom. This entails an extension of that individualization of justice presumably begun at the sentencing stage. But the exercise of discretion in individualizing releases on parole and in the revocation of parole-permits for violation of conditions calls, just as the sentencing function does, for some sort of disciplinary apparatus—a system of judicial review or some technique of science—lest it lapse into ineptitude. The soundly constructed prediction table is such a device.

Prediction tables should prove of considerable value to a parole board in determining whether a prisoner should be released on extramural supervision, that is, whether, according to past experience with similar cases, he will probably do well on parole and for a reasonable period thereafter.[31] The predictive device should be of aid also in deciding whether a prisoner should be paroled for a lengthy period or for only a brief span sufficient to bridge the gap between the penal institution and unsupervised freedom. It should, moreover, be of value in determining the type of parole supervision best adapted to various classes of cases—whether essentially of a policing nature or a case-work type, psychotherapeutic type, and the like.[32]

Other Uses of Prediction Tables

In addition to their employment at the sentencing and paroling stages, prediction instruments could be of great value to social workers and forward-looking legislators in establishing the true utility of existing punitive or reformative institutions and techniques. When offenders with a certain combination of traits and factors are demonstrated to fail, in large measure, under *all* forms of existing peno-correctional

[31] A predictive device has been successfully employed in Illinois for a number of years. See L. E. Ohlin, *Selection for Parole*, New York, Russell Sage Foundation, 1951; S. Glueck, book review of "Selection for Parole," 66 *Harvard Law Review* (1952), pp. 368–373.

[32] In considering the use of prediction tables by parole boards, it must be borne in mind that such administrative bodies are constantly faced with a dilemma arising out of the fact that existing legislation does not provide for a *wholly indeterminate* sentence for felons. Consequently, even though a prediction score in an individual case may show that the probability of satisfactory behavior of a particular prisoner on parole is extremely low, the members of the parole board may still decide to release him before the end of his sentence, on the assumption that it is preferable that he be supervised even for a brief time, during the dangerous transitional period from imprisonment to complete freedom, than that he spend his full time in the artificial environment of a prison. Nevertheless, prediction tables can be of aid in assessing the choices to be made.

treatment, intensive study of their characteristics and examination of the various corrective techniques now employed could lead to the development of new forms of treatment better calculated to reduce recidivism.

Prediction tables can, moreover, be very valuable as screening devices in selecting early in life those children whose makeup and background are such as to indicate, in the trustworthy reflection of systematically organized past experience, a high *delinquency potential*.[33] This would permit timely clinical and social intervention, which gives the greatest promise of redirecting the endangered child.

But the predictive approach to the problems of delinquency and crime is not limited either to its immediate practical utility in the more realistic administration of criminal justice or to its value as a screening device for discovery of potential delinquents early in life. Prediction also opens the doorway to a more fruitful management of the *etiologic* problem than has yet been advanced by any other method or theory. The predictive approach to the causal problem isolates, from a widespread and confusing network of *possible* biologic and sociocultural influences, those relatively few crucial ones that have actually been demonstrated to be markedly associated with antisocial behavior tendency. By thus narrowing the field, it permits more intensive exploration of the dynamics of causation in the most relevant areas. It gives the clinician a clearly defined starting point, rescuing him from the morass of numerous *possible* influences on behavior. He can go forward from that point more surely. Of course, the traits and factors found to be of the most potent predictive capacity are not all directly "causal" of delinquency or recidivism; they may be only surrogates of more ultimate etiologic forces. But they are important in focusing attention on the areas in which further and deeper exploration of causal involvements is most likely to be fruitful. For example, the so-called Social Prediction Table initially presented in *Unraveling Juvenile Delinquency* involves such factors[34] as: *Discipline of Boy by Father* (72.5% of the boys whose discipline was classifiable as overstrict or erratic having turned out to be delinquents compared to but 9.3% of the cases in which discipline was firm but kindly); *Supervision of Boy by Mother* (83.2% of the cases in which maternal oversight had been unsuitable having proved to be delinquents compared to but 9.9% of the cases in which it was suitable); *Affection of Father for Boy* (the delinquency incidence being

[33] See Chapter IX.
[34] How these categories are defined is shown in Appendix B, pp. 245–255.

16

75.9% where the father's attitude was one of indifference or hostility as contrasted with 33.8% where it was warm and affectionate); *Affection of Mother for Boy* (where the similar contrast is between 86.2% and 43.1%); *Cohesiveness of Family* (in respect to which factor 96.9% of boys from unintegrated families were delinquent as opposed to 20.6% of those reared in cohesive families). Such factors clearly "separate the sheep from the goats" in the vast majority of instances. By contrast, it would be of little value to employ such a factor as residence in an underprivileged area as a predictive factor since, even as to the most markedly deteriorated urban region, some 80% or 90% of the boys therein resident somehow manage *not* to become delinquents; and a factor that is etiologically operative in but a small number of instances can obviously not be employed either in the prediction of delinquency or as a particularly fruitful target for causal exploration.

Some device has long been necessary in the field of criminology to subject to a reasonable conceptual discipline the sprawling mass of fact, theory, and dictum developed in numerous investigations and writings. We know of no more promising disciplinary device than the carefully constructed prediction table. Its very essence consists of a focusing on the relevant and a cutting away of the adventitious and incidental.

* * *

We have discussed the general nature and expectable values of predictive devices in contrast with traditional methods in the administration of criminal justice.

Can such instruments be devised? If so, how would they be employed in the day-to-day work of judges and parole boards? How would they be used in screening potential delinquents at a stage early enough in life to permit promising intervention by clinician and social worker?

Some answers to these questions, in the light of a battery of prediction tables developed in our numerous researches, are given in the succeeding chapters.

II

Glueck Prediction Tables

Introduction

The theory behind prediction tables underlies any kind of actuarial work; it represents objectified and tabulated experience. Insurance companies have constructed actuarial tables out of the thousands of cases which they have handled or studied, from which they can determine the chances of longevity for persons of different sexes and various ages, occupations, and physical conditions. On the basis of such tables they are able to determine whether or not a person is a good insurance risk. The theory is sound and has worked satisfactorily in the insurance field. It is as yet new in the administration of criminal justice, but sufficient analysis of the methods involved and some tests of their operation have demonstrated their feasibility in the field of parole,[1] and suggest their practicability both in the imposition of sentence and in the screening of potentially delinquent children at a very early age.

In comparing the characteristics and backgrounds of delinquents and non-delinquents,[2] and of recidivists and non-recidivists,[3] it has been established that certain characteristics and circumstances in the makeup and background of the different types of juvenile and adult offenders bear a significant relationship to variations in their behavior during and following peno-correctional treatment. The fact that such significant differences exist and that these differences are related to behavior makes

[1] See L. E. Ohlin, *Selection for Parole*, New York, Russell Sage Foundation, 1951.
[2] See S. and E. T. Glueck, *Unraveling Juvenile Delinquency*, New York, The Commonwealth Fund, 1950.
[3] See S. and E. T. Glueck, *500 Criminal Careers*, New York, Knopf, 1930; *Five Hundred Delinquent Women*, New York, Knopf, 1934; *One Thousand Juvenile Delinquents*, Cambridge, Mass., Harvard University Press, 1934; *Later Criminal Careers*, New York, The Commonwealth Fund, 1937; *Juvenile Delinquents Grown Up*, New York, The Commonwealth Fund, 1940; *Criminal Careers in Retrospect*, New York, The Commonwealth Fund, 1943.

18

possible the use of such information in the construction of prognostic instruments. The use of a small number of the most highly differentiative factors has made it possible to construct a battery of predictive devices which give promise of improving the administration of criminal justice at the sentencing and paroling levels and also furnishing a means for the timely recognition of children whose delinquency *potential* makes prophy- lactic intervention desirable.

Before presenting a brief resumé of the development of our prediction tables since the beginning of our researches in 1925, it should be stated that these tables have been a byproduct and not the main objective of our researches, which have dealt primarily with making evaluations, through follow-up studies, of the effectiveness of various forms of peno- correctional treatment given to juvenile and adult offenders,[4] and, later, with investigation of the causes of juvenile delinquency.[5] Had our studies been primarily directed to the development of prognostic instruments, their design and content might have been different, and the resulting tables more discriminative. As it is, they are constructed on the basis of samples of true delinquents (as opposed to pseudodelinquents) and not on the "run-of-the-mill" of juvenile and adult offenders;[6] and some

[4] See note 3 in this chapter.

[5] *Unraveling Juvenile Delinquency.*

[6] In the case of children, some persistency of antisocial behavior is a necessary indication of "true delinquency" as opposed to "pseudodelinquency." The object is to distinguish between an occasional transient childish prank and more serious and fixed antisocial behavior. In *Unraveling Juvenile Delinquency* (p. 13), the boys included as delinquents had committed repeated acts of a kind which when committed by persons beyond the sixteen year statutory juvenile court age are punishable as crimes—except for a few instances of persistent stubbornness, truancy, running away, associating with immoral persons, comprising a course of behavior also within juvenile court jurisdiction. We did not include children who once or twice during the period of growing up in an excitingly attractive urban milieu stole a toy, sneaked into a subway or motion picture theatre, played hooky, and the like, but who shortly abandoned such peccadilloes, even though, technically, they had violated the law; their misconduct cannot be deemed either habitual or symptomatic of deep-rooted causes. The boys included in *One Thousand Juvenile Delinquents* were those appearing before the Boston Juvenile Court and sent by the judge for examination to the Judge Baker Guidance Center. Not all boys appearing in the court were so studied. Some persons have therefore assumed that the sample of cases was highly atypical. However, a subsequent study showed a quite similar rate of recidivism on the part of a run-of-the-mill sample as had been found in the thousand boys sent to the clinic. See W. Healy, A. F. Bronner, and M. E. Shimberg, "The Close of Another Chapter in Criminology," 19 *Mental Hygiene* (1935), pp. 208–222.

The youths and young women included in *500 Criminal Careers* and *Five Hundred Delinquent Women* were largely persistent offenders. For example, 84.9% of the 510 youths were known to have been arrested for crimes prior to the offense for which

contain factors that are subjective in nature, or difficult to gather; and some of the tables are regrettably based on too few cases. Nevertheless, as this is the first attempt to develop a *network* of predictive instruments to take account of the variety of peno-correctional treatments, it seems to us not inadvisable to assemble within the compass of this volume most of the tables we have constructed, as illustrative of the potentialities of a system of predictive devices. The fact that some of these tables have been subjected to checking on other samples of cases and show promise of validity should encourage experimentation with them as well as with those not yet checked; and certainly other investigators may profit from such shortcomings in our tables as further experience may reveal, and design researches specifically directed toward the construction of better predictive devices.

Evolution of Glueck Prediction Tables

How did the idea of prediction tables evolve in our thinking in the late 1920's when our first research, *500 Criminal Careers*, was being completed? That inquiry was a follow-up study of 510 men who had been committed to the Massachusetts Reformatory and traced over a period of five years after the expiration of their reformatory sentences. We had learned in the course of investigation that some offenders reacted differently during some forms of peno-correctional treatment than during others, and that although 30% of the ex-inmates of the Massachusetts Reformatory were noncriminal during parole supervision, a lower proportion, 21.1%, were noncriminal during a five-year period following the end of parole.[7] We also observed that 17.5% of the group

---

they were sentenced to the Massachusetts Reformatory, 86.7% of 1,944 prior arrests having resulted in convictions. At least 54.2% of the youths were first delinquent at fourteen or younger. Of these, 266 (61.5%) had been afforded one or more "constructive opportunities" (foster home placement, commitment to children's homes, schools for feebleminded, state hospitals, as opposed to ordinary penal institutions) before sentence to the Reformatory. In 1,451 out of the 1,688 prior convictions, sentences followed, of which 15.3% were fines, 37.8% probation, 41.6% commitments to penal or correctional institutions, the balance divided among other dispositions. See *500 Criminal Careers*, pp. 140 *et seq.* In the case of the women, 333 had been arrested at least 1,261 times prior to sentence to a reformatory; and 70.9% had been placed on probation at one time or another. See *Five Hundred Delinquent Women*, pp. 98 *et seq.* It will be observed, therefore, that because of the nature of the follow-up researches involved, the samples under study did not include substantial numbers of "accidental" or first offenders.

[7] *500 Criminal Careers*, Table 16, p. 190.

did not violate any of the institution's rules and were in other ways "model prisoners"; but the remainder, 82.5%, were in varying degrees not amenable to the institutional regime. Some 86% of those who misbehaved committed serious offenses in the institution, such as rebellion against authority, violence against the person, offenses against property, and sex offenses; while about 14% could be designated minor offenders. We further noted in our more intensive studies of individual delinquents that particular offenders, although behaving very well in a reformatory, misbehaved during periods of probation or parole; and that other offenders did not respond well either in institutions or during periods of extramural treatment.

In comparing the behavior patterns of offenders, we observed that some offenders who underwent frequent periods of institutionalization responded very poorly in their earlier years but later grew more amenable to institutional regimes. We also noted that some offenders who misbehaved during probation or parole proved most responsive to life in the Army or Navy; and that others who behaved well during probation or parole came into conflict with legal authorities very shortly after such supervision ceased. We found, in addition, that some offenders, though not behaving satisfactorily in reformatories and prisons where the regimes are strict, got along acceptably under the more permissive atmosphere of jails; and that some always behaved well during probation or parole, while others behaved satisfactorily under these forms of treatment only when the supervision was very strict.

From these observations of variation in behavior during different forms of peno-correctional treatment, we were impelled to ascertain the differences in the *characteristics* of offenders who responded variously to extramural and intramural supervision, and to construct tables predicting behavior during each form of peno-correctional treatment. In *500 Criminal Careers*, *Later Criminal Careers*, and *Five Hundred Delinquent Women*, the prediction tables constructed dealt largely with conduct *after* expiration of sentence to a reformatory; and in *One Thousand Juvenile Delinquents* the prediction tables constructed dealt largely with conduct *after* expiration of the sentence imposed by the juvenile court. It was from this series of studies that we came more and more to see the importance of determining probable behavior not only following, but *during*, treatment.

21

In order to provide the foundations for the construction of prediction tables covering behavior during each of several forms of peno-correctional treatment, as well as for a study of the characteristics of what might be called "treatment types," we decided to record in chronological order, in the succeeding follow-up of *One Thousand Juvenile Delinquents*, namely *Juvenile Delinquents Grown Up*, all forms of peno-correctional treatment to which each boy had been subjected from the earliest onset of delinquency through the juvenile court "treatment period," and to secure information concerning the behavior of these offenders during their various "treatments." These treatments consisted of ordinary probation; probation under suspended sentence; incarceration in correctional (or truant) schools, reformatories, prisons, or jails; and parole. In some cases, of course, an offender had only one or two modes of peno-correctional experience during this span of twenty to twenty-five years (covering, as already indicated, not only the years prior to appearance in the Boston Juvenile Court but also the original "treatment period" and the fifteen years thereafter). A very large proportion, however, had been subjected to many experiences of probation, parole, or imprisonment.

Somewhat later in the evolution of our thinking, we began to see that we might extend the scope and usefulness of prediction tables, not only by covering longer follow-up periods to determine the probability of ultimate reformation of offenders by the time they were approximately forty years old, but also, by breaking down the responses, to analyze the reaction of offenders to treatment at various age levels. We were led to this type of analysis because we had learned that some offenders began to adapt themselves to certain forms of treatment as they grew older—that is, for example, a turbulent adolescent may have become a model parolee in his middle thirties.

Still later, faced by the high rate of recidivism revealed in our follow-up investigations and by the all-too-slow decline of criminalism with advancing years, we began to turn our attention to the problem of crime causation as exemplified in our study, *Unraveling Juvenile Delinquency*. As a by-product of this investigation we were able to construct four prediction tables (one of which is newly published in the current volume), designed to select at an early age those children who are likely to develop into true delinquents unless suitable intervention occurs.

Any reader interested in a chronological listing of all the tables we

22

have constructed in the course of our follow-up and causation researches should consult "Status of Glueck Prediction Studies."[8]

Glueck Method of Constructing Prediction Tables

Two basic methods for the construction of prediction tables have been developed in the United States—that of Ernest W. Burgess,[9] and that of the authors of the present work.[10] The Burgess method gives equal weight to numerous factors found to be differentially related to success or failure on parole; the Glueck method employs in a prediction table only those few factors (usually five) that have been demonstrated through follow-up studies to bear a high relationship to subsequent behavior. By the Glueck method, each case is scored on the basis of the actual violation rate (variously referred to as maladaptation, recidivism, or delinquency rate) of the particular subclass of each predictive factor to which the individual belongs. His total score on the group of five factors yields his chance of success or failure during the particular period for which a prediction of behavior is desired.

There have been modifications of these basic methods in the United States and England. As adequate documentation exists on other methods of prediction, we leave to the reader an exploration of them without any further reference to them here.[11]

[8] E. T. Glueck, in 47 *J. Crim. L., Criminology & Police Science* (1956), pp. 18–32.

[9] E. W. Burgess, "Factors Determining Success or Failure on Parole," in *The Workings of the Indeterminate-Sentence Law and the Parole System in Illinois*, by Bruce, Harno, Burgess, and Landesco, Illinois State Board of Parole, Springfield, 1928, Chapter XXX.

[10] "Predictability in the Administration of Criminal Justice," 42 *Harvard Law Review* (1929), pp. 297–329; reprinted in 13 *Mental Hygiene* (1929), pp. 678 *et seq.*; this article is the substance of Chapter XVIII of *500 Criminal Careers* (a five-year post-sentence follow-up study of 500 Massachusetts Reformatory inmates). See, also: Chapter XII of *Later Criminal Careers* (a ten-year follow-up study); Chapters XIV, XV, and XVI of *Criminal Careers in Retrospect* (a fifteen-year follow-up study of these same cases); Chapter XI of *One Thousand Juvenile Delinquents* (a follow-up of delinquents during a five-year period); Chapter XIX of *Juvenile Delinquents Grown Up*, covering these same delinquents during a fifteen-year follow-up; Chapter XVII of *Five Hundred Delinquent Women* (a five-year follow-up of 500 inmates of the Massachusetts Reformatory for Women); Chapter VI of *After-Conduct of Discharged Offenders*, Macmillan Company, London, 1945 (summary of the various findings of these studies of recidivism). In *Unraveling Juvenile Delinquency*, Chapter XX, prediction tables are presented, designed to forecast delinquency on the part of children, these being based on the traits and factors found to differentiate most markedly between a sample of 500 delinquents and 500 non-delinquents.

[11] See Appendix A, "Historical Survey of Prediction Studies in the Field of Criminology," from *Prediction Methods in Relation to Borstal Training*, by Dr. Hermann

Although, as an introduction to the prediction tables themselves, it is well to give the reader a conception of how these tables are constructed, it is not our purpose to enter into great detail. The preparation of prediction tables by our method is a long process based on intensive follow-up studies, and although there may be many who would wish to use such devices, there are few who will want to construct them.

It needs, first, to be emphasized that unless the raw materials entering into the construction of a predictive instrument have been carefully defined, competently gathered, and thoroughly verified, and the follow-up of conduct (be it during or after treatment) has been equally adequate, the resultant prediction table will be at best a useless and even deceptive, albeit interesting, exercise in mathematics. Obviously, no mathematical procedure, however refined and sophisticated, can erase the inadequacy of raw data.[12]

It should also be pointed out that until a prediction table is applied to samples of cases other than the one on which it was constructed, it is more accurate to regard it as an "experience" table; for at this stage it records merely an existing situation with reference to the particular sample from which it is derived. Testing for validity by applying an experience table to other samples of cases is clearly necessary to determine whether the interconnection of factors and behavior is quite general.

Turning now to the method of constructing our prediction tables, the first step is to relate each factor encompassed in the particular inquiry to the behavior of the offenders during or following that form of peno-correctional treatment for which a prediction device is desired. Obviously, the greater the difference in the incidence of a subclass of a particular factor between those who do and those who do not behave acceptably during (or following) a particular form of treatment, the more potent is that factor as a predictor.

Mannheim and Leslie T. Wilkins, London, H. M. Stationery Office, 1955. Here will be found detailed reference to the Burgess and the Glueck methods and to all the other predictive techniques so far developed.

In addition we call attention to excellent papers prepared by Lloyd E. Ohlin and Elio D. Monachesi for the Third International Congress of Criminology, London, 1955 (thus far these have not appeared in print). See, also: 7 *British Journal of Delinquency* (1956); and S. Glueck, *Prognosis of Recidivism*, General Report Section IV, Third International Congress of Criminology, London, 1955.

[12] See Lloyd E. Ohlin, book review of "Prediction Methods in Relation to Borstal Training," by Hermann Mannheim and Leslie T. Wilkins, 70 *Harvard Law Review* (1956), pp. 398–400.

From among the completed correlations, those factors are selected for possible use in the prediction table which are found to bear the highest relationship to behavior during or following the particular form of correction for which a table is to be constructed.[13] Experience has shown,

[13] In our earliest studies, we relied on the Pearsonian coefficient of mean-square contingency ("C") to determine the degree of relationship between a factor and behavior during or after treatment, "The greatest possible value of the coefficient" (Karl Pearson's "mean-square contingency coefficient") "is . . . only unity if the number of classes be infinitely great; for any finite number of classes the limiting value of C is the smaller, the smaller the number of classes," quoted by G. Udny Yule, *An Introduction to the Theory of Statistics*, 1922, p. 65. In a twofold table, C cannot exceed 0.71; in a threefold, 0.82; in a fourfold, 0.87; etc. (*ibid.*, p. 66). The coefficient used is a mathematical device for indicating the associations shown in tables by means of a single convenient figure. For the mathematical process involved in ascertaining this coefficient, see Yule, pp. 66–67; *500 Criminal Careers*, pp. 239–240.

In *Five Hundred Delinquent Women* (p. 286), we resorted to a simpler, less time-consuming computation suggested by the late Professor Earnest A. Hooton of Harvard University. This consisted in establishing the degree of association between any particular factor and behavior by the simple determination of the maximum percentage difference between any subclass of a particular factor and the expectancy of recidivism for the entire group of cases involved. By comparing the total degree of relationship to recidivism by this method with that yielded by the more elaborate computation in the use of the mean-square contingency coefficient, the following scale was established (see *Five Hundred Delinquent Women*, p. 287):

Maximum Difference in Percentages Between Category of a Factor and Expectancy of Recidivism	Degree of Relationship Indicated Between the Factor and Recidivism
Less than 4	None
4–7	Slight
7–15	Appreciable
15–26	Considerable
26 or Over	High

Reference to this table of values facilitated the selection of the predictive factors.

Considerably later in our work, i.e., when we came to preparing the prediction tables in *Unraveling Juvenile Delinquency* (see Chap. XX of that volume), we pursued an even simpler method. We inspected those factors in which significant differences ($P < 0.01$ as determined by the computation of the chi-square) occurred between the delinquents and their matched non-delinquents; and from among these, we selected as predictive factors those showing the *widest range of differences* between the delinquents and non-delinquents in the subclasses of each factor. For example, although there is statistical significance in the differences between the delinquents ("failures") and non-delinquents ("successes") in their ordinal rank among their brothers and sisters (see *Unraveling Juvenile Delinquency*, Table XI–5, p. 120), the actual differences are not nearly as great as the differences between the delinquents and non-delinquents as to *Affection of Father for Boy* (see *Unraveling Juvenile Delinquency*, Table XI–13, p. 125). The latter factor became one of a cluster of five factors in a table designed to differentiate at an early age—at school entrance—between those youngsters who are likely to become delinquents and those who are not.

however, that it is not indispensable to utilize the five factors bearing the very highest association with behavior; even the cumulative effect of small differences can result in a competent predictive device. It is essential, however, that the factors selected make, when combined, a workable prognostic device; and this is best determined by testing it on other samples of cases.

There are other considerations in choosing the five factors out of a range of possibilities. We find it advisable, for example, to consider whether the factors chosen are mutually exclusive and, if possible, to select from among all the possibilities those that are relatively independent of one another. However, a small amount of overlap is not necessarily objectionable.

Also, the practical question has to be considered, whether peno-correctional authorities who might use such tables would have the needed data readily available. Great expertness in the gathering of data by probation officers is not likely to be generally found; hence data that are more, rather than less, easily obtained by those who staff peno-correctional systems are preferable when selecting the factors to be included in the prediction instrument. In a number of our tables we have sometimes through early inexperience, and at other times because of the limited number of the factors from among which choices could be made, included items that should be avoided, such as, for example, *Intelligence of Offender* or *Mental Condition of Offender*. Obviously, the ascertainment of these requires expert skills not possessed by peno-correctional staffs and is dependent on the availability of psychological and psychiatric services that are still rarely at hand.

In brief, given a sufficiently wide choice of factors of fairly equal prognostic power, it is best to select from among them the ones that are least difficult to assemble in the day-to-day practice of courts and associated agencies.

After the selection of the factors, the next step in the construction of prediction tables by our method is to set down the percentage of offenders actually misbehaving within each subclass of a factor (the appropriate definitions of violation, maladaptation, recidivism, etc. are provided in Appendix B). For example, in Exhibit A are presented the five factors selected as the basis for a table predicting the behavior of juvenile delinquents on parole, with their subcategories and the percentage incidence (within each of these subcategories) of those who actually had shown clear evidences of antisocial behavior during parole.[14]

The next step is to determine what are the highest and the lowest violation scores it is possible for an offender to obtain on the five factors involved. (It should be clear to the reader by now that the scores represent

Exhibit A. Factors Predictive of Behavior of Juvenile Offenders during Parole

Predictive Factors and Subcategories*	Percentage Incidence of Parole Violators
BIRTHPLACE OF FATHER	
Foreign Countries other than Ireland	64.3
United States	77.9
Ireland	89.7
BIRTHPLACE OF MOTHER	
United States, Poland, Russia, Lithuania, Italy	66.9
Foreign Countries other than Poland, Russia, Lithuania, Italy, Ireland	72.7
Ireland	86.7
DISCIPLINE BY FATHER	
Firm but Kindly	40.3
Erratic	63.9
Overstrict or Lax	74.1
DISCIPLINE BY MOTHER	
Firm but Kindly	50.0
Erratic	61.7
Overstrict or Lax	73.8
SCHOOL MISCONDUCT	
None	55.2
Some	72.2

* Whatever contractions have been made of the original, more detailed, subcategories of the factors are based on an examination of the raw tables, from which it could readily be determined which subcategories to combine. Definitions of the factors will be found in Appendix B, pp. 245–255.

the actual percentage of offenders [in each subclass of a factor and in the sample from which the table is being constructed] who failed to respond satisfactorily during parole.) By adding the smallest percentages in the subcategories of the five factors, the *lowest possible parole violation score* is obtained; by summating the five largest percentages of the subcategories of the five factors, the *highest possible parole violation score*

[14] *Juvenile Delinquents Grown Up*, Table 73, p. 206.

is determined. For example, Exhibit A shows that summation of the lowest scores—64.3, 66.9, 40.3, 50.0, and 55.2—provides one extreme of the range of scores, namely, 276.7; summation of the highest possible scores—89.7, 86.7, 74.1, 73.8, and 72.2—gives us the other, namely,

Exhibit B.   Social Factors Identifying Potential Juvenile Delinquents

Predictive Factors and Subcategories	Percentage Incidence of Delinquents
DISCIPLINE OF BOY BY FATHER	
Firm but Kindly	9.3
Lax	59.8
Overstrict or Erratic	72.5
SUPERVISION OF BOY BY MOTHER	
Suitable	9.9
Fair	57.5
Unsuitable	83.2
AFFECTION OF FATHER FOR BOY	
Warm (including overprotective)	33.8
Indifferent or Hostile	75.9
AFFECTION OF MOTHER FOR BOY	
Warm (including overprotective)	43.1
Indifferent or Hostile	86.2
COHESIVENESS OF FAMILY	
Marked	20.6
Some	61.3
None	96.9

Note: Those who wish to apply the table are asked to note that the determination of the particular category into which a case falls is based on the situation generally prevailing in a child's life up to the point at which the prediction is made. In cases in which one or another parent has left or been removed from the home before a child was three years old, and there is no parent surrogate (stepparent, foster parent), discipline of the missing parent is graded as "lax," affection as "indifferent," and supervision as "unsuitable." But if there has been a substitute parent, at least since the child was three years old, the discipline, affection, and supervision of the parent substitute is rated.

396.5. Between these minimal and maximal limits, score classes are first established in narrow, equidistant intervals. Within this tabular framework, each offender in the group is placed according to his total score on the five predictive factors.

Another illustration might be helpful. This one deals with the prediction table constructed in *Unraveling Juvenile Delinquency* which was designed to identify potential delinquents at the time of school entrance and is known as the Glueck Social Prediction Table (Appendix B, Table IX–1).

In Exhibit B are presented the five factors selected as the basis for a table for predicting who, among young school children, are potential delinquents, with the subcategories of the factors and the percentage incidence (within each of these subcategories) of those who actually became delinquents.[15]

Again, by adding the smallest percentages in the subcategories of the five factors, the *lowest potential delinquency score* was obtained; by summating the five largest percentages of the subcategories of the five factors, the *highest potential delinquency score* was determined. For example, from the series of factors just presented, summation of the lowest scores—9.3, 9.9, 33.8, 43.1, and 20.6—provides one extreme of the range of scores, namely, 116.7; summation of the highest possible scores—72.5, 83.2, 75.9, 86.2, and 96.9—gives us the other, namely, 414.7. Between these minimal and maximal limits, score classes were first established in narrow, equidistant intervals. Within this tabular framework, each individual in the group was placed according to his total score on the five predictive factors, on the one hand, and in respect to whether he was a delinquent or a non-delinquent, on the other.

Exhibit C. Detailed Prediction Table from Five Factors of Social Background

Weighted Failure Score Class	Number of Delinquents	% of Delinquents within Respective Score Classes	Number of Non-Delinquents	% of Non-Delinquents within Respective Score Classes
Less than 150	5	2.9%	167	97.1%
150–199	19	15.7	102	84.3
200–249	40	37.0	68	63.0
250–299	122	63.5	70	36.5
300–349	141	86.0	23	14.0
350–399	73	90.1	8	9.9
400 or Over	51	98.1	1	1.9
Total	451		439	

An illustration of such a distribution of cases within class intervals is given in this prediction table which, as already stated, is designed to

[15] *Unraveling Juvenile Delinquency*, p. 261.

identify at an early age those children who are likely to become delinquents unless suitable intervention occurs. To review, the factors involved are: *Discipline of Boy by Father, Supervision of Boy by Mother, Affection of Father for Boy, Affection of Mother for Boy*, and *Cohesiveness of Family;* and the resulting distribution of the 890 cases from among the original 1,000 (500 delinquents and 500 non-delinquents) who could be categorized on all five factors is seen in Exhibit C.[16]

Inspection of the percentages shows that the first two groupings might well be combined, and also the last three, resulting in a four score-class table.[17]

Exhibit D.   Four-Class Prediction Table from Five Factors of Social Background

Weighted Failure Score Class	Delinquency Rate	Non-Delinquency Rate
Less than 200	8.2%	91.8%
200–249	37.0	63.0
250–299	63.5	36.5
300 or Over	89.2	10.8

To summarize the Glueck method of constructing prediction tables:

(1) From among the highly differentiating factors, five are selected, taking into consideration whether or not these factors are mutually exclusive. If possible, those are selected that are relatively independent of one another. The practical matter of the ease or difficulty of gathering the data by those who would be charged with the task is also considered in making the selection.

(2) The percentages of subclass incidence of violation, or maladaptation, or recidivism, or delinquency, as the case may be, are next set down for each of the five selected factors.

(3) The next step is to determine the lowest and the highest possible scores by adding all the smallest percentages of the subcategories of the five factors, on the one hand, and all the largest percentages of the subcategories of the five factors, on the other.

(4) Next, score classes are established in equidistant intervals between the minimum and maximum score limits.

[16] *Ibid.*, Table XX–2.
[17] *Ibid.*, p. 262, Table XX–3.

(5) Then, each case in the group is scored on the five factors and placed in the appropriate score class and appropriate behavior category, the number falling into each score class being converted into percentages.

(6) The resulting distribution of percentages is the basis for the predictive instrument.

(7) Finally, the distribution of the percentages is examined to determine what combinations of the score classes provide the sharpest predictive instrumentality.[18]

Illustrative Interpretation of a Prediction Table

To understand how to interpret a prediction table, the reader is asked to examine the following table designed to predict the behavior of juvenile offenders on probation (Appendix B, III–1):

Score Class*	Probation Violation Rate	Probation Non-Violation Rate
Less than 240	36.0%	64.0%
240–270	66.7	33.3
270 or Over	85.6	14.4

* The factors involved, together with their subcategories and definitions and the "violation score" for each subcategory of a factor, are also in Appendix B.

This shows that an offender scoring less than 240 on the five factors involved has 36/100 chances of violating probation (see the definition of "violation" in Note of Explanation to Appendix B); while if he scores between 240–270 his chances of violation rise to 67/100; and if he scores more than this his chances are 86/100.

With this explanation, the reader should be able to interpret all of the prediction tables in Appendix B.

* * *

The use of prediction tables as aids in the administration of criminal justice does not carry with it any commitment to a new form of "mechanical jurisprudence." It must be borne in mind that we are dealing here with an instrument in aid, not in replacement, of the judgmental process. An authority in the practical application of predictive devices has put

[18] For the reader who would profit from a more detailed illustration of the selection of factors and the construction of prediction tables than is given in this chapter, see E. T. Glueck, "Identifying Juvenile Delinquents and Neurotics," 40 *Mental Hygiene* (1956), pp. 24–43.

the matter very clearly as regards parole, and this is equally applicable to all forms of peno-correctional treatment:

> An evaluation of the risk of violation involved in the decision to grant parole is helpful to the parole board. Whether or not the risk should be taken in an individual case remains a matter of judgment on the part of the board since there are many other considerations which may be of equal or even of greater importance. Thus the fear that use of an experience table may lead to the automatic granting of parole is unfounded. The table covers only a portion of the factors entering into the parole decision, and affords a statement of violation risk useful only in conjunction with these other considerations.[19]

Whether the relevant factors derive from psychiatric examinations, personality tests, or assessments of parent-child relationships, the resultant predictive instrument is not to be used mechanically, any more than the case history is to be blindly followed by the judge or parole board. What we said a quarter of a century ago is still true today:

> The wise judge does not surrender the judging process to the specialist in psychiatry, psychology, sociology, or education. It is his domain to pass their contributions through the alembic of his mind and distil them into a workable program that takes account of legal demands and social limitations, as well as clinical findings.[20]

[19] Ohlin, pp. 68–69.
[20] *One Thousand Juvenile Delinquents*, p. 114.

III

Prediction of Behavior of Male
Juvenile Delinquents

Introduction

In this chapter a series of tables is presented dealing with the probable behavior of juvenile offenders during various forms of peno-correctional treatment and for a considerable follow-up span thereafter. Illustrations of the application of these tables are given in Chapter VIII. The immediate aim, however, is to review the factors that were found in our researches to have predictive potential in the case of boy offenders and to suggest reasons for their discriminative power.

Summary of Juvenile Court Prediction Tables

Attention is called to the fact that some of the prediction tables (see Appendix B) have four score classes, others three, and still others two. Examination of the "violation," or "maladaptation," or "recidivism," or "delinquency" rate, as the case may be, reveals that it is possible to find a *common base line* for all these tables; namely, *more than an even chance* as opposed to *less than an even chance* of violation, maladaptation, recidivism, or delinquency. The more detailed score classes are contained in Appendix B. Although there is value of knowing, for example, that a particular offender falls into a group that has sixty in a hundred chances of acceptable (or unacceptable) behavior under a particular form of treatment rather than ninety in a hundred chances, comparison of his chances of good (or poor) conduct under various alternative treatments is rendered easier for textual presentation by dichotomizing the score classes.

Errors in classification (whether in a dichotomized table or one with a greater number of score classes) obviously can be avoided only if the data entering into the scoring of the factors that comprise the table are accurate. And it goes without saying that the prediction table itself stands

33

or falls on the strength of the data that initially entered into its construction.

In presenting textual summaries of the prediction tables, it is to be noted that the numbers in parentheses to the right of the treatment or post-treatment period in question refer to the detailed tables in Appendix B; the Roman numerals represent the chapter numbers and thus facilitate cross-reference. Definitions of all factors appear in alphabetical order at the end of Appendix B.

Prediction of Behavior on Probation

Summary Table III–A. Prediction of Behavior of Male Juvenile Offenders during Straight Probation and Probation with Suspended Sentence

Type of Treatment		Less than Even Chance of Violation		More than Even Chance of Violation	
		Score Class	(Rate)	Score Class	(Rate)
Straight Probation[1]	(III–1)	Less than 240	(36.0%)	240 or Over	(82.9%)
Probation with Suspended Sentence[2]	(III–2)	Less than 300	(50.0)*	300 or Over	(81.6)

* Even chance.

[1] Predictive Factors: Birthplace of Father; Discipline by Father; Discipline by Mother; School Retardation; School Misconduct.

[2] Predictive Factors: Birthplace of Father; Discipline by Father; Discipline by Mother; Affection of Father for Offender; School Misconduct.

Note: Numbers in parentheses to right of type of treatment refer to table numbers in Appendix B; definitions of the predictive factors and the scores for the respective subcategories will also be found in Appendix B.

The first two tables deal with probation, that is, the extramural oversight of delinquents whether in their own homes or in a foster home. Even when the judge has made his basic decision to keep the particular delinquent in the community instead of committing him to some institution he is still faced with a choice between straight probation and probation accompanied by a suspended sentence to an institution. Tables III–1 and III–2 are designed to aid him in making this important decision which involves the possible role of deterrence where the added pressure of a threatened incarceration may be needed. It will be seen from Tables III–1 and III–2 that four of the five factors used in constructing these two prediction tables are the same. The fifth predictor is *School Retardation*, in the case of straight probation, and *Affection of Father for Offender*, in the table designed to reflect response to probation accompanied by suspended sentence.

34

Prediction of Behavior in Correctional Schools

Summary Table III–B. Prediction of Behavior of Male Juvenile
Offenders in Correctional Schools

Type of Treatment		Less than Even Chance of Maladaptation		More than Even Chance of Maladaptation	
		Score Class	(Rate)	Score Class	(Rate)
Correctional School[1] (irrespective of age)	(III–3)	Less than 210	(45.0%)	210 or Over	(65.5%)
Correctional School under 17 Years of Age[2]	(III–4)	Less than 290	(20.0)	290 or Over	(72.2)
Correctional School at 17–21 Years of Age[3]	(III–5)	Less than 380	(*)	380 or Over	(79.1)

* Rate not available.

[1] Predictive Factors: Moral Standards of Home; Number of Children in Family of Offender; Conjugal Relations of Parents; Bad Habits in Childhood; Time Between Onset of Antisocial Behavior and First Arrest.

[2] Predictive Factors: Family Relationships; Age at Onset of Antisocial Behavior; School Retardation; Age First Left Home; Age Began Work.

[3] Predictive Factors: Nativity of Parents and Offender; Economic Status of Childhood Home; Family Relationships; Economic Responsibility of Offender; School Retardation.

Note: Numbers in parentheses to right of type of treatment refer to table numbers in Appendix B; definitions of the predictive factors and the scores for the respective subcategories will also be found in Appendix B.

Table III–3 deals with the probable response of juvenile offenders of differing backgrounds, as reflected in the five predictive factors, to the regime of an average industrial or correctional school for youthful delinquents. The institutions for juvenile offenders involved in the investigation on which these prediction tables are based are the Lyman School and the Shirley School in Massachusetts. Their regimes, while tending to be more disciplinary than permissive,[1] may be regarded as quite similar to the regimes generally found in such institutions in different parts of the United States.[2] In this connection, it may be mentioned that institutional practices in the field of penology and correction do not tend to vary greatly over considerable periods of time. The changes that can be expected in institutions are, rather, variations in directive and treatment personnel;

[1] See W. McCord and J. McCord, "Two Approaches to the Cure of Delinquents," 44 *J. Crim. L., Criminology & Police Science* (1953), pp. 442–467; W. McCord and J. McCord, *Psychopathy and Delinquency*, New York, Grune & Stratton, 1956, pp. 123–176.

[2] For confirmation of this, see H. Ashley Weeks, *Youthful Offenders at Highfields*, Univ. of Michigan Press, Ann Arbor, 1958.

and while these are sooner or later reflected in modifications of regimes, the process is likely to be slow and uneven. At all events, the prediction table in question (Table III–3), like the other tables, is not intended to be a definitive reflector of the behavior to be expected in all industrial schools for delinquents. To what extent it is, can only be determined by testing it.

It will be noted that the factors emerging as the most intimately related to adaptation to the regime of a correctional school are quite different from those predictive of non-violation or violation of probation. While the two tables having to do with behavior during probation (Tables III–1 and III–2) involve the disciplinary practices of the parents and school misconduct, Table III–3 is made up largely of factors dealing with the quality of family life—*Number of Children in Family, Moral Standards of Home, Conjugal Relations of Parents*. However, *Time Between First Misbehavior and First Arrest*—a factor reflective of the lag between the typically early beginnings of juvenile delinquency and official intervention to cope with it—is also associated with failure to respond to a correctional school regime.

The two other tables summarized in III–B, based on another sample of cases[3] of young-adult offenders originally investigated in *500 Criminal Careers*,[4] should be of value in aiding a decision regarding the wisdom of commitment to a correctional school. Since the juvenile court ordinarily has oversight of youthful offenders committed to industrial schools until the age of twenty-one, it becomes important to determine whether a delinquent has a greater or lesser likelihood of adapting satisfactorily to a correctional school regime when he is under or over seventeen, the usual statutory dividing line for original jurisdiction. If the youthful offender is not likely to make a reasonably good adjustment during the years seventeen through twenty-one, consideration may well be given to transferring him to a reformatory (see Table III–9).

Table III–4 deals with behavior in industrial schools when delinquents are under seventeen years of age. The first factor in Table III–4, *Family Relationships*, is not specifically included in any of the tables thus far considered. However, it is reflected in certain other factors of some of the preceding tables, such as *Affection of Father for Offender* and, more

---

[3] S. and E. T. Glueck, *Criminal Careers in Retrospect*, New York, The Commonwealth Fund, 1943, pp. 258–259.

[4] S. and E. T. Glueck, New York, Knopf, 1930.

specifically, *Conjugal Relations of Parents*. It also appears or is reflected, as will be seen below, in Tables III–5 (behavior in correctional schools at ages seventeen through twenty-one), III–9 (behavior in reformatories), and III–10 (behavior in prisons), yet to be discussed. The second predictive factor in Table III–4, *Age at Onset of Antisocial Behavior*, is similar to *Time Between First Misbehavior and First Arrest* (Table III–3, behavior in correctional schools) and occurs also in Table III–7 (behavior during five-year follow-up span) and Table III–8 (behavior during fifteen-year follow-up span), and as *Age of Offender at First Arrest* in Table III–10 (behavior of former juvenile offenders in prisons), to be discussed below. The third factor in Table III–4, *School Retardation*, echoes a like factor in Table III–1 (straight probation), in Table III–5 (correctional schools at ages seventeen through twenty-one), and in Table III–7 (behavior during five-year follow-up span). The fourth factor in Table III–4, *Age First Left Home*, is not specifically included in any of the other tables; so also regarding *Age Began Work*. However, these factors, reflective of an early breakaway from the moorings of the home, are more or less involved in some of the other factors previously discussed having to do with early delinquency and arrest.

In Table III–5, which deals with the behavior of the youths studied in *500 Criminal Careers* and in *Criminal Careers in Retrospect*, in correctional schools during the age-span seventeen through twenty-one, the first predictor, *Nativity of Parents and Offender*, is similar to the datum, *Birthplace of Father*, which has been used in Table III–1 (straight probation), Table III–2 (probation with suspended sentence), in Table III–6 (parole), Table III–8 (behavior during fifteen-year follow-up period), and Table III–9 (behavior of former juvenile offenders in reformatories), which are discussed below. The second factor in Table III–5, *Economic Status of Childhood Home*, is new in the series of prediction tables. The third factor, *Family Relationships*, is specifically involved in Table III–4 (behavior in correctional schools when under seventeen years of age) and is similar to *Conjugal Relations of Parents* in Table III–3 (behavior in correctional schools), Table III–9 (behavior of former juvenile offenders in reformatories), and Table III–10 (behavior of former juvenile offenders in prisons). The next factor in Table III–5, *Economic Responsibility of Offender*, is a new predictor. The final one, *School Retardation*, has been previously employed in Table III–1 (straight probation) and Table III–4 (response to correctional schools when under seventeen years of age),

37

and is also involved in Table III–7 (behavior at end of five-year follow-up); and is of course related to *Intelligence of Offender*, which is used as a predictor in Table III–9 (behavior of former juvenile delinquents in reformatories).

Prediction of Behavior on Parole

Summary Table III–C.   Prediction of Behavior of Male
Juvenile Offenders during Parole

Type of Treatment	Less than Even Chance of Violation		More than Even Chance of Violation	
	Score Class	(Rate)	Score Class	(Rate)
Parole[1] (III–6)	Less than 290	(0.0%)	290 or Over	(89.8%)

[1] Predictive Factors: Birthplace of Father; Birthplace of Mother; Discipline by Father; Discipline by Mother; School Misconduct.

Note: Number in parentheses to right of type of treatment refers to table number in Appendix B; definitions of the predictive factors and the scores for the respective subcategories will also be found in Appendix B.

Table III–6 is intended to predict non-violation or violation of parole from an institution for juvenile delinquents. The parole regime on the basis of which the table was constructed may be regarded as typical, both regarding parole board hearings and nature of supervision of parolees;[4] and here, as in respect to probationary supervision and the institutional regime, behavior during exceptional systems of parole (not as good as or better than usual) may not be as competently predicted by the table as in run-of-the-mill regimes. But, once again, it should be emphasized that we present these tables not as final predictive instruments to cover a wide variety of regimes but rather as a basis for further testing on other and varied samples of cases in order to determine their value, their limitations, and how they can be improved. Already, however, one significant check of these tables has been carried out and is reported in the next chapter.

Although illustrations of the use of these tables are given in Chapter VIII, it may make the Summary Tables more intelligible if we present a brief example of their use here. For example, if an offender has *more than an even chance* of behaving acceptably in a correctional school but less than an even chance on probation, or under a suspended sentence, or on parole, a judge would have to consider the wisdom of committing

[4] See *500 Criminal Careers*, pp. 165–181.

such an offender to a correctional school without the oft-resorted-to intermediate step of probation under suspended sentence; and in view of the poor prospect of acceptable conduct on parole, it might be that the parole authorities would wish to consider a longer rather than a shorter period of institutional treatment for such a boy or intensive supervision during parole.

Prediction of Behavior after End of Treatment Imposed by Juvenile Court

Summary Table III–D.   Prediction of Behavior of Male Juvenile Offenders after Completion of First Sentence Imposed by Juvenile Court

Period	Less than Even Chance of Recidivism		More than Even Chance of Recidivism	
	Score Class	(Rate)	Score Class	(Rate)
Five Years after Completion of First Sentence[1] (III–7)	Less than 476	(50.0%)*	476 or Over	(†)
Fifteen Years after Completion of First Sentence[2] (III–8)	Less than 180	(27.2)	180 or Over	(56.6%)

* Even chance.
† Rate not available for a dichotomized table; see Table III–7, Appendix B, for more detailed table.
[1] Predictive Factors: Discipline by Father; Discipline by Mother; School Retardation; School Misconduct; Age at Onset of Antisocial Behavior; Time Between Onset of Antisocial Behavior and First Arrest.
[2] Predictive Factors: Birthplace of Father; Birthplace of Mother; Time Parents Were in United States; Religion of Parents; Age at Onset of Antisocial Behavior.
Note: Numbers in parentheses to right of period refer to table numbers in Appendix B; definitions of the predictive factors and the scores for the respective subcategories will also be found in Appendix B.

One of the contentious aspects of assessing the ultimate efficacy of various forms of peno-correctional treatment is the element of time. Can it be determined that a particular regime is successful in "curing" a criminalistic tendency if the test period embraces but a short span beyond the termination of the treatment period? We have always believed that such a period should cover at least five years if the effect of a regime is to be reasonably assessed;[5] and an even longer time is desirable if the probable permanence of a change in behavior is to be established.

[5] But see Mannheim and Wilkins, *Prediction Methods in Relation to Borstal Training*, London, H.M. Stationery Office, 1955, p. 152, in which it is said: "The equations for prediction based on an average of $3\frac{1}{2}$ years' exposure give almost equally good results for predicting success or failure within one year."

Table III–7 is therefore designed to predict behavior five years beyond completion of the first treatment (other than mere filing of a case, or a fine) imposed by the juvenile court (straight probation, probation with suspended sentence, or commitment to a correctional school with its attendant parole system); and Table III–8 may be used to forecast results by the end of a substantially longer period of fifteen years, which brings youthful offenders well beyond the generally unsettled adolescent stage.[6] In Table III–7, in which six predictive factors are used, four of them— *Discipline by Father*, *Discipline by Mother*, *School Retardation*, and *School Misconduct*—have been met with in the table predicting success or failure on straight probation; and a fifth factor—*Time Between First Misbehavior and First Arrest*—enters into Table III–3, dealing with adaptation to an industrial school regime. A highly suggestive associated factor—*Age at Onset of Antisocial Behavior*—is also involved. These last two factors of course reflect the relative deep-rootedness of the delinquency pattern and the timeliness or belatedness of official intervention.

In Table III–8 (behavior fifteen years after end of first treatment by juvenile court), *Age at Onset of Antisocial Behavior* is also involved. The remaining factors largely reflect the subtle influence of ethnic origin on the delinquency of children. It is to be noted that, contrary to frequent allusion to the criminogenic role of culture conflict, the highest incidence of recidivism at the end of a fifteen-year span does not occur among the native-born delinquents of foreign-born parents but rather among the antisocial youngsters whose parents were born in the United States.

Prediction of Behavior of Former Juvenile Delinquents in Reformatories and Prisons

In addition to the foregoing tables which deal with the ordinary dispositions by juvenile courts, we present Tables III–9 and III–10, dealing with the behavior of former juvenile delinquents in reformatories and prisons. Having traced the careers of the delinquents involved in *One Thousand Juvenile Delinquents* and in *Juvenile Delinquents Grown Up* for a period of fifteen years beyond the end of juvenile court treatment, we were able to obtain data regarding the behavior of those who, as

---

[6] Such tables would be of particular value to the youth correction authorities and similar court devices in several states. See Official Draft, *Youth Correction Authority Act*, The American Law Institute (1940); K. Holton, "The California Youth Authority," in *Society's Stake in the Offender*, 1946 Yearbook of the National Probation Association, 1947, p. 126; J. R. Ellingston, *Protecting Our Children from Criminal Careers*, New York, Prentice-Hall, 1948; B. M. Beck, *Five States*, American Law Institute, Philadelphia, 1951.

young adults, were sentenced to the Massachusetts Reformatory and to the Massachusetts State Prison. We include these tables in this chapter because some judges, bearing in mind how often "the child is father to the man," may wish to cast an anticipatory eye on the behavior of juvenile delinquents in institutions for adults. Also, certain states remove from the jurisdiction of the juvenile court children who commit

Summary Table III–E. Prediction of Behavior of Former Male Juvenile Offenders in Reformatories and Prisons

Type of Treatment		Less than Even Chance of Maladaptation		More than Even Chance of Maladaptation	
		Score Class	(Rate)	Score Class	(Rate)
Reformatory[1]	(III–9)	Less than 210	(41.0%)	210 or Over	(69.1%)
Prison[2]	(III–10)	120 or Over	(34.3)	Less than 120	(66.7)

[1] Predictive Factors: Birthplace of Father; Conjugal Relations of Parents; Intelligence of Offender; School Misconduct; Member of Gang or Crowd.

[2] Predictive Factors: Age of Younger Parent at Marriage; Conjugal Relations of Parents; Discipline by Father; Affection of Father for Offender; Age of Offender at First Arrest.

Note: Numbers in parentheses to right of type of treatment refer to table numbers in Appendix B; definitions of the predictive factors and the scores for the respective subcategories will also be found in Appendix B.

one or another of the more serious felonies, and in the majority of states the juvenile court has some concurrent jurisdiction with the criminal court. Such children, although tried and sentenced in courts for ordinary adult offenders, are, from a clinical point of view, not relevantly different from the ordinary run of juvenile delinquents; yet they can be sentenced to reformatories and prisons. And it has already been suggested that on occasion it may be desirable to transfer an offender from one kind of an institution to another. In such various connections, then, Tables III–9 and III–10, dealing with the probable adaptation of former juvenile offenders to reformatories and prisons, should be helpful.

It will be seen that Table III–9, reflecting success or failure in responding to the regime of the reformatory, employs *Birthplace of Father* as considerably related to behavior in the reformatory. This factor was also relevant in Table III–1 (straight probation), Table III–2 (probation with suspended sentence), Table III–6 (parole), and Table III–8 (behavior at end of a fifteen-year follow-up period). A second factor in Table III–9, *Conjugal Relations of Parents*, is a predictor in Table III–3 (behavior in correctional schools) and Table III–10 (behavior in prisons). *Intelligence of Offender* and *Membership in Gang or Crowd* are two new factors which were not

41

found to be sufficiently related to other forms of behavior to be included in the tables already discussed. However, *School Misconduct*, here shown to differentiate youths who adapt successfully or adversely to the regime in a reformatory, has been previously found useful in connection with Table III–1 (straight probation), Table III–2 (probation with suspended sentence), Table III–6 (parole), and Table III–7 (behavior five years after end of treatment). It is clear that maladaptation in the school, the first authoritarian regime outside the home, is strongly prodromal of later maladjustment to various regimes imposed by the juvenile and adult courts.

Table III–10 deals with behavior of former juvenile delinquents during a prison regime. Here a new predictive factor, *Age of Younger Parent at Marriage*, is significant, though it is difficult to explain why. *Conjugal Relations of Parents* is a predictor not only with reference to response to a prison regime, but, as has been shown, in regard to adjustment in correctional schools for boys (Table III–3) and in reformatories (Table III–9). *Discipline by Father* has also been found to be related to types of response to straight probation (Table III–1), probation with suspended sentence (Table III–2), parole (Table III–6), and behavior at the end of a five-year follow-up period (Table III–7). Another factor in Table III–10, *Affection of Father for Offender*, was found to be relevant in Table III–2 (probation with suspended sentence). It will be seen in a later chapter[7] that certain of the elements in parent-child relationships (such as discipline and affection), that run like a thread throughout most of the tables dealing with the behavior of juvenile offenders under various peno-correctional regimes, are also highly significant in predicting delinquency in the first place. *Age of Offender at First Arrest*, although not specifically involved in prior tables, is closely related to such other factors which have been employed in some of the foregoing predictive instruments as *Time Between First Misbehavior and First Arrest* (response to correctional school regime and behavior during five-year follow-up) and *Age at Onset of Antisocial Behavior* (Tables III–3, III–7, and III–8).

Summary of Incidence of Predictive Factors

The following chart brings out clearly the incidence of the different predictive factors involved in the ten foregoing tables for use by juvenile courts.

[7] See Chapter IX.

Factors	Tables
A. Factors Pertaining to Nativity:	
Birthplace of Father	1—Straight Probation 2—Probation with Suspended Sentence 6—Parole 8—Fifteen Years after Completion of Sentence Imposed by Juvenile Court 9—Reformatories
Birthplace of Mother	6—Parole 8—Fifteen Years after Completion of Sentence Imposed by Juvenile Court
Nativity of Parents and Offender	5—Correctional Schools at 17 through 21 Years of Age
Time Parents Were in United States	8—Fifteen Years after Completion of Sentence Imposed by Juvenile Court
B. Factors Pertaining to Religious Affiliations:	
Religion of Parents	8—Fifteen Years after Completion of Sentence Imposed by Juvenile Court
C. Economic Factors:	
Economic Status of Childhood Home	5—Correctional Schools at 17 through 21 Years of Age
Economic Responsibility of Offender	5—Correctional Schools at 17 through 21 Years of Age
Age Began Work	4—Correctional Schools under 17 Years of Age
D. Factors Pertaining to Family Life:	
Number of Children in Family	3—Correctional Schools
Family Relationships	4—Correctional Schools under 17 Years of Age 5—Correctional Schools at 17 through 21 Years of Age
Conjugal Relations of Parents	3—Correctional Schools 9—Reformatories 10—Prisons
Moral Standards of Home	3—Correctional Schools
Age of Younger Parent at Marriage	10—Prisons
E. Factors Pertaining to Parent-Child Relationships:	
Affection of Father for Offender	2—Probation with Suspended Sentence 10—Prisons

Discipline by Father

1—Straight Probation
2—Probation with Suspended Sentence
6—Parole
7—Five Years after Completion of Sentence Imposed by Juvenile Court
10—Prisons

Discipline by Mother

1—Straight Probation
2—Probation with Suspended Sentence
6—Parole
7—Five Years after Completion of Sentence Imposed by Juvenile Court

F. *Factors Pertaining to School Life of Boy:*

School Retardation

1—Straight Probation
4—Correctional Schools under 17 Years of Age
5—Correctional Schools at 17 through 21 Years of Age
7—Five Years after Completion of Sentence Imposed by Juvenile Court

School Misconduct

1—Straight Probation
2—Probation with Suspended Sentence
6—Parole
7—Five Years after Completion of Sentence Imposed by Juvenile Court
9—Reformatories

Intelligence of Offender

9—Reformatories

G. *Factors Pertaining to Early Habits, Leisure, or Conduct:*

Bad Habits in Childhood

3—Correctional Schools

Age First Left Home

4—Correctional Schools under 17 Years of Age

Age at Onset of Antisocial Behavior

4—Correctional Schools under 17 Years of Age
7—Five Years after Completion of Sentence Imposed by Juvenile Court
8—Fifteen Years after Completion of Sentence Imposed by Juvenile Court

Time Between Onset of Antisocial Behavior and First Arrest

3—Correctional Schools
7—Five Years after Completion of Sentence Imposed by Juvenile Court

Member of Gang or Crowd

9—Reformatories

Age of Offender at First Arrest

10—Prisons

As we reflect on the various predictive factors involved in the ten tables, some striking indications emerge. First and foremost is the *permeative influence of certain elements in the family life.*[8] This is illustrated by the fact that *Conjugal Relations of Parents* is found to be predictive of response to as wide a variety of regimes as correctional schools, reformatories, and prisons (Tables III–3, III–9, and III–10). And, a broader aspect of family life, *Family Relationships*, is predictive in two additional tables: Table III–4 (behavior in correctional schools when under seventeen years of age) and Table III–5 (behavior in correctional schools at ages seventeen through twenty-one). It is also illustrated by the widespread influence of paternal and maternal discipline in connection with response to treatment. Thus, *Discipline by Father* is found to have a bearing upon the response of the boy to straight probation, probation with suspended sentence, parole from a correctional institution, behavior at end of a five-year span following handling by the juvenile court, and behavior in prisons (Tables III–1, III–2, III–6, III–7, and III–10); and *Discipline by Mother* is relevant to the behavior of the boy on straight probation, probation with suspended sentence, parole, and behavior at end of a five-year follow-up span (Tables III–1, III–2, III–6, and III–7).

Secondly, the role of early childhood maladjustment in forecasting unfavorable response to a wide variety of peno-correctional treatments and over a considerable span of years is evident. Thus, *School Misconduct*

[8] It is interesting to note that despite the emphasis by certain sociologic criminologists upon neighborhood and cultural factors, one of the best factors in the Illinois experience with prediction of parole among adults was *Family Interest*. "Parole workers have often observed the controlling and supporting effect of close family ties. Theoretical and research results have emphasized the important role of the parolee's family in easing the transition between prison life and life in the outside community. Close family relationships help the parolee feel that he is wanted and that society accepts him. His adjustment is made easier because he finds a clearly defined place for himself and a conventional role to play. . . . The extent of family interest in the imprisoned offender has been found to be a good index of the effect of close family ties in the parole situation, and bears a significant relation to parole outcome." L. Ohlin, *Selection for Parole*, New York, Russell Sage Foundation, 1951, p. 49. On the other hand, when the necessary tests were applied to the twenty-seven parole prediction factors developed by the University of Chicago sociologic criminologists, which resulted in excluding fifteen from use "because none of the subclasses of the factors adequately met the statistical tests" of "a sufficient degree of association with outcome, or statistical significance, or reliability, or stability," *Neighborhood at Offense* and even *Parole Neighborhood* turned out to be among the factors that had to be dropped. "The Chicago area was divided into eleven subclasses on the basis of crime and delinquency rates," yet this greatly emphasized factor of residence in a "delinquency area" had to be discarded. *Ibid.*, pp. 122–123.

turns up as a predictor in five tables (III–1, III–2, III–6, III–7, and III–9) dealing with straight probation, probation with suspended sentence, parole, behavior at the end of a five-year follow-up span, and behavior of former juvenile offenders in reformatories. Again, *School Retardation* is predictive in four tables (III–1, III–4, III–5, and III–7): straight probation, behavior in correctional schools when under seventeen years of age, behavior in correctional schools at ages seventeen through twenty-one, and behavior at end of a five-year follow-up span. Related to this is the frequency with which early maladjustments are prodromal of later difficulties, illustrated by the fact that *Age at Onset of Antisocial Behavior* is a predictor in Table III–4 (behavior in correctional schools when under seventeen years of age), Table III–7 (behavior at end of five-year follow-up span), and Table III–8 (behavior at end of fifteen-year follow-up span after first treatment prescribed by juvenile court).

One factor, *Birthplace of Father*, and its related factor, *Nativity of Parents*, occurs very frequently in the tables; but the relationship of these to recidivism is not clear. It may be that these factors reflect a special kind of culture conflict arising out of the clash of ideals, standards, and values between parents with old world backgrounds and children plunged into new world demands.

* * *

The tables presented, like other tables in this work, are not to be taken as final and definitive, until they have been subjected to checking against other samples of cases. However, we are able in the next chapter to present the results of one such checking of the entire series of tables described in this chapter.

IV

Checkup of Prediction Tables Dealing
with Juvenile Offenders

Introduction

As already stressed, until the tables constructed from the correlation of background factors and behavior are tested on other samples of cases, it would be more correct to regard them as tentative summaries of experience rather than as definitive predictive instruments. The aim must therefore be to check our tables against other samples of cases in order to determine the extent of their practical utility. We are now able to report that one such checking has recently been completed in connection with the tables in Chapter III.

The tables summarized in the prior chapter and presented in detail in Appendix B, III–1 through III–10, one of which was constructed from the data of *One Thousand Juvenile Delinquents*[1] and the others from *Juvenile Delinquents Grown Up*,[2] have in fact been applied to the group of 500 delinquents embraced in *Unraveling Juvenile Delinquency*.[3]

When the boys included in *Unraveling* were initially examined (for a research comparing 500 delinquents and 500 non-delinquents, matched, case by case, for age, intelligence, ethnic origin, and residence in under-privileged areas), the data required for the prediction of behavior of the delinquents (on straight probation, on probation with suspended sentence, in correctional schools, in reformatories, in prisons, on parole, and at the end of five-year and fifteen-year periods after the treatment imposed by a juvenile court) were assembled for each boy. These predictions were then set aside pending a long-term follow-up of the young offenders to see how closely their predicted behavior would correspond

---

[1] S. and E. T. Glueck, Cambridge, Mass., Harvard University Press, 1934.
[2] S. and E. T. Glueck, New York, The Commonwealth Fund, 1940.
[3] S. and E. T. Glueck, New York, The Commonwealth Fund, 1950.

47

to their actual behavior during and following the first treatment by the juvenile court. We set ourselves to record the behavior of the 500 delinquents from the onset of their criminal careers until age twenty-three. We deemed this to be indispensable to an evaluation of the practical utility of our prediction tables.

Method of Inquiry

The necessary field inquiries were begun in 1940 (the boys ranging from ten to seventeen years of age when taken on for study) and were carried on until 1956, when all 500 boys had reached the age of twenty-three years. Had the investigation been continued until they were thirty, the results would have encompassed many more reformatory and prison incarcerations. However, as our focus was essentially on the years of juvenile court and correctional jurisdiction, we were mainly concerned with ages up to twenty-one, because the boys we studied in *Unraveling Juvenile Delinquency* had, with rare exceptions, already been committed to correctional schools in Massachusetts and were therefore under the jurisdiction of the correctional school and parole authorities, and, later, the Youth Service Board, until the twenty-first birthday. We followed them until their twenty-third birthday, however, in order to get at least some gleanings of their behavior during various forms of treatment as adult offenders.

Examination of Appendix A of *Unraveling Juvenile Delinquency* will reveal that, when first taken on for study, all but forty-nine of the boys had already had two or more court appearances and the average number of such appearances was 3.66. Therefore, it was necessary first to "followback" over each boy's court and correctional school history. An elaborate system of inquiry was established, with the cooperation of the Trustees of the Massachusetts Training Schools (a Division of the Department of Public Welfare); the Boys' Parole Division of the same Department (now the Youth Service Board, Division of Youth Service, Massachusetts Department of Education); the Massachusetts Board of Probation (a central clearing file for court records); the superintendents and certain staff members of the correctional schools, including psychologists, teachers, and house-parents; the Massachusetts Department of Correction and Parole Board; the superintendents and personnel of the Massachusetts Reformatory (now the Massachusetts Correctional Institution, Concord), Massachusetts State Prison (now the Massachusetts Correctional Institution, Walpole), State Prison Colony (now the Massachusetts

Correctional Institution, Norfolk), and the Massachusetts Bureau of Criminal Identification of the Department of Public Safety (for fingerprint records); and many out-of-state and Federal courts, institutions, and parole authorities.

In addition to copying essential data from already-recorded sources of information in the court, institution, and parole files, it was the practice of our staff, before the end of a period of peno-correctional treatment, to interview probation and parole officers and institutional officials about a particular offender's behavior and to talk with the offender himself. In the case of out-of-state treatment periods, the necessary information was secured from some official in close contact with the offender. The advantage to be gained by this kind of *essentially contemporaneous follow-up* was realized in the greater accuracy and richer detail of the information obtained while the experience was still fresh in mind.

The amount of effort expended on the part of our staff and of the cooperating juvenile, peno-correctional, and court authorities, both within and outside Massachusetts, may be surmised from the fact that during the years, 1940–1956, complete reports were gathered on 3,397 "treatment periods." Actually, many more periods were studied; but in instances where the data were found wanting in one respect or another, these reports were not utilized in the final analysis. We had, for example, initially included consideration of behavior in jails and houses of correction, but after studying several hundred investigational reports we abandoned the quest since the data available in the records were found to be too meagre, interviews with personnel of such institutions were often of little value, and the periods of confinement were usually of very short duration. This applied also to brief returns to institutions for medical treatment or relocation.

The most important aid in keeping abreast of changes in the treatment history of the 500 offenders resulted from an arrangement which was concluded with the Boys' Parole Department, which is charged with the supervision of all youngsters committed to the correctional schools of Massachusetts until they are twenty-one (unless, for special reasons, discharged from custody prior to age twenty-one). By this arrangement, as soon as a boy was ready for follow-up, our staff secretary was permitted to "flag" the boy's folder to signify our interest in the case. It was arranged that the Boys' Parole authorities would notify us promptly by post card if (1) the offender was paroled; (2) the offender was rearrested; (3) parole was revoked; (4) a marked change occurred in the offender's home conditions, such as going to live with relatives; (5) the parole period was terminated.

The institutional authorities also extended their cooperation in ways that made it possible for us to obtain full and accurate reports promptly after the treatment periods were completed. For example, they would inform us of a boy's running away from the correctional school, of his return, or of his transfer to another institution. By this system, it was possible to schedule interviews with the authorities and the offenders soon after termination of a treatment period.

As regards the reformatories and prisons, the authorities in the Massachusetts Department of Correction and the Parole Board for adult offenders also gave their full cooperation, the arrangement being much the same as with the Boys' Parole Department. For example, as soon as we learned through fingerprint files or other sources of the commitment of an offender to one of the institutions for adult offenders, we informed the institution of our interest. The institution personnel would, in turn, notify us of any serious offenses committed by the inmate, such as attempt to escape, assault on an officer, and so on. They agreed also to notify us of the date of parole. We in turn notified the adult parole authorities of our special interest; they too informed us of any unusual circumstances or behavior arising during parole, especially those happenings which would terminate a parole period.

In order not to miss any treatment periods to which our 500 offenders might have been subjected, we adopted the safeguard of annually clearing certain cases through the files of the Massachusetts Board of Probation, especially offenders already discharged from the oversight of the Boys' Parole Department, those already once committed to reformatories or prisons in or out of the State, and those who entered the armed services.

We also cleared our cases through individual fingerprint files in Massachusetts and elsewhere. Special arrangements had to be made with several official agencies in order to accomplish this.

Because of the ever-increasing number of treatment periods, it was necessary to keep progress charts. Alongside the name of each boy were entered all the assignments to staff members on an individual case. This was kept up to date by the office secretary. As assignments were completed they were checked off, so that the work yet to be carried out was always in clear view.

Although throughout the sixteen years of this project (which represents only a small aspect of our over-all research program) a number of different field workers, secretaries, and part-time clerks participated, it was necessary to use the services of only one male field investigator and one secretary at any one time.[4]

As each case was completed, the data were summarized by Mrs. Glueck, with some assistance from Richard E. Thompson, on a special form designed for this purpose; the findings were coded and punched on I.B.M. cards to permit tabulation and correlation, the objective being to determine the extent of *agreement between the predicted and the actual behavior*. The detailed findings will be found in Appendix C. Here we present a summary only.

Agreement Between Predicted and Actual Behavior[5]

Four hundred and ninety-seven boys, whose behavior during various forms of peno-correctional treatment was followed from the onset of their criminal careers until their twenty-third birthday, had a total of 3,397 peno-correctional experiences for which sufficient data were available (Appendix C, Tables 1, 2, and 3).

The average number of treatment experiences was six per boy (Appendix C, Table 1).

Regarding the number of types of peno-correctional treatments (straight probation, probation with suspended sentence, correctional school, parole, reformatory, prison), 10 offenders had only one type of peno-correctional treatment; 53 had two; 156, three; 191, four; 76, five; and 11, six (Appendix C, Table 2).

Two hundred and ninety-seven boys had 380 straight probation experiences; 356 boys had 548 probations under suspended sentences; 488 boys, 1,055 correctional school experiences; 461 boys, 1,053 parole periods;

---

[4] Ralph Whelan, now Director of the New York City Youth Board, was the first investigator engaged in the follow-up project. He was shortly succeeded by George F. McGrath, whose Army service interrupted his work for three years, during which time it was taken over by Samuel C. Lawrence and John E. Burke. We wish here to acknowledge our very special indebtedness to Mr. McGrath for his competent supervision of this project; to Mr. Burke for carrying on a good portion of the interviews; and to our very capable secretary, Esther Ghostlaw, who assumed the major responsibility, under Mr. McGrath's direction, for assembling the criminal records and performing numerous other secretarial and clerical tasks.

[5] This, and all the other tabulations in Appendix C, was carried out independently in the Bureau of Business Research of the Harvard Business School under the personal direction of Rose W. Kneznek, Executive Secretary of the Bureau.

157 boys, 320 reformatory commitments; and 35 boys had 41 prison terms (Appendix C, Table 3).

There are, in our files, 497 charts covering the predicted behavior for each boy under each of the above types of treatment. As stated, these predictions were made when each boy was first taken on for study during the years 1940–1945, in connection with the work on *Unraveling Juvenile Delinquency*. The distribution by score class of boys predicted as having more than an even chance of behaving unacceptably during each type of treatment is presented in Appendix C, Table 4, in juxtaposition with that referring to the particular group of offenders who actually experienced a given type of treatment. A close correspondence is shown in predicted behavior as between the total group and the particular group of delinquents who underwent the form of treatment involved.

In interpreting the following findings, it is necessary to bear in mind that, in our particular sample of cases, the proportion of offenders predictable as *good risks* under straight probation, probation with suspended sentence, in correctional schools, or on parole, is small, for the boys were already serious and persistent offenders when selected for inclusion in *Unraveling Juvenile Delinquency*, and do not therefore represent the run-of-the-mill juvenile offenders.

With these preliminaries, we are in a position to give consideration to the *extent of agreement between the behavior predicted for a delinquent and his actual behavior.*

In order to make more intelligible the findings that follow, concerning agreement between predicted and actual behavior, we present a case summary (Exhibit F, pp. 54–55) which indicates, in chronological order, the peno-correctional treatments in a given case; length of each treatment; age of the offender at the time; the prediction score for chance of violation in the case of straight probation, probation with suspended sentence, parole, and of maladaptation in correctional school, reformatory, or prison, as the case may be; a summary of misbehavior during each treatment as derived from the follow-up investigation; a classification of the boy's behavior during each treatment period in terms of whether it was serious, persistent minor, occasional minor, or whether the boy was a non-offender; and, on the basis of all these data, a determination of agreement or disagreement between the predicted and the actual behavior.

First, in regard to various forms of *extramural treatment*, it is seen in Appendix C, Table 6, that of 286 delinquents predicted as having more than an even chance of violating *straight probation*, 94.4% actually committed serious or persistent minor offenses during probation; of 344 offenders similarly predicted as failures during *probation under suspended sentence*, 98.0% actually turned out to be serious or persistent minor offenders; of 458 offenders predicted as violating *parole*, 91.0% actually were later found to be parole violators.

As regards *intramural treatment*, of 465 offenders predicted as not adapting well to a *correctional school regime*, 78.7% proved to be serious or persistent minor offenders in correctional schools; and of 39 boys predicted as not adapting well to a *reformatory regime*, 53.8% proved to be serious or persistent minor offenders in a reformatory. Although three of the four offenders predicted as not doing well in *prison* were found to be serious or persistent minor offenders, the number involved is so small that no conclusion can be reached about agreement between predicted and actual behavior.

Looking now at the other side of the shield, i.e., at those few delinquents predicted as *adapting well* during extramural treatments and in correctional schools, only a guarded conclusion can be drawn about these, because of the smallness of numbers. But of 118 offenders predicted as adapting well to a *reformatory regime*, 67.8% actually proved to be non-offenders or to have committed only an isolated minor offense; while of 31 offenders predicted as good risks in *prison*, 80.6% were in fact found to have been such.

We turn next to a consideration of the extent of agreement and disagreement between the predicted and actual behavior during each of the *treatment periods* experienced by the offenders. Agreement between predicted and actual behavior is considered to have occurred if an offender was predicted as having *more than an even chance of delinquency* during a particular form of peno-correctional treatment and was actually found to have committed *serious, or persistent minor, offenses* thereon; or if an offender was predicted as having *more than an even chance of non-delinquency* and was later found to have been a *non-offender* or to have committed only an isolated minor offense, such as violating traffic regulations.

Of 380 *straight probation periods*, the predicted and the actual behavior were in agreement in 92.1% of such periods; of 545 periods on *probation with suspended sentence*, agreement was found in 93.6%; as to 1,053 *parole periods*, the predicted and the actual result agreed in 91.9%; of 1,054 *correctional school experiences*, agreement occurred in 78.8%. As to

Exhibit F. Illustrative Case Analysis of Follow-up Investigation

ROBERT
Born: 6/8/26

Peno-Correctional Treatment	Dates	Age	Prediction Score	Violation or Maladaptation Rate	Chance of Violation or Maladaptation	Misbehavior	Type of Behavior	Agreement Between Predicted and Actual Behavior
STRAIGHT PROBATION	6/8/39– 11/29/39 (6 Months)	13	310.6	85.6%	More than Even Chance	Away from home for 4 days; truancy; associating with gang of delinquents, arrested on B & E & L charge	Serious	Yes
PROBATION WITH SUSPENDED SENTENCE	11/29/39– 6/27/40 (7 Months)	13	383.1	86.7%	More than Even Chance	B & E & L; violation of probation; B & E	Serious	Yes
CORRECTIONAL SCHOOL	6/27/40– 2/12/41 (8 Months)	14	227.4	62.9%	More than Even Chance	Very minor misdemeanors; i.e., talking back and just plain talking; took cards from desk	Occasional Minor	No
PAROLE	2/12/41– 7/11/41 (5 Months)	15	364.9	84.6%	More than Even Chance	None, until 7/11/41; B & E (night)	Serious	Yes
CORRECTIONAL SCHOOL	7/11/41– 9/9/42 (14 Months)	15	227.4	62.9%	More than Even Chance	Runaway once; mutual masturbation; minor rule breaking	Serious	Yes
PAROLE	9/9/42– 12/31/42 (4 Months)	16	364.9	84.6%	More than Even Chance	Stealing; bad companions; late hours; attempted suicide in cell at police station	Serious	Yes

54

Institution	Dates (Duration)	Age		%	Prognosis	Conduct	Severity	
CORRECTIONAL SCHOOL	1/21/43–2/17/43 (1 Month)	17	227.4	62.9%	More than Even Chance	Runaway; stole $1,000 from a home; poor attitude	Serious	Yes
REFORMATORY	3/24/43–6/21/44 (15 Months)	17	186.9	33.3%	Less than Even Chance	None	None	Yes
PAROLE	6/21/44–8/18/44 (2 Months)	18	364.9	84.6%	More than Even Chance	Bad companions; loafing; drinking; late hours; failing to report; court appearance for broken glass; parole revoked for running away when seen with a parolee by a P.O.	Persistent Minor	Yes
REFORMATORY	8/18/44–9/17/45 (13 Months)	18	186.9	33.3%	Less than Even Chance	Destroying or injuring state property; boy claims machine broke accidentally	Serious	No
PAROLE	9/17/45–10/11/45 (1 Month)	19	364.9	84.6%	More than Even Chance	Never slept at home since release; falsifying report to P.O.; left home and worked without permission; associated with parolee; arrested on suspicion of B & E & L	Serious	Yes
REFORMATORY	10/11/45–6/2/47 (20 Months)	19	186.9	33.3%	Less than Even Chance	Damaging state property; agitating; carelessness	Serious	No
REFORMATORY	11/23/48–5/26/49 (6 Months)	22	186.9	33.3%	Less than Even Chance	Disturbance in hospital	Occasional Minor	Yes

periods in *reformatories* and *prisons*, agreement was found in 73.1% and 75.6%, respectively (Appendix C, Table 7).

To what extent does the *age* factor play a role in predicting delinquent behavior? Examination of Appendix C, Table 8, will indicate that *agreement between predicted and actual behavior is progressively lower as the boys grow older*, ranging from 96.7% of those treatments occurring when the offenders are under eleven years old to 76.9% when they were twenty-one to twenty-three years old. This appears to indicate the wisdom of refining the prediction tables to take account of the age of the offenders. However, it should be pointed out that for use in juvenile courts (normally involved up to the seventeenth birthday) there would not appear to be too great a need to provide for the age breakdown, since it is evident that agreement between predicted and actual behavior is 99% in the age span seven to ten years; 90% in the age span eleven to fourteen years; and 85% in the age span fifteen to sixteen years.

Of special interest in this connection is the series of tables in Appendix C, 9–15, which deal with the actual behavior of our offenders during 3,397 treatment periods, broken down by age—first for all treatments (Appendix C, Table 9) and then for each type of treatment (Appendix C, Tables 10–15). The results confirm findings made by us in other researches,[6] that as delinquents advance in age there is some decline in their recidivism.

Without going into detail, it is seen in the over-all summary that there is a gradual reduction in the commission of serious or persistent minor offenses, ranging from 95.9% during treatment periods in the age span seven to ten years to 56.6% in the age span twenty-one to twenty-two years. However, in the age span in which juvenile court authorities would be mainly concerned (i.e., usually up to the seventeenth birthday), the reduction of serious or persistent minor offenses during treatment periods ranges from 95.9% of all treatments in the age span seven to ten years to 89.8% at eleven to twelve years, to 88.4% at thirteen to fourteen years, to 80.9% at fifteen to sixteen years (Appendix C, Table 9).

The decline in recidivism rates is reflected in behavior in correctional schools, in reformatories, and on parole.

Does difference in the *length of the treatment periods* affect determination of behavior during treatment? Because of the variation in the length of the treatment periods, ranging from less than seven months to more than

---

[6] *Juvenile Delinquents Grown Up*; and *Criminal Careers in Retrospect*, New York, The Commonwealth Fund, 1943.

twenty-four months, some readers might express skepticism about a determination on such a varied base of the behavior of the offenders during the 3,397 treatment periods. From Appendix C, Table 16, it will be seen that 1,375 treatment periods were less than seven months in length, 1,167 were seven to twelve months in duration, 392 were thirteen to eighteen months long, 179 were nineteen to twenty-four months in length, and 284 were twenty-five months and longer. Contrary to what some might expect, namely, that the *shorter* the treatment period the less likelihood there is for accurately predicting the commission of serious or of persistent minor offenses, the facts are just the reverse: for in a higher proportion of treatment periods of less than seven months' duration (83.1%) the unlawful behavior was serious or persistent minor in nature than during treatments of twenty-five months and over (73.6%). On the whole, the actual length of the treatment periods has made very little difference in the proportion of those found to have been serious or persistent minor offenders during such periods.

In addition to determining the extent of agreement between the predicted and the actual behavior of the offenders *during* peno-correctional treatments, we have taken the opportunity which this inquiry provided to check a prediction table developed in the volume, *One Thousand Juvenile Delinquents*,[7] designed to predict the behavior of offenders *at the end of a five-year follow-up span after a treatment imposed by a juvenile court* and presented in Appendix B, Table III–7. As applied to this group of offenders for the five-year period following the end of the first period of treatment in each case (and this was possible in 441 cases), it will be seen, by consulting Appendix C, Table 17, that 435 offenders, or 98.6%, were predicted as having more than an equal chance of serious or persistent minor delinquency during the five-year period following the end of the first treatment period, and that actually 419 of these 435 offenders, or 96.3%, proved to be serious or persistent minor offenders in the five-year span.

Some Reasons for Disagreement Between Predicted and Actual Results

We have not made an exhaustive exploration of the few cases *incorrectly* predicted to see whether it is possible to determine why the predicted behavior and the actual behavior of an offender during one or another

[7] Table 39, p. 188.

type of treatment were not in agreement. But we have kept notes of the more striking instances:

(a) In at least ten treatment periods where consistently good behavior occurred during a form of treatment despite the predictive indication of bad conduct, there was especially suitable treatment.

(b) In at least eight cases there was especially resourceful supervision.

(c) In at least twenty instances there was a radical change of residence of the family to a more wholesome environment.[8]

(d) In at least ten instances there was a psychologic "transference" to an adult whom the boy especially liked.

(e) In at least twenty-six instances the ultimate reformation was related to a delayed maturation which finally was achieved.

(f) In at least eleven instances there was an especially strong incentive for good conduct.

On the other hand, there are a few illustrations of the kinds of *counteractive influences* that apparently played a determining role in bringing about consistently poor behavior during one or more periods of treatment despite a prediction of good behavior:

(a) In at least five treatment periods the offenders were influenced by markedly antisocial companions.

(b) In at least three instances there was a developing psychosis.

(c) In at least three treatment periods the maladapted behavior was the result of some deep-seated personality difficulty.

(d) In at least three treatment periods the exceptionally low mentality of the offenders appeared to account for the inaccurate prediction.

These findings are clearly suggestive of the fact that predictive devices are not to be used mechanically and without consideration of the circumstances of the individual case as disclosed in the probation officer's investigation report and the clinician's report.

Evidences of Wide Applicability of Juvenile Court Prediction Tables

It is to be noted that the 1,000 juvenile delinquents on whom the juvenile court tables were initially constructed appeared in the Boston Juvenile Court in the years 1917–1922. The boys on whom the tables were tested

[8] Compare footnote 8, Chapter III.

first appeared in juvenile courts throughout the Boston area in the years 1938–1940, and some even in other cities and towns of Massachusetts. It cannot be said, therefore, that the juvenile court prediction tables have a narrow applicability because constructed on boys who passed through such courts in 1917–1922. It is to be noted, also, that a comparison of the background of *One Thousand Juvenile Delinquents* (followed over a fifteen-year span in *Juvenile Delinquents Grown Up*), from whose case histories the juvenile court prediction tables were initially constructed, and the 500 delinquents of *Unraveling Juvenile Delinquency* reveals that although they resemble each other in certain aspects of their background, they differ in other ways. Among the resemblances in the two groups are the size of the families in which the offenders were reared, the poor disciplinary practices of the father and/or of the mother (either overstrict or lax), and in the low moral standards of the homes in which these boys grew up.

The fact that prediction tables constructed on one group of cases check on another group despite *marked differences* in the background of the two sets of delinquents broadens the base of their usefulness. For example, there is a considerable difference in the birthplace of the mothers, for a much lower proportion of the mothers of the boys of *Unraveling* were born in Russia, Poland, or Lithunia (5.6% as contrasted with 19% of the mothers of the boys of *One Thousand Juvenile Delinquents*); and 15.8% of the former were Italian born as contrasted with 30.8%. Likewise, half the proportion of the mothers of the boys in *Unraveling* were of Irish birth (8.6% as contrasted with 15.3% of the mothers of the boys of *One Thousand Juvenile Delinquents*), but over twice as great a proportion of mothers of the boys in *Unraveling* were born in the United States (55.8% as contrasted with 20.2% of the mothers of the boys in *One Thousand Juvenile Delinquents*). Differences are found likewise in the birthplace of the fathers of the boys, for a third as many of the fathers of the boys of *Unraveling* were born in Poland, Russia, or Lithuania as were the fathers of *One Thousand Juvenile Delinquents*. Lower proportions of the fathers of the boys of *Unraveling* were born in Italy or Ireland, and two and one-half times as many were born in the United States.

Differences are to be noted, also, in the religious background of the two groups of boys, for a far higher proportion of the parents of the boys of *One Thousand Juvenile Delinquents* were both Hebrew (13.3 : 1.2%); and a far greater proportion were of two different religions (17% as contrasted with 2.5% of the parents of the boys of *One Thousand Juvenile Delinquents*).

59

There are differences, also, in the affection of the fathers for the boys, for a considerably higher proportion of the fathers of the boys on whom the prediction tables were tested were not warm in their relationship to the boys (59.8 : 32.0%). There is also a marked difference in the relationship of the parents of both groups of boys toward one another, a far lower proportion of the parents of the boys of *Unraveling* living together in harmony (36.8% as contrasted with 62.4% of the parents of *One Thousand Juvenile Delinquents*).

Still another difference is found in the higher proportion of boys of *Unraveling* who were not retarded in school or not more than one year behind grade (59.0 : 38.9%). And, finally, a difference was found in the proportion of school truants among the boys of *Unraveling* as contrasted with *One Thousand Juvenile Delinquents* (94.8 : 74.8%).

These evidences of the applicability of prediction tables despite differences in the background of offenders would appear to enhance their value. There is further confirmation of this regarding other prediction tables presented in this volume (see Chapter V, section entitled "Evidences of Validity of Prediction Tables Dealing with Adult Offenders"; and Chapters IX and X concerned with applications of the Social Prediction Table).

* * *

From the foregoing results it would appear that the prediction tables for use in juvenile courts have met one test of practical effectiveness as instrumentalities for forecasting the response of offenders to the traditional peno-correctional treatments prescribed by such courts.

V

Prediction of Behavior of Adult Male Offenders

Introduction

Turning now to a battery of prediction tables relating to adult offenders, it is necessary at the outset to advert to the basic difficulty of publishing them before they have been tested. The checking of these tables on one sample of cases would be a lengthy process. The reader will recall that it took sixteen years of follow-up to make one check of the juvenile court prediction tables.

As the offenders for whom the adult series of tables have been prepared span the ages from seventeen to thirty-five, it would take even longer to follow up a new set of cases for purposes of checking the tables since we personally would prefer to apply them to one group of adult offenders from the time of their first appearance in an adult court at least until age forty rather than to segmentize the tables by applying each one to a different set of offenders. Although this method would be more economical in time, it would not result in a rounded picture of the utility of predictive devices in mapping out for a judge the probable course of behavior of a particular offender from his first adult court appearance to age forty.

Added to the difficulty of presenting tables, as yet unchecked, is our inability to define the extent to which the regimes involved are typical of those in other jurisdictions. However, we do describe in *500 Criminal Careers*[1] the main features of the institutional and parole regimes prevailing at the time the offenders in question passed through the Massachusetts Reformatory and parole system, to which experimenters with the tables can refer. In the final analysis, however, the extent of the practical utility of the prediction tables about to be presented is best determined through testing on a variety of regimes. Clearly, until checking of these tables has been made, they are to be regarded as "experience tables." However,

[1] S. and E. T. Glueck, New York, Knopf, 1930, pp. 25–51, 165–181.

61

judging from the partial validation of one of the tables in the series about to be presented (Table V–28, Prediction of Behavior of Civilian Delinquents in Armed Forces[2]), there is reason to hope that other tables in this series would also be found to be workable predictive devices, because the raw materials on which the tables in this chapter are based are from the same pool of data.

In constructing this series of tables from the data in *Criminal Careers in Retrospect*[3] (a follow-up of the cases originally presented in *500 Criminal Careers*) we did the best we could with the available data. In a few tables, the very narrow differences in the failure scores of the subcategories of each factor are explained by the fact that the cases on which the tables were constructed were serious or persistent minor offenders and therefore did not include the run-of-the-mill of adult offenders of a less serious category. We consider it advantageous to publish the tables, nevertheless, since for the first time in the history of criminology an entire battery of predictive devices has been constructed dealing with every form of traditional peno-correctional treatment.

As in Chapter III, pertaining to juvenile delinquents, so in this chapter, on adult male offenders, our aim is to present in the text the summary prediction tables and to comment on the nature of the discriminative factors involved. The detailed tables will be found in Appendix B.

Prediction of Behavior on Probation

The tables in the present section deal with extramural oversight provided by a court: namely, probation, with and without suspended sentence; and they have the added feature of taking into account the expectable response of adult offenders during various age spans.

Table V–1 is intended to predict the chances of violation of straight probation, irrespective of the age of the offender when placed on probation. Table V–2 takes account of the age factor, in providing predictions for ordinary probationers under twenty-seven years of age. The selection of this age-line was of course not arbitrary, but grew inductively out of analysis of the intercorrelations. Table V–3 deals with the expectable behavior on straight probation of offenders at ages twenty-seven or older. Table V–4 is designed to predict the varied responses to be expected from adult offenders with different characteristics, when placed on probation

---

[2] See Appendix B.
[3] S. and E. T. Glueck, New York, The Commonwealth Fund, 1943.

Summary Table V–A. Prediction of Behavior of Adult Male
Offenders during Straight Probation and Probation with
Suspended Sentence

Type of Treatment		Less than Even Chance of Violation		More than Even Chance of Violation	
		Score Class	(Rate)	Score Class	(Rate)
Straight Probation[1] (irrespective of age)	(V–1)	Less than 440	(0.0%)	440 or Over	(98.0%)
Straight Probation under 27 Years of Age[2]	(V–2)	Less than 460	(0.0)	460 or Over	(95.7)
Straight Probation at Ages 27 or Older[3]	(V–3)	Less than 410	(25.0)	410 or Over	(92.1)
Probation with Suspended Sentence[4]	(V–4)	*	(*)	*	(*)
Probation with Suspended Sentence under 32 Years of Age[5]	(V–5)	Less than 440	(0.0)	440 or Over	(99.0)
Probation with Suspended Sentence at Ages 32 or Older[6]	(V–6)	Less than 410	(*)	410 or Over	(85.7)

* Score classes and/or rates not available.
[1] Predictive Factors: Family Relationships; Education of Parents; Church Attendance; Age at Onset of Antisocial Behavior; Number of Children in Family.
[2] Predictive Factors: Age at Onset of Antisocial Behavior; Bad Habits in Childhood; Church Attendance; Family Relationships; Industrial Skill of Offender.
[3] Predictive Factors: Number of Children in Family; Economic Status of Childhood Home; Adequacy of Childhood Home; Age at Onset of Antisocial Behavior; Mental Disease or Distortion.
[4] Predictive Factors: Nativity of Offender; Intelligence of Offender; Grade Attained in School; Age at Onset of Antisocial Behavior; Industrial Skill of Offender.
[5] Predictive Factors: Nativity of Offender; Age at Onset of Antisocial Behavior; Intelligence of Offender; Mobility; Use of Leisure.
[6] Predictive Factors: Number of Children in Family of Offender; Economic Status of Childhood Home; Intelligence of Offender; Age at Onset of Antisocial Behavior; Industrial Skill of Offender.
Note: Numbers in parentheses to right of type of treatment refer to table numbers in Appendix B; definitions of the predictive factors and the scores for the respective subcategories will also be found in Appendix B.

with suspended sentence. Table V–5 covers response to probation under suspended sentence of offenders who are less than thirty-two years old; and Table V–6 deals with behavior on probation under suspended sentence of offenders who are thirty-two years or older.

Examination of this series of tables concerned with the extramural treatment and behavior of adult male offenders shows, first of all, the crucial significance of the factor of *Age at Onset of Antisocial Behavior*; for this datum has been found to be a predictor of behavior under straight probation and probation with suspended sentence, and in all the age spans involved. Thus the relative deep-rootedness of the antisocial tendency, which we have seen in Chapter III to play a marked role in predicting the response of young delinquents to various forms of correction, is now shown to extend its influence well into adult life. This finding is all the more significant since it is derived from two different samples of cases.

Three other factors turn up as predictive in three of the six tables in this series dealing with probation: *Number of Children in Family* (in Tables V–1, V–3, and V–6); *Industrial Skill of Offender* (in Tables V–2, V–4, and V–6); and *Intelligence of Offender* (in Tables V–4, V–5, and V–6). The first of these factors indicates that the larger the family from which the offender springs the less the likelihood of his failing to adapt to probation, both irrespective of age and on straight probation at twenty-seven years of age or more, or on probation with suspended sentence at age thirty-two years or more. The second of the factors—*Industrial Skill of Offender*—indicates a lower violation rate on the part of the skilled workers than of others during straight probation under twenty-seven years of age and probation with suspended sentence irrespective of age; but during probation with suspended sentence at thirty-two years of age or older, a lower violation rate is found for the semiskilled or unskilled workers. This obvious erraticism is attributable to smallness of numbers in the subcategories of the factor, for all but three of the offenders on whom the table was constructed were semiskilled or unskilled workers.

The third factor which appears in three of the six tables dealing with the probation of adult offenders—*Intelligence of Offender*—shows a lower violation rate in the case of mentally immature offenders under suspended sentence irrespective of their age.

The other predictive factors are not duplicated in more than two of the six tables dealing with probation.

We want again to stress that in some of these tables the differences in percentage incidence of the cases having the lowest and of those having the highest violation scores are narrow, the violation rates being high in *all* the subcategories. These tables should therefore be viewed with special caution, bearing in mind that they are intended as an experimental starting point toward more efficient instruments of prediction based on local experience.[4]

Prediction of Behavior in Reformatories

Among the choices open to a judge in sentencing young adult offenders is commitment to a reformatory. We have expressed the view that the Massachusetts Reformatory, one of the pioneer institutions in the reformatory movement, provides a regime similar to most such institutions in different parts of the country. The interested reader can turn to our *500 Criminal Careers* for a detailed description of the procedures and facilities of the Massachusetts Reformatory during the period when the young offenders who were the subjects of that follow-up investigation were in the Reformatory. It might be mentioned, however, that the impression of the parent reformatory (that at Elmira, New York), gained in 1929 by the Osborne Association, would not be too far afield as a description of the Massachusetts institution:

> The history of Elmira raises the question, significant for every state, of how successful a reformatory program is likely to be which stresses regimentation, even though the routine is in worthwhile pursuits. At Elmira, as in many other American reformatories, the inmates are walking a chalk-line as surely as though they were in a prison. The chalk-line is broader than in some prisons, and it leads along more interesting paths: academic instruction, trade school, gymnasium work, etc. It is nevertheless the chalk-line of routine, with all the old-time stress on regimentation, which so easily becomes stereotyped and futile and which is doubly monotonous for the young.[5]

Apart from the disclosure in *500 Criminal Careers* of the high rate of recidivism of "graduates" of the Massachusetts Reformatory, there have been other, more generalized, criticisms.

> Criticism of the reformatory has been widespread. Reports and surveys are full of caustic condemnation of plant, program, personnel, release methods, and basic philosophy. In short, the reformatory is just another prison.[6]

[4] While we would not go as far as the following suggestion, since we believe that sound prediction tables can be developed which will have utility in a wide diversity of institutions, it is wise to keep it in mind: "Each institution, department, and community needs to develop its own experience tables and not rely upon those of other groups, which may strongly reflect unique elements in their peculiar situations," P. V. Young, *Social Treatment in Probation and Delinquency*, New York, McGraw-Hill, 1937, pp. 621–622.

[5] *American Prisons and Reformatories*, Handbook, 1929, New York, p. 692.

[6] Negley K. Teeters and J. O. Reinemann, *The Challenge of Delinquency*, New York, Prentice-Hall, 1950, p. 526.

In 1930 we made the following observation about the admixture of reformatory and prison offenders in the sentencing practices of judges; and the observation remains, we believe, valid:

> Whether the original scheme of the proponents of the reformatory system to have a special institution for "young adults" is sound depends on what modern biology and psychology can tell us as to the special characteristics of adolescents and early post-adolescents. We leave this question to specialists in the fields mentioned. But assuming that there have definitely been established certain vital distinguishing marks of the ages of, say, eighteen to twenty-five, and that these are intimately related to character development and deterioration, the specialized "young men's" reformatory should obviously be confined to young men, instead of being used for prisoners varying in age from fifteen to forty. Moreover, if it be intended to have a reformatory for young inexperienced criminals who for some good reason are probably unsuited to probational supervision, it should be the policy of judges and correctional authorities strictly to limit the reformatory population to those who are still, relatively speaking, amateurs in criminality. No hard and fast definition of this can be given, nor should it ever have been attempted. It is a question to be decided in the individual case after careful study by the social and psychiatric investigators attached to the court. The technical line now drawn between reformatory and state-prison inmates should be eliminated; and all cases where study of the individual personality and the soil in which it grew indicates promise of reorientation by a reformative regime should be committed to a reformatory.[7]

All we would add to this is that in the process of individualization, prediction tables should be of value.

Despite the claim that the American reformatory is in most places just as mechanically administered and as nonrehabilitative an institution as the traditional "penitentiary," or prison, some distinction remains between a prison and a reformatory; the latter is still dedicated theoretically to the younger and presumably more hopeful offenders, and the distinction is somewhat reflected in a variation in the predictive factors governing response to these two types of institution.

We present now an analysis of four tables dealing with the response of different age groups of offenders to the reformatory regime.

Examination of the predictive items discloses one factor running through three of the series of four tables dealing with behavior in the reformatory. This factor has been shown to be predictive in other connections also:

---

[7] *500 Criminal Careers*, pp. 315–316.

Age at Onset of Antisocial Behavior, which is found to be markedly related to adjustment in the reformatory regardless of age, and in the age spans seventeen to twenty-two years (Table V–8), and twenty-two to twenty-seven years (Table V–9), and which, it will be recalled, was also found to be a predictive factor in Tables V–1 to V–6, inclusive, of the present chapter,

Summary Table V–B.   Prediction of Behavior of Adult Male
Offenders in Reformatories

Type of Treatment		Less than Even Chance of Maladaptation		More than Even Chance of Maladaptation	
		Score Class	(Rate)	Score Class	(Rate)
Reformatory[1] (irrespective of age)	(V–7)	Less than 270	(29.2%)	270 or Over	(71.7%)
Reformatory at 17–21 Years of Age[2]	(V–8)	Less than 350	(34.3)	350 or Over	(78.4)
Reformatory at 22–26 Years of Age[3]	(V–9)	Less than 300	(37.5)	300 or Over	(69.1)
Reformatory at Ages 27 or Older[4]	(V–10)	Less than 160	(37.9)	160 or Over	(*)

* Rate not available.
[1] Predictive Factors: Nativity of Parents and Offender; Education of Parents; Adequacy of Childhood Home; Age at Onset of Antisocial Behavior; Industrial Skill of Offender.
[2] Predictive Factors: Intelligence of Offender; Age at Onset of Antisocial Behavior; Grade Attained in School; Family Relationships; Industrial Skill of Offender.
[3] Predictive Factors: Delinquency in Family; Adequacy of Childhood Home; Occupation of Mother; Age at Onset of Antisocial Behavior; Intelligence of Offender.
[4] Predictive Factors: Education of Parents; Economic Status of Childhood Home; Work Habits of Offender; Economic Responsibility of Offender; Use of Leisure.
Note: Numbers in parentheses to right of type of treatment refer to table numbers in Appendix B; definitions of the predictive factors and the scores for the respective subcategories will also be found in Appendix B.

as well as in several tables in Chapter III, dealing with juvenile delinquents. Here, then, there is further evidence from two different samples of cases of the crucial significance of the extent of the deep-rootedness of the tendency to delinquency. We shall see, in subsequent tables, that the importance of this factor for predictive purposes can hardly be overemphasized.

Other factors having to do with the offender himself and which are found to be predictive in at least two of the series of four tables dealing with behavior in reformatories are *Intelligence of Offender,* predictive in Tables V–8 and V–9,[8] and *Industrial Skill of Offender,* predictive in

[8] Note here the turnaround from Tables V–4, V–5, and V–6, where low intelligence has the low score.

Tables V–7 and V–8. The two remaining factors appearing at least twice in the battery of prognostic instruments having to do with behavior in reformatories are concerned with family environment—*Adequacy of Childhood Home*, predictive in Tables V–7 and V–9, and *Education of Parents*, in Tables V–7 and V–10.

We shall advert to these factors again in the next chapter where the entire list of predictive factors pertaining to adult offenders is summarized and discussed.

Prediction of Behavior in Prisons

Despite the view of some that reformatories for young men are usually no different in basic outlook and regime than the typical prison, the views of legislatures as expressed in statutes, the sentencing practices of judges, and the releasing policies of parole boards do draw a distinction between the two types of institution. Moreover, the distinction is reflected, to some extent, in the difference in the factors predicting adjustment to the prison regime as opposed to that of the reformatory.

Examination of the tables dealing with behavior in prison discloses the interesting fact that *Intelligence of Offender* is predictive in *all* five. This is to be expected. Good intelligence probably conditions the resourcefulness necessary to adhere, outwardly, to the prison routine and rules, and the capacity to be a "good prisoner." Being a good prisoner does not, of itself, indicate that the person will also be a good ex-prisoner. Intelligence is likewise predictive in two of the tables dealing with behavior in reformatories (Tables V–8 and V–9). In all these, prisoners of normal or dull intelligence chalk up a better record of "adjustment" than those of borderline or downright defective intelligence.

Three of the factors predictive of adjustment to the prison regime have been found to be prognostic in three of the tables. One of these, *Age at Onset of Antisocial Behavior* (appearing in Tables V–11, V–12, and V–15), has already been commented on in connection with preceding tables as highly significant and widely permeative in its influence. The other two have to do with the childhood home: *Adequacy of Childhood Home* is significant in forecasting behavior in Tables V–11, V–12, and V–14; and *Education of Parents* is predictive in Tables V–11, V–12, and V–13.

Two factors are operative in the five tables in the series under discussion: *Industrial Skill of Offender* turns up in Tables V–12 and V–15; *Grade Attained in School*, in Tables V–14 and V–15; *Number of Children in Family*,

68

in Tables V–13 and V–14; *Nativity of Parents and Offender*, in Tables V–11 and V–13; *Conjugal Relations of Parents*, in Tables V–13 and V–14. (These will be adverted to more comprehensively in the next chapter.)

Summary Table V–C.   Prediction of Behavior of Adult Male
Offenders in Prisons

Type of Treatment		Less than Even Chance of Maladaptation		More than Even Chance of Maladaptation	
		Score Class	(Rate)	Score Class	(Rate)
Prison[1] (irrespective of age)	(V–11)	Less than 130	(33.9%)	130 or Over	(63.0%)
Prison under 27 Years of Age[2]	(V–12)	Less than 230	(11.1)	230 or Over	(58.3)
Prison at 27–31 Years of Age[3]	(V–13)	Less than 200	(16.7)	200 or Over	(56.2)
Prison at 32–36 Years of Age[4]	(V–14)	Less than 180	(10.0)	180 or Over	(69.2)
Prison at Ages 37 or Older[5]	(V–15)	Less than 140	(18.4)	140 or Over	(100.0)

[1] Predictive Factors: Nativity of Parents and Offender; Education of Parents; Adequacy of Childhood Home; Intelligence of Offender; Age at Onset of Antisocial Behavior.

[2] Predictive Factors: Education of Parents; Intelligence of Offender; Adequacy of Childhood Home; Age at Onset of Antisocial Behavior; Industrial Skill of Offender.

[3] Predictive Factors: Nativity of Parents and Offender; Education of Parents; Conjugal Relations of Parents; Number of Children in Family of Offender; Intelligence of Offender.

[4] Predictive Factors: Number of Children in Family of Offender; Intelligence of Offender; Grade Attained in School; Conjugal Relations of Parents; Adequacy of Childhood Home.

[5] Predictive Factors: Rank of Offender among Siblings; Intelligence of Offender; Grade Attained in School; Age at Onset of Antisocial Behavior; Industrial Skill of Offender.

Note: Numbers in parentheses to right of type of treatment refer to table numbers in Appendix B; definitions of the predictive factors and the scores for the respective subcategories will also be found in Appendix B.

Prediction of Behavior in Jails and Houses of Correction

It is common knowledge that the jails in many parts of the United States accomplish little or nothing in the way of reconstruction and reformation of offenders. Indeed, the influence of these short-term institutions is often more harmful than good. The evils of the jail system have been emphasized in numerous surveys and in all standard texts on criminology. Writing in 1923, a well-informed authority depicted the evils of the jail in terms which, with very few exceptions, are in large measure applicable in many places down to today, and which he puts into the mouth of a judge engaged in sentencing men to typical short-term institutions of the jail type:

I not only sentence you to confinement for thirty days in a bare, narrow cell in a gloomy building, during which time you will be deprived of your family, friends, occupation, earning power, and all other human liberties and privileges; but in addition I sentence you to wallow in a putrid mire demoralizing to body, mind and soul, where every rule of civilization is violated, where you are given every opportunity to deteriorate, but none to improve, and where your tendency to wrong-doing cannot be corrected, but only aggravated.[9]

Houses of correction, also institutions for short-term offenders, are, occasionally, of better quality in that they sometimes have outdoor farming facilities and an opportunity for some work. Those in Massachusetts are not as benighted as many jails in the thousands of county units of the United States in downright evils (such as grossly insanitary conditions and oppression of inmates through the "kangaroo court")[10] but afford little opportunity for employment, guidance, or other constructive activities of a truly reformative regime. Yet jails and houses of correction are with us; and although respected authorities have long cried, "the jail must be abolished,"[11] the chances are that short-term institutions will be part of the peno-correctional apparatus for a long time to come. Any help which judges may be given in determining the probable response of petty offenders to short periods of incarceration in jails and houses of correction should be welcome. It will be seen from the following tables that, although "adjustment" to the regime does not necessarily indicate any fundamental reform and rehabilitation, there are significant differences in failure rates dependent upon the background and characteristics of the prisoners.

Again, the reader is reminded that we publish the tables in this chapter largely as suggestive for serious-minded administrators of justice who are interested in experimenting with predictive instruments with a view to improving them in the light of experience in their own courts, institutions, and administrative agencies.

With these explanations and qualifications, let us proceed to examine the series of five tables reflective of response to incarceration in jails and houses of correction.

Examination of the discriminative factors in this series of tables shows that not a single one of them is predictive in all of the five tables involved, or even in four of them. The following factors are predictive of behavior in three of the five tables in the series:

[9] J. Fishman, *Crucibles of Crime*, New York, Cosmopolis Press, 1923, p. 21.
[10] S. Bates, *Prisons and Beyond*, New York, Macmillan, 1936, p. 52.
[11] This is the title of a section in the excellent analysis of the jail problem in H. E Barnes and N. K. Teeters, *New Horizons in Criminology*, p. 861.

Number of Children in Family of Offender is related to conduct in Table V–17 (behavior in jails or houses of correction under twenty-two years of age), Table V–18 (in such institutions at ages twenty-two through twenty-six), and Table V–19 (in age span twenty-seven through thirty-one). This factor was also a predictor in Tables V–1, V–3, V–6, V–13, and V–14 (probation and prison).

Summary Table V–D.   Prediction of Behavior of Adult Male
Offenders in Jails and Houses of Correction

Type of Treatment	Less than Even Chance of Maladaptation		More than Even Chance of Maladaptation	
	Score Class	(Rate)	Score Class	(Rate)
Jail and House of Correction[1] (irrespective of age) (V–16)	Less than 140	(29.4%)	140 or Over	(64.0%)
Jail and House of Correction under 22 Years of Age[2] (V–17)	Less than 240	(40.0)	240 or Over	(62.5)
Jail and House of Correction at 22–26 Years of Age[3] (V–18)	Less than 180	(4.2)	180 or Over	(53.6)
Jail and House of Correction at 27–31 Years of Age[4] (V–19)	Less than 230	(32.3)	230 or Over	(66.7)
Jail and House of Correction at 32–36 Years of Age[5] (V–20)	Less than 130	(0.0)	130 or Over	(71.4)

[1] Predictive Factors: Nativity of Parents and Offender; Economic Status of Childhood Home; Rank of Offender among Siblings; Grade Attained in School; Age Began Work:
[2] Predictive Factors: Number of Children in Family of Offender; Adequacy of Childhood Home; Grade Attained in School; Age at Onset of Antisocial Behavior; Age First Left Home.
[3] Predictive Factors: Number of Children in Family of Offender; Economic Status of Childhood Home; Mobility; Age Began Work; Industrial Skill of Offender.
[4] Predictive Factors: Number of Children in Family of Offender; Intelligence of Offender; Economic Status of Childhood Home; Age Began Work; Industrial Skill of Offender.
[5] Predictive Factors: Conjugal Relations of Parents; Adequacy of Childhood Home; School Misconduct; Industrial Skill of Offender; Mental Disease or Distortion.
Note: Numbers in parentheses to right of type of treatment refer to table numbers in Appendix B; definitions of the predictive factors and the scores for the respective subcategories will also be found in Appendix B.

Industrial Skill of Offender is another factor that turns up in at least three of the tables in the series of five dealing with behavior in jails and houses of correction (Tables V–18, V–19, and V–20). Industrial skill had also been found to be discriminative in Tables V–2, V–4, V–6, V–7, V–8, V–12, and V–15, dealing with the prediction of behavior on probation, in reformatories, and in prisons. There are exceptions, but by and large, the less skilled the offender, the greater is the likelihood that he will not adapt himself to the peno-correctional treatment involved.

Economic Status of Childhood Home is another factor that is found to be discriminative in three tables in the present series (Tables V–16, V–18, and V–19). This factor was also a predictor in Tables V–3, V–6, and V–10 (straight probation, probation with suspended sentence, and reformatories).

One final factor found to be associated in at least three tables with behavior in jails or houses of correction is *Age Began Work* (Tables V–16, V–18, and V–19). This has not been involved in any of the tables previously discussed and is relevant in only one other table, which deals with the behavior of civilian delinquents in the Armed Forces (see Appendix B, Table V–28).

Prediction of Behavior on Parole

Continuing the presentation and analysis of the battery of predictive tables dealing with the administration of criminal justice in relation to adult male offenders, we next consider parole.

Summary Table V–E.   Prediction of Behavior of Adult Male
Offenders during Parole

Type of Treatment		Less than Even Chance of Violation		More than Even Chance of Violation	
		Score Class	(Rate)	Score Class	(Rate)
Parole[1] (irrespective of age)	(V–21)	Less than 290	(50.0%*)	290 or Over	(79.1%)
Parole under 22 Years of Age[2]	(V–22)	Less than 390	(45.2)	390 or Over	(88.9)
Parole at 22–26 Years of Age[3]	(V–23)	Less than 300	(28.6)	300 or Over	(74.3)
Parole at Ages 27 or Older[4]	(V–24)	Less than 340	(†)	340 or Over	(68.9)

* Even chance.
† Rate not available.
[1] Predictive Factors: Education of Parents; Number of Children in Family of Offender; Adequacy of Childhood Home; Intelligence of Offender; Grade Attained in School.
[2] Predictive Factors: Delinquency in Family; Age at Onset of Antisocial Behavior; Bad Habits in Childhood; Industrial Skill of Offender; Physical Condition.
[3] Predictive Factors: Delinquency in Family; Economic Status of Childhood Home; Adequacy of Childhood Home; Work Habits of Offender; Economic Responsibility of Offender.
[4] Predictive Factors: Nativity of Offender; Rank of Offender among Siblings; Age at Onset of Antisocial Behavior; Use of Leisure; Physical Condition.
Note: Numbers in parentheses to right of type of treatment refer to table numbers in Appendix B; definitions of the predictive factors and the scores for the respective subcategories will also be found in Appendix B.

Release of prisoners on parole oversight is nowadays recognized as a very important adjunct to the correctional system. Parole serves both as an incentive to the prisoner and as an important proving ground when he leaves the institution.

Examination of the tables in this series indicates that the subcategories involved in the predictive factors are among the most clearly discriminative in the entire battery of tables included in this chapter. However, no single factor runs through all four or even three of these tables. Four factors are involved in two of the relevant tables: the already emphasized *Age at Onset of Antisocial Behavior* (Tables V–22 and V–24), *Delinquency in Family* (Tables V–22 and V–23), *Adequacy of Childhood Home* (Tables V–21 and V–23), and *Physical Condition of Offender* (Tables V–22 and V–24).

Prediction of Behavior in Age Spans Twenty-five to Forty

While behavior on parole is of great importance for the administrators of justice, it does not, in itself, give sufficient indication of the relative permanence of reform or recidivism. For that purpose it is necessary to follow the inquiry several years beyond official control, to learn how

Summary Table V–F. Prediction of Behavior of Male Offenders
after Completion of First Reformatory Sentence

Period	Less than Even Chance of Recidivism		More than Even Chance of Recidivism	
	Score Class	(Rate)	Score Class	(Rate)
Five Years after Completion of First Sentence[1] (V–25)	Less than 296	(5.0%)	296 or Over	(*)
Ten Years after Completion of First Sentence[2] (V–26)	Less than 350	(26.1)	350 or Over	(72.4%)
Fifteen Years after Completion of First Sentence[3] (V–27)	Less than 180	(31.2)	180 or Over	(66.7)

* Rate not available for a dichotomized table; see Table V–25, Appendix B, for more detailed table.
[1] Predictive Factors: Work Habits Preceding Sentence; Seriousness and Frequency of Prereformatory Crimes; Arrests Preceding Offense for Which Sentenced; Penal Experiences Prior to Reformatory Sentence; Economic Responsibility Preceding Sentence; Mental Disease or Distortion on Entrance to Reformatory.
[2] Predictive Factors: Work Habits Preceding Sentence; Economic Responsibility Preceding Sentence; Age at Onset of Antisocial Behavior; Arrests Preceding Offense for Which Sentenced; Mental Disease or Distortion on Entrance to Reformatory.
[3] Predictive Factors: Number of Children in Family of Offender; Economic Status of Childhood Home; Industrial Skill of Father; Intelligence of Offender; Age at Onset of Antisocial Behavior.
Note: Numbers in parentheses to right of period refer to table numbers in Appendix B; definitions of the predictive factors and the scores for the respective subcategories will also be found in Appendix B.

various types of offenders conduct themselves when they are presumably on their own. With this in view, we have constructed a series of tables extending the behavioral outcomes over three follow-up periods of five years each.

The three tables here summarized were constructed on 500 former inmates of the Massachusetts Reformatory, whose average age at commitment to that institution was 20.2 years. They were initially designed to predict the behavior of adult offenders after the end of an official period of reformatory treatment, which includes parole in most cases. As the average period of treatment in this series was five years, the tables should be generally useful in determining the behavior of adult offenders (of the type usually sent to reformatories) in the age spans twenty-five to thirty, thirty to thirty-five, and thirty-five to forty years. Thus these tables deal with a significant segment of the lives of offenders, carrying the story of their careers well beyond adolescence and young manhood.

None of the relevant factors is discriminative in all three of these tables; but the following ones do reflect a significant difference in the recidivism rate among the subcategories involved in two of the tables: first is the factor that again and again has been shown to be of prime importance —*Age at Onset of Antisocial Behavior*, which is operative in Tables V–26 and V–27. Another factor affecting outcomes in two tables is *Work Habits of Offender* (Tables V–25 and V–26). A third is *Economic Responsibility of Offender* (Tables V–25 and V–26). A fourth is *Mental Disease or Distortion* (Tables V–25 and V–26); and the final factor involved in two of the three tables predicting post-treatment behavior is *Arrests Preceding Offense for Which Sentenced* (Tables V–25 and V–26).

Prediction of Behavior of Civilian Delinquents in Armed Services

The final series of tables presented in this chapter does not deal directly with the behavior of delinquents or criminals while undergoing one or another mode of peno-correctional treatment or thereafter. However, these tables are pertinent both in showing the relationship of a background of delinquency to the prediction of good or poor performance in the armed services—a matter of great importance to the military authorities in the selection and assignment of recruits—and in the fact that one of these tables has been at least partially checked[12] and suggests that this kind of predictive device is likely to be of real value in practice.

[12] See pp. 75–76.

One factor, *Industrial Skill of Offender,* occurs in all three tables (**Tables** V–28, V–29, and V–30). Two factors appear in two of the three tables: *Economic Status of Childhood Home* (Tables V–29 and V–30) and *Conjugal Relations of Parents* (Tables V–29 and V–30).

Summary Table V–G.   Prediction of Behavior of Civilian
Delinquents in Armed Forces

Period		Less than Even Chance of Maladaptation		More than Even Chance of Maladaptation	
		Score Class	(Rate)	Score Class	(Rate)
Armed Forces[1]	(V–28)	Less than 190	(30.6%)	190 or Over	(64.6%)
Armed Forces under 22 Years of Age[2]	(V–29)	Less than 280	(27.3)	280 or Over	(78.6)
Armed Forces at Ages 22 or Older[3]	(V–30)	Less than 200	(24.1)	200 or Over	(58.4)

[1] Predictive Factors: Education of Parents; Intelligence of Offender; Age at Onset of Antisocial Behavior; Age Began Work; Industrial Skill of Offender.

[2] Predictive Factors: Economic Status of Childhood Home; Conjugal Relations of Parents; Number of Children in Family of Offender; Grade Attained in School; Industrial Skill of Offender.

[3] Predictive Factors: Nativity of Offender; Economic Status of Childhood Home; Conjugal Relations of Parents; Adequacy of Childhood Home; Industrial Skill of Offender.

Note: Numbers in parentheses to right of period refer to table numbers in Appendix B; definitions of the predictive factors and the scores for the respective subcategories will also be found in Appendix B.

One Evidence of Validity of Prediction Tables Dealing with Adult Offenders

We should have liked to be able to report that the tables in the present chapter had been sufficiently validated to transform them from experience tables into prediction instrumentalities. However, thus far we have had an opportunity to check only one aspect of the table evolved to cover response to service in the Armed Forces. The test—and this was the first one among all the tables we have constructed to be subjected to checking—is based on 200 men in the United States Army who had been delinquents in civilian life and who then committed military offenses while in the Army. The problem posed was the extent to which it could have been foreseen, on the basis of our prediction table, that these men, formerly delinquents, would be military offenders. Since an article has been published describing this checking, those interested can refer to it.[13] It need only be said here

[13] A. J. N. Schneider, C. W. LaGrone, Jr., E. T. and S. Glueck, "Prediction of Behavior of Civilian Delinquents in the Armed Forces," 28 *Mental Hygiene* (1944), pp. 456–475.

that the data required to prepare the prediction scores on the 200 men were gathered by Army personnel. (The factors are *Education of Parents, Intelligence of Offender, Age at Onset of Antisocial Behavior, Age Began Work,* and *Industrial Skill of Offender.*) The final result indicated that the prediction table would have foretold that 168 of the 200 soldiers (84%) would be poor risks for the Armed Forces, in the sense that they would commit military offenses (absence without leave, desertion, theft, forgery, assault, etc.) and an additional 10.5% had about a fifty-fifty chance of committing military offenses.

Of particular encouragement in pursuing further checks on our prediction method is the discovery that certain important differences in the background of offenders seem not to affect the efficiency of the Army Prediction Table. For example, in the original series of 131 cases on which the Army table was constructed: all were residents of Massachusetts; 64.8% were Catholics; 31.3%, Protestants; and 3.9%, Hebrews. In the Army Rehabilitation Center series, on the other hand, the soldiers were residents of twenty-four different states; 20% were Catholics and 80%, Protestants. Another difference in the background of the two series is revealed in the fact that in the original series, 82.4% of the men came from large cities, 6.2% from small towns, and 11.4% from rural areas; while in the Army Rehabilitation Center series, 24.5% were from large cities, 37.0% came from small towns, and 38.5% from rural areas.

A weakness of the checkup on the efficiency of the Army table is that it deals with only "one side of the fence;" that is, while it shows a high incidence of correct predictions for those previously delinquent who also became delinquent in the Army, it does not cover the situation of those previously delinquent who stayed out of trouble in the Army. Thus far, such a test has not been made.

* * *

The foregoing discussion—dealing with tables that are to be regarded as experience tables until validated—has nevertheless yielded several clues to the special significance of certain factors in forecasting the probable behavior of adult offenders during various forms of peno-correctional treatment and for fifteen years after reformatory incarceration.

In the next chapter we examine the role of each of the predictive factors more intensively.

VI

Distribution of Predictive Factors Relating to Adult Male Offenders

Summary of Predictive Factors

In the analysis in the preceding chapter it became evident that certain factors play a much more permeative role in prognostication of behavior under various forms of peno-correctional treatment and thereafter than do others. The following chart brings out clearly the varying incidence of the different factors in the series of prediction tables presented in Chapter V.

Exhibit G.   Nature and Frequency of Predictive Factors in Series of Prediction Tables Dealing with Adult Male Offenders*

Factors	Tables
A. *Factors Pertaining to Nativity:*	
1. Nativity of Parents and Offender	7—Reformatories
	11—Prisons
	13—Prisons at 27 through 31 Years of Age
	16—Jails and Houses of Correction
2. Nativity of Offender	4—Probation with Suspended Sentence
	5—Probation with Suspended Sentence under 32 Years of Age
	24—Parole at Ages 27 or Older
	30—Civilian Delinquents in Armed Forces at Ages 22 or Older
B. *Economic Factors:*	
1. Economic Status of Childhood Home	3—Straight Probation at Ages 27 or Older
	6—Probation with Suspended Sentence at Ages 32 or Older
	10—Reformatories at Ages 27 or Older
	16—Jails and Houses of Correction
	18—Jails and Houses of Correction at 22 through 26 Years of Age

* Definitions of terms are alphabetically arranged in Appendix B, pp. 245–255.

Exhibit G (Continued)

Factors	Tables
1. Economic Status of Childhood Home (Continued)	19—Jails and Houses of Correction at 27 through 31 Years of Age 23—Parole at 22 through 26 Years of Age 27—Fifteen Years after Completion of First Reformatory Sentence 29—Armed Forces under 22 Years of Age 30—Armed Forces at Ages 22 or Older
2. Economic Responsibility of Offender	10—Reformatories at Ages 27 or Older 23—Parole at 22 through 26 Years of Age 25—Five Years after Completion of First Reformatory Sentence 26—Ten Years after Completion of First Reformatory Sentence
3. Work Habits of Offender	10—Reformatories at Ages 27 or Older 23—Parole at 22 through 26 Years of Age 25—Five Years after Completion of First Reformatory Sentence 26—Ten Years after Completion of First Reformatory Sentence
4. Industrial Skill of Offender	2—Straight Probation under 27 Years of Age 4—Probation with Suspended Sentence 6—Probation with Suspended Sentence at Ages 32 or Older 7—Reformatories 8—Reformatories at 17 through 21 Years of Age 12—Prisons under 27 Years of Age 15—Prisons at Ages 37 or Older 18—Jails and Houses of Correction at 22 through 26 Years of Age 19—Jails and Houses of Correction at 27 through 31 Years of Age 20—Jails and Houses of Correction at 32 through 36 Years of Age 22—Parole under 22 Years of Age 28—Armed Forces 29—Armed Forces under 22 Years of Age 30—Armed Forces at Ages 22 or Older
C. *Factor Pertaining to Religious Affiliation:*	
1. Church Attendance	1—Straight Probation 2—Straight Probation under 27 Years of Age
D. *Factors Pertaining to Family Life:*	
1. Number of Children in Family of Offender	1—Straight Probation 3—Straight Probation at Ages 27 or Older

78

Factors	Tables
1. Number of Children in Family of Offender (Continued)	6—Probation with Suspended Sentence at Ages 32 or Older 13—Prisons at 27 through 31 Years of Age 14—Prisons at 32 through 36 Years of Age 17—Jails and Houses of Correction under 22 Years of Age 18—Jails and Houses of Correction at 22 through 26 Years of Age 19—Jails and Houses of Correction at 27 through 31 Years of Age 21—Parole 27—Fifteen Years after Completion of First Reformatory Sentence 29—Armed Forces under 22 Years of Age
2. Rank of Offender among Siblings	15—Prisons at Ages 37 or Older 16—Jails and Houses of Correction 24—Parole at Ages 27 or Older
3. Family Relationships	1—Straight Probation 2—Straight Probation under 27 Years of Age 8—Reformatories at 17 through 21 Years of Age
4. Conjugal Relations of Parents	13—Prisons at 27 through 31 Years of Age 14—Prisons at 32 through 36 Years of Age 20—Jails and Houses of Correction at 32 through 36 Years of Age 29—Armed Forces under 22 Years of Age 30—Armed Forces at Ages 22 or Older
5. Education of Parents	1—Straight Probation 7—Reformatories 10—Reformatories at Ages 27 or Older 11—Prisons 12—Prisons under 27 Years of Age 13—Prisons at 27 through 36 Years of Age 21—Parole 28—Armed Forces
6. Industrial Skill of Father or Father Substitute	27—Fifteen Years after Completion of First Reformatory Sentence
7. Occupation of Mother	9—Reformatories at 22 through 26 Years of Age
8. Delinquency in Family	9—Reformatories at 22 through 26 Years of Age 22—Parole under 22 Years of Age 23—Parole at 22 through 26 Years of Age
9. Adequacy of Childhood Home	3—Straight Probation at Ages 27 or Older

Factors	Tables
9. Adequacy of Childhood Home (Continued)	7—Reformatories 9—Reformatories at 22 through 26 Years of Age 11—Prisons 12—Prisons under 27 Years of Age 14—Prisons at 32 through 36 Years of Age 17—Jails and Houses of Correction under 22 Years of Age 20—Jails and Houses of Correction at 32 through 36 Years of Age 21—Parole 23—Parole at 22 through 26 Years of Age 30—Armed Forces at Ages 22 or Older
10. Mobility	5—Probation with Suspended Sentence under 32 Years of Age 18—Jails and Houses of Correction at 22 through 26 Years of Age
E. *Factors Pertaining to Physical and Mental Condition of Offender:*	
1. Physical Condition	22—Parole under 22 Years of Age 24—Parole at Ages 27 or Older
2. Intelligence of Offender	4—Probation with Suspended Sentence 5—Probation with Suspended Sentence under 32 Years of Age 6—Probation with Suspended Sentence at Ages 32 or Older 8—Reformatories at 17 through 21 Years of Age 9—Reformatories at 22 through 26 Years of Age 11—Prisons 12—Prisons under 27 Years of Age 13—Prisons at 27 through 31 Years of Age 14—Prisons at 32 through 36 Years of Age 15—Prisons at Ages 37 or Older 19—Jails and Houses of Correction at 27 through 31 Years of Age 21—Parole 27—Fifteen Years after Completion of First Reformatory Sentence 28—Armed Forces
3. Mental Disease or Distortion	3—Straight Probation at Ages 27 or Older 20—Jails and Houses of Correction at 32 through 36 Years of Age 25—Five Years after Completion of First Reformatory Sentence

80

Factors	Tables
3. Mental Disease or Distortion (Continued)	26—Ten Years after Completion of First Reformatory Sentence
F. *Factors Pertaining to School Life of Offender:*	
1. Grade Attained in School	4—Probation with Suspended Sentence 8—Reformatories at 17 through 21 Years of Age 14—Prisons at 32 through 36 Years of Age 15—Prisons at Ages 37 or Older 16—Jails and Houses of Correction 17—Jails and Houses of Correction under 22 Years of Age 21—Parole 29—Armed Forces under 22 Years of Age
2. School Misconduct	20—Jails and Houses of Correction at 32 through 36 Years of Age
G. *Factors Pertaining to Early Habits, Leisure, Work, or Conduct:*	
1. Bad Habits in Childhood	2—Straight Probation under 27 Years of Age 22—Parole under 22 Years of Age
2. Age First Left Home	17—Jails and Houses of Correction under 22 Years of Age
3. Age Began Work	16—Jails and Houses of Correction 18—Jails and Houses of Correction at 22 through 26 Years of Age 19—Jails and Houses of Correction at 27 through 31 Years of Age 28—Armed Forces
4. Use of Leisure	5—Probation with Suspended Sentence under 32 Years of Age 10—Reformatories at Ages 27 or Older 24—Parole at Ages 27 or Older
5. Age at Onset of Antisocial Behavior	1—Straight Probation 2—Straight Probation under 27 Years of Age 3—Straight Probation at Ages 27 or Older 4—Probation with Suspended Sentence 5—Probation with Suspended Sentence under 32 Years of Age 6—Probation with Suspended Sentence at Ages 32 or Older 7—Reformatories 8—Reformatories at 17 through 21 Years of Age

Exhibit G (Concluded)

Factors	Tables
5. Age at Onset of Antisocial Behavior (Continued)	9—Reformatories at 22 through 26 Years of Age 11—Prisons 12—Prisons under 27 Years of Age 15—Prisons at Ages 37 or Older 17—Jails and Houses of Correction under 22 Years of Age 22—Parole under 22 Years of Age 24—Parole at Ages 27 or Older 26—Ten Years after Completion of First Reformatory Sentence 27—Fifteen Years after Completion of First Reformatory Sentence 28—Armed Forces
H. *Factors Pertaining to Prior Criminal Record:*	
1. Seriousness and Frequency of Prereformatory Crimes	25—Five Years after Completion of Reformatory Sentence
2. Arrests Preceding Offense for Which Sentenced	25—Five Years after Completion of First Reformatory Sentence 26—Ten Years after Completion of First Reformatory Sentence
3. Penal Experiences Prior to Reformatory Sentence	25—Five Years after Completion of First Reformatory Sentence

Permeative Predictive Factors

Some very interesting facts are revealed in the foregoing Exhibit.

First and foremost, it will be observed that the factor, *Age at Onset of Antisocial Behavior*, which we have emphasized at various stages in the preceding discussion, appears in the largest proportion of the prediction tables: that is, in no fewer than *eighteen* of the thirty tables dealing with adult offenders. Granting that some of these tables involve rather small numbers, the phenomenon in question cannot be due to chance. It will be recalled that *Age at Onset of Antisocial Behavior* was also found in three of the ten tables concerned with the behavior of juvenile delinquents. In all but four of the tables dealing with adult offenders, *the earlier the onset of delinquency, the higher the failure score* under one or another form of peno-correctional treatment and thereafter;[1] or, to put it differently, the deeper the roots of childhood maladjustment, the smaller the chance of

[1] Tables V–1, V–2, V–3, and V–17 show a reverse trend.

adult adjustment. Thus it can be taken as quite clearly established that the deep-rootedness of the antisocial behavioral manifestations exerts a continuing influence throughout the careers of delinquents and criminals. One would be justified in inferring that this factor must also be crucially significant in connection with the *etiology* of delinquency. This inference is supported by our researches which have demonstrated that some nine-tenths of a sample of 500 persistent delinquents (compared with a matched sample of 500 true non-delinquents, all resident in underprivileged urban areas) first showed signs of behavioral maladjustment that could be interpreted as prodromal of delinquency when they were but ten years of age or younger,[2] while the average age of first known misbehavior of another large sample of urban delinquents investigated by us previously was also low—nine years and seven months.[3]

When it is borne in mind that the juvenile court (with or without clinical and other adjuncts) does not normally take hold of delinquents until they are about twelve to fifteen years of age,[4] the crying need for much earlier preventive and therapeutic intervention is apparent. But more timely concern involves the determination of which children, among all those showing signs of behavioral and emotional maladjustment, are true delinquents and which are pseudodelinquents, or youngsters who are merely trying their wings and finding it difficult for a time to adjust their impulses to the prohibitions of the social and legal codes, but destined finally to master a legally acceptable balance between desire and prohibition. More timely concern with the problem of delinquency also involves the determination of which children who do not yet display any overt signs of maladjustment, whether of a kind that will disappear with time or of a kind prodromal of later habitual antisocial behavior, are probably headed for delinquent careers in the absence of early therapy and re-education. And for these purposes prediction tables are of the utmost promise. Relevant devices to discover *potential* delinquents or

[2] S. and E. Glueck, *Unraveling Juvenile Delinquency*, New York, The Commonwealth Fund, 1950, p. 28. The mean age was 8.35 years (S.D. 2.39 years).

[3] For 643 boys about whom the age of first or early delinquency was known (out of a sample of 1,000). S. and E. T. Glueck, *One Thousand Juvenile Delinquents*, Cambridge, Mass., Harvard University Press, 1934, p. 95.

[4] The average age of the delinquents in *Unraveling Juvenile Delinquency* at the time of their first court appearance was 12.4 years (±2.1), and 25.8% were first summoned at the ages of 14, 15, or 16. *Unraveling Juvenile Delinquency*, p. 27. The mean age at first arrest of the boys involved in *One Thousand Juvenile Delinquents* was 11 years, 11 months (A. D. ±2). *One Thousand Juvenile Delinquents*, p. 97.

predelinquents very early in life—at five or six years of age—are presented in Chapter IX.

Another factor that has been found to be permeatively associated with maladaptation of adult offenders is *Intelligence of Offender* which is involved in *fourteen* of the thirty tables. With the exception of three tables,[5] *the poorer the intellect of offenders, the higher the failure score*, both during and after various forms of peno-correctional treatment. As is true in other walks of life, this finding shows that the role of intelligence is important in connection with the response of offenders to efforts to correct and rehabilitate them. (The consistency of the results indicates the reliability of the mental tests to which these men were subjected at various stages in their careers.)

Another factor—*Industrial Skill of Offender*—is involved in *fourteen* of the thirty tables concerning adult offenders. With the exception of two of the tables,[6] *the lower the industrial capacity of offenders, the higher their failure rate in various forms of peno-correctional treatment and beyond.*

Two factors—*Number of Children in Family of Offender* and *Adequacy of Childhood Home*—are involved in *eleven* of the thirty tables dealing with adult offenders.

In regard to *Number of Children in Family of Offender*, it is found that in seven of the eleven tables,[7] *the larger the family in which an offender was reared, the lower the probability of misbehavior during adult life under various forms of peno-correctional treatment.*

In regard to *Adequacy of Childhood Home*, in six of the eleven tables, offenders who came from broken or distorted households have the highest misbehavior scores;[8] in five, the reverse is true.

One factor—*Economic Status of Childhood Home*—is associated with behavioral outcomes in *ten* of the tables. With the exception of three tables,[9] *offenders whose childhood homes were of poorer economic status turned out to be the better risks under various forms of peno-correctional treatment than those who came from more comfortable homes.* Thus, poor economic influences in childhood do not necessarily affect adult behavior adversely. Indeed, it may well be that an institution provides a level of

[5] The exceptions are Tables V–4, V–5, and V–6.
[6] Tables V–6 and V–15.
[7] Tables V–1, V–3, V–6, V–17, V–21, V–27, and V–29.
[8] Tables V–3, V–7, V–9, V–17, V–21, and V–23; Tables V–11, V–12, V–14, V–20, and V–30 indicate an opposite trend.
[9] Tables V–3, V–10, and V–23.

comfort and security greatly needed by those who have been denied them in childhood, for there affairs of life are planned and ordered by a protective authority.

Two factors—*Education of Parents* and *Grade Attained in School*—are related to failure scores in *eight* of the tables. In regard to *Education of Parents*, with the exception of one table,[10] *the lower the educational achievement of the parents of adult offenders, the higher the failure score of the latter under various modes of peno-correctional treatment.* Thus, education of parents, and all that this implies and reflects, turns out to be frequently prodromal of the kind of behavior that is to be expected by adult offenders under various forms of peno-correctional treatment.

In regard to *Grade Attained in School*, in four of the eight tables, *the lower the grade achieved by offenders during their school days, the higher their misbehavior scores as adults under various forms of peno-correctional treatment;*[11] in the remaining four, the reverse is true.[12] Here, as in other factors, what appears to be an erratic result may well be a statistical artifact due to smallness of numbers in some of the tables.

Conjugal Relations of Parents turns up as a predictive factor in *five* of the tables. One might expect that where the relationship of the parents of the offender to each other had been poor, the response of the latter to the types of peno-correctional treatment involved would be worse than where the conjugal relations were good or at least fair. This holds true in only one table (Table V–29). With this exception, the opposite occurs. The explanation might well be that modes of peno-correctional treatment, however poor they may be, are nevertheless a matrix of security and protection badly missed by offenders in childhood and to some extent belatedly supplied by prison, jail, and military service.

The following six factors have been found to be related in *four* of the prediction tables to behavioral response to the various forms of treatment involved:

> *Nativity of Parents and Offender*
> *Nativity of Offender*
> *Economic Responsibility of Offender*
> *Work Habits of Offender*
> *Mental Disease or Distortion*
> *Age Began Work*

[10] Table V–28.
[11] Tables V–8, V–14, V–15, and V–21.
[12] Tables V–4, V–16, V–17, and V–29.

85

In respect to *Nativity of Parents and Offender*, it would appear that whatever inference there may be about the role of culture conflict in originating delinquency, this factor is not of great importance as a predictor.

In respect to *Nativity of Offender* himself, native-born offenders appear less likely to adapt well to correctional treatment than foreign-born offenders.[13] Perhaps the latter have a greater regard for authority as part of their cultural experience.

In regard to *Economic Responsibility of Offender*, criminals classifiable as failing to meet their financial obligations to the family are the ones who have the highest rate of misbehavior.

With reference to *Work Habits of Offender*, in the four tables involved[14] the situation is as expected: those with poor work habits have a higher failure score than the others.

As to *Mental Disease or Distortion*, offenders with a background of mental disease or distortion have, as is to be expected, a higher misbehavior rate than normal offenders in the four tables involved.[15]

In respect to *Age Began Work*, offenders who began work early might perhaps be anticipated to have a higher misbehavior score than those who were not subjected to the attendant hazards until a later age; yet, in the four tables involved,[16] the reverse is true. It may well be that the boys who "get out and hustle" early in life are the more enterprising ones and of better "stuff." We can only speculate about this and hope that studies by others will be more definitive.

Some Generalizations Concerning Predictive Factors

It will be helpful now to draw together the principles respecting the role of various factors which have been found to be relevant in a considerable number of the tables:

1. The earlier the onset of delinquency, the greater the chances of misbehavior during treatment.
2. The poorer the intellect of offenders, the greater the chances of misbehavior during treatment.

[13] Tables V–4, V–5, V–24, and V–30.
[14] Tables V–10, V–23, V–25, and V–26.
[15] Tables V–3, V–20, V–25, and V–26.
[16] Tables V–16, V–18, V–19, and V–28.

3. The lower the industrial capacity of offenders, the greater the chances of misbehavior during treatment.
4. The smaller the family from which offenders stem, the greater the chances of misbehavior during treatment.
5. Within the rather limited financial situation of our cases, the better the economic status of the childhood homes, the greater the chances of misbehavior during treatment.
6. The lower the educational achievement of the parents, the greater the chances of misbehavior during treatment.

It is to be borne in mind that these generalizations have been derived from the considerable majority, but not necessarily from all, of the tables involved.

There are a few other generalizations that emerge from the foregoing analysis, but inasmuch as these are based on small numbers of tables we prefer to present them separately:

1. Offenders with a background of mental disease or distortion have a greater chance of misbehaving during treatment.
2. Offenders who began to work *later* in life rather than earlier have a greater chance of misbehaving during treatment.
3. Offenders who fail to meet their family economic obligations have a greater chance of misbehaving during treatment.

In connection with the foregoing summation, it should be pointed out that while certain valuable general principles have emerged inductively from analysis of a network of prediction tables covering a considerable variety of samples of delinquents and criminals, there may well be additional ones. Our researches are based only on samples of cases; and samples are necessarily but a fraction of the entire universe of phenomena under study. Moreover, it will be recalled that we have sometimes allowed certain practical considerations to dictate the inclusion in a table of a factor which is not quite as differentiative of acceptable and unacceptable behavior under a particular form of peno-correctional treatment as some other factor might have been.

VII

Prediction of Behavior of Female Offenders

Introduction

Predictive instrumentalities are of no less promise in making judicial, institutional (classification), and parole decisions in respect to female offenders than in the case of male criminals.

The prediction tables in this chapter, while not as comprehensive in scope as the ones dealing with male adult criminals, are the first instruments for forecasting the behavior of women offenders that have been developed. They are based on our follow-up study, *Five Hundred Delinquent Women*,[1] an analysis of the make-up, treatment, and significant aspects of the careers of female offenders sentenced to the Massachusetts Reformatory for Women. Offenders are sent to that institution for a variety of offenses running the entire gamut of crimes.

Certain comments about institutions devoted to the peno-correctional treatment of female offenders which we made at the threshold of *Five Hundred Delinquent Women* are perhaps still relevant and bear repetition:

Despite the fact that there are substantially fewer female than male offenders in penal and correctional institutions and under parole oversight, they bulk large in any statement of the weighty problems of social policy and social engineering dealt with by penologists. The more progressive correctional institutions for women have served as experiment stations in testing various correctional practices which many penal institutions for men might, with appropriate modification, profitably take over.[2] However, not all of the institutions for women offenders are of this nature. In some penal institutions,

[1] New York, Knopf, 1934.

[2] "These reformatories represent a marked advance in methods of caring for women prisoners. From many of them, particularly those of Massachusetts, New York, New Jersey, Pennsylvania, Connecticut, and the Federal Reformatory, the institutions for men can learn valuable lessons." P. W. Garrett and A. H. MacCormick, *Handbook of American Prisons and Reformatories*, New York, 1929, p. xxxiii. Quoted in *Five Hundred Delinquent Women*, p. 4, note 5.

correctional farms, and training schools both male and female prisoners are housed and varying degrees of classification are applied to them. There are some separate correctional and reformatory institutions for women which, regardless of their names, are essentially prisons in both spirit and regime.[3]

As concerns the Massachusetts Reformatory for Women, we think it probable that its regime, under the late Mrs. Jessie D. Hodder, was well above the average among reformatories in the United States. Readers who desire details about the procedure at the Massachusetts Reformatory and the accompanying parole practices in the 1920s, when the women who formed the subject of *Five Hundred Delinquent Women* were inmates, are invited to consult Chapter I of that volume.

A major aspect of the influence of a reformatory regime to which we gave special emphasis refers to the role of native endowment in the reformative process. After detailed analyses of numerous factors, certain conclusions emerged which are relevant to the background against which the tables to be presented in this chapter are projected. The Conclusion of Chapter XV of *Five Hundred Delinquent Women* is as follows:

> The foregoing analysis has shown that even where the rehabilitation of our women may be credited to the efforts of the Reformatory, the peculiarly favorable make-up and background of these women largely contributed to the good result. Consequently, the rehabilitation of those offenders whose good behavior after the expiration of sentence cannot fairly be assigned at all to the Reformatory (or to the parole system) must even more markedly be due to their advantageous background and traits. *Per contra*, recidivism for all or part of the post-parole period must be charged largely to the unfavorable characteristics of this particular group.
>
> It is to the delineation of the traits and background of these various types of women as related to their conduct during the post-parole period that we now turn our attention. Through such analyses are reflected the major reasons for continued recidivism or for such reformation in conduct after expiration of sentence as obviously cannot be attributed to the influence of the Reformatory.[4]

And after analyzing the relevant traits and background characteristics of the women in Chapter XVI of *Five Hundred Delinquent Women*, "Other Reformative Influences," we arrived at the following conclusion:

> What is the significance of these findings? They reveal that the reformation of an offender is dependent upon at least two sets of variables, (a) an endowment (native and acquired) which is favorable to reform, and (b) particular treatments or conditions to which offenders having certain characteristics are

[3] *Five Hundred Delinquent Women*, p. 4.
[4] *Ibid.*, p. 263.

most likely to respond. The fact that certain of our women and not others responded to Reformatory treatment or to parole treatment is proof of this point.

In the second place, our findings bring us closer to the intricate problem of crime-causation as contrasted with recidivism, in giving us a means of isolating in what seems to be a logical manner, causative factors from others. We have pointed out, for example, that certain influences in the lives of offenders may be of considerable significance in criminogenesis, but probably bear only a doubtful relationship to recidivism or reform.

Thirdly, findings like the foregoing furnish an approach to a better management of the crime problem (particularly as concerns women offenders) than at present exists; for they indicate that it is possible to fit to any specific type of offender the treatment most promising to her, thereby substituting a scientific methodology for the existing practice of working more or less in the dark. Obviously, it is not the Reformatory or the parole system or any incidental experience or treatment such as marriage, absorbing work, or "rule by an iron hand," or living in a protected environment, *alone*, that brings about the desired result of reformation, but rather the interaction of such experiences with certain characteristics found in the background and careers of certain offenders who respond to them.

Findings such as these (some of which have not been worked out in detail because further research materials are necessary) should enable the authorities to tell *in advance* of sentence or of release of prisoners, which types of offenders are likely to recidivate (under the existing regime), which are likely to respond immediately to Reformatory and parole treatment, and which may reform later, provided certain circumstances become operative in their lives. This should aid in distinguishing the offenders who require lengthy incarceration (or even lifelong isolation and control) from those who may profitably be handled on probation rather than by the more stringent and expensive method of incarceration; and more thought and time might well be expended by all concerned on offenders of the type of our up-grade delinquents than upon those who are very likely to be permanent offenders.

An instrumentality which is practicable in forecasting recidivism as well as the treatment likely to be most suitable to various types of offenders is presented . . . , to be used as a possible model in furthering the development of this phase of the new penology.[5]

Method of Constructing Prediction Tables

An examination of Tables VII–1, VII–2, and VII–3 in Appendix B, will indicate that in *Five Hundred Delinquent Women* we employed a method of constructing the prediction tables different from the other methods thus far presented: the five factors constituting the table predicting behavior in the reformatory are repeated in the table predicting the

[5] *Ibid.*, pp. 282–283.

behavior of female offenders during parole from the reformatory and also in the table predicting their behavior five years after the completion of the reformatory sentences, but in Table VII–2 a sixth factor has been added, and in Table VII–3 the six factors of Table VII–2 are repeated and a seventh is added. An examination of the prediction tables in our first volume, *500 Criminal Careers*,[6] will reveal that there, also, we had utilized this additive method of constructing predictive devices. Although after the publication of *Five Hundred Delinquent Women* we no longer continued to construct prediction tables in this way, there is no reason to believe that the method is not a sound one; on the contrary, it brings out the cumulative effect of certain influences with the passage of time and the subjection of offenders to various forms of correction and supervision. Students of delinquency prediction will want to experiment with these and other methods.

The three tables comprising the present chapter are summarized in Summary Table VII–A.

Summary Table VII–A. Prediction of Behavior of Female Offenders

Type of Treatment or Period		Less than Even Chance of Maladaptation, Violation, or Recidivism		More than Even Chance of Maladaptation, Violation, or Recidivism	
		Score Class	(Rate)	Score Class	(Rate)
Reformatory[1]	(VII–1)	Less than 325	(0.0%)	325 or Over	(78.6%)
Parole[2]	(VII–2)	Less than 400	(0.0)	400 or Over	(78.1)
Five Years after Completion of First Reformatory Sentence[3]	(VII–3)	Less than 475	(0.0)	475 or Over	(82.5)

[1] Predictive Factors: Mental Disease or Distortion; School Retardation; Neighborhood Influences; Steadiness of Employment; Economic Responsibility of Offender.
[2] Predictive Factors: Same five as in footnote (1), above; plus Kind of Worker in Reformatory.
[3] Predictive Factors: Same six as in footnote (2), above; plus Recreations and Interests during Parole.
Note: Numbers in parentheses to right of type of treatment or period refer to table numbers in Appendix B; definitions of the predictive factors and the scores for the respective subcategories will also be found in Appendix B.

Prediction of Behavior in Reformatories

Table VII–1 of the present series deals with the response of female offenders to the reformatory regime. From such a table, a judge, in questioning whether or not to sentence a woman to an institution of this same general type, can be aided in determining the advisability of such

[6] S. and E. T. Glueck, New York, Knopf, 1930. See Chapter 18.

disposition, providing of course the investigation report furnished by his probation officer contains reliable data on the five relevant factors in the defendant's history. If, for example, the offender scores less than 325, it will be evident to the judge that the woman before him for sentence has a very good chance of a successful adaptation to the reformatory regime. If, on the other hand, the score is 325 or greater the judge will see at a glance that the probabilities of the woman's maladaptation are considerable. If the judge should have similar prognostic tables for each of the other possible forms of treatment at his command (straight probation, probation with suspended sentence, incarceration in a jail, or imprisonment in an institution of severer and more mechanical regime than the reformatory), he would (as in the case of male offenders) be in a position to determine which, among alternative remedies provided by society, is on the whole the most promising. Unfortunately, we have not developed tables for female offenders to cover all existing forms of treatment. But with Table VII–1 of the present series before him, the judge can at least rule out commitment to a reformatory type of institution if the probabilities of poor response to such a regime are very high.

Prediction of Behavior on Parole

Tables VII–2 and VII–3 are intended for the use of parole boards in determining which inmates of a reformatory for women to release on parole[7] and how long to keep various types of female parolees under extramural oversight. Table VII–2 is based on the same five factors which entered into composition of the first table, plus the most significant factor in the reformatory life of the women, namely, their work habits in the institution. Other factors in the reformatory experience might have been used in the construction of the table; but *Kind of Worker in Reformatory*

[7] As long as a system of completely indeterminate sentences does not exist, it is preferable that *all* prisoners, since they must be released from prison at some time, be placed under some parole supervision rather than sent out into the community without any oversight during the hazardous transitional period from imprisonment to freedom. However, society may before long evolve other forms of extramural treatment in addition to parole or release without any supervision at all; for example, oversight by the police; or "preventive detention," as applied in Continental countries; or a system analogous to the indenture practices formerly employed in certain cases by the Reformatory for Women in Massachusetts; or the more recent practice of allowing some inmates to go out into the community to work during the day. In such an event, prediction tables based on a statistical transcription of experience with hundreds of women treated extramurally by these various methods will be of value to the authorities charged with releasing prisoners from correctional institutions.

bears the most marked relationship to recidivism, and information regarding such a factor is readily available. Since inclusion of but one additional factor yields an adequately high measure of predictability, there is little point in using additional factors for this purpose.[8]

From Table VII–2, parole authorities can see at a glance that a woman inmate of a reformatory whose violation score mounts to 400 has more than an even chance of misbehaving on parole; while one whose total rating on the six factors involved is less than 400 is likely to do well under extramural oversight.

In addition to determining whether to release a prisoner on parole, the authorities may want to decide, from time to time, which parolees to continue further on parole and which to discharge from supervision. Too often, parole boards have to rely upon rather meagre reports they receive from their agents regarding the conduct of parolees, whose supervision is generally terminated if they have apparently abided by the rules of the parole permit. Our research has shown, however, that some offenders, though good parolees, are still dangerous when released from official oversight.[9] Table VII–3 ought, therefore, to be of practical value to parole boards in administering a wholly indeterminate sentence, if such type of statute be enacted, and also (under existing upper-limit sentences) in determining which offenders can be released from a reformatory with only brief or casual supervision. For the purpose of this predictive instrument we might have used any one of several other factors in the parole experiences of our women which were found to bear a considerable relationship to recidivism.[10] But, again, in the light of practical considerations, and because the factor, *Recreations and Interests during Parole*, was found to bear the highest association with recidivism after expiration of sentence, this factor alone was added to those used in Table VII–2.

We have not yet mentioned those women who served their full sentence in the reformatory without any parole. In order to make the prognostic

---

[8] Some critics of prediction methods in sentencing have erroneously assumed that prediction tables will replace the probation officer's investigation report. On the contrary, much of the information helpful in framing a plan of treatment in the individual case will be retained in the investigation report, but the report will be more realistic if it includes the factors found to be significant for prediction purposes.

[9] *Five Hundred Delinquent Women*, footnote 2, pp. 252–253.

[10] These were (in parentheses is the subclass of each factor having the *lowest* proportion of recidivists): *Recreations and Interests* (constructive); *Leisure and Habits* (constructive); *Industrial History* (successful); *Work Habits* (good); *Economic Responsibility* (responsible); *Steadiness of Employment* (regular).

table more useful, provision was made for this class of female offender also. From Table VII–3, a parole board can see that an inmate of a reformatory who is to be released only after expiration of the full sentence, as well as one already on parole, whose score on the seven factors mounts to 475 or over, has more than an even chance of engaging in further criminality. On the other hand, one whose total score on the seven factors is less than 475 will very probably not recidivate. In this connection, it should be borne in mind that the test span involved is five years after end of parole (or sentence, where no parole was granted). Regrettably, we did not follow our female offenders beyond the five-year period.

Under the existing administration of criminal justice, a substantial proportion of defendants of all types appearing before criminal courts are already, or will become, recidivists. Under a wholly indeterminate sentence, which some criminologists have regarded as a necessary adjunct to a modern system of peno-correctional treatment (with appropriate protections against abuse), it might be advisable to remove many of the repeated offenders from the horde of recidivists who today stumble in and out of courts and institutions. This does not mean that society will abandon and forget them, any more than it will stop research on the chronically and incurably ill among hospital patients. However, some means of reasonably accurate detection of the *chronically maladjusted offender*, from the point of view of the penal code, should be of value. As a rule, authorities are not concerned with the conduct of offenders after the outside limits of the sentence have been reached. Such an attitude, while natural enough in busy officials burdened with current cases, is, from the point of view of the protection of society, shortsighted. It is an illustration of what, we venture to assert, is probably a major weakness in the process of administering criminal justice; namely, that each official, stationed at one point on the offender's *via dolorosa* from arrest to his return to society, regards his particular post as the all-important one, and his part in the process as a specific and isolated end in itself. He is all too prone to overlook the fact that his function is intimately related to those which precede and succeed his and that, whatever may be stressed as the major aim of the criminal law, it cannot be denied that the ultimate object of it all is to prevent further depredations on social values protected by law. Of what use to society are good parolees, for example, if they relapse into delinquency and crime as soon as parole supervision is removed? Obviously, therefore, parole boards and courts should take into account the behavior of

94

offenders not only when behind lock, bar, and wall, or under parole super-vision, but during a reasonable period—in the study on which the tables in this chapter are based, five years—after the expiration of sentence. This will be especially important if the suggestion is adopted that *all* ex-prisoners—including those not released on parole before expiration of sentence—are placed in the community under some form of oversight for a time.

A very important principle is suggested by the three tables under dis-cussion. A basic weakness in the administration of criminal justice is the lack of planning and continuity in the correctional process. If the informa-tion gathered at the first court appearance of an offender could be centralized so that not only the parole board but subsequent courts would have the benefit of it, investigative time and effort would be saved and better planning and consistency would evolve in the treatment of each offender. A continuing dossier on each offender, with emphasis placed on relevant predictive factors, might turn out to be an important instrument of integration of the processes of criminal justice.

Comparison of Predictive Factors for Female and Male Offenders

Comparing the factors found to be associated with varied behavioral response to the reformatory and parole regimes among women with those found to be relevant in the prediction tables pertaining to male offenders, the following interesting points emerge.

Mental Disease or Distortion, included in all the tables of the present series, was previously found to be relevant to male offenders in Tables V–3 (straight probation at ages twenty-seven or older); V–20 (jail and house of correction at thirty-two to thirty-six years of age); V–25 (five-year follow-up); and V–26 (ten-year follow-up). In the tables in this chapter, as in those on male criminals, it was established that offenders classifiable as not mentally abnormal had less likelihood of maladapted behavior than those suffering from identifiable mental aberrations.

School Retardation, included in the three tables of the series dealing with female offenders, was also found to be relevant in the following tables pertaining to juvenile delinquents: III–1 (straight probation); III–4 (correctional school under seventeen years of age); III–5 (correctional school at seventeen through twenty-one years of age); and III–7 (five-year follow-up). In all these tables, the offenders who had not been retarded in school had a lower chance of misbehavior than those who had been.

95

Neighborhood Influences, a factor included throughout the present series, had not been found to be sufficiently associated with future behavior of either male juvenile delinquents or male adult offenders to be included in any of the tables presented in Chapters III and V. In the case of female offenders, unwholesome neighborhood influences in childhood were found to result in poorer adaptation to the reformatory regime, to parole, and thereafter. It is conceivable that environmental influences have a greater bearing on the course of behavior of female offenders than of male.

Steadiness of Employment (from beginning of work history to first arrest) is included in Tables VII–1, VII–2, and VII–3 of this series; and it was found that the steady workers have a lesser likelihood of maladapted behavior. While this specific factor has not appeared in prior prediction tables, analogous or related factors have. One of these is *Work Habits of Offender*, which appeared previously in Tables V–10 (reformatory at ages twenty-seven or older); V–23 (parole at twenty-two to twenty-six years of age); V–25 (five-year follow-up); and V–26 (ten-year follow-up). Another related factor previously shown to be associated with behavior is *Industrial Skill of Offender* which has been found relevant in no fewer than fourteen of the tables dealing with male adult offenders.[11]

Economic Responsibility is associated with the behavior of female offenders in the three tables of the series to which this chapter is devoted. The women who met their economic obligations to the family are less likely to misbehave than the others. This factor was found to be predictive among adult male offenders in Tables V–10 (reformatory at ages twenty-seven or older); V–23 (parole at twenty-two to twenty-six years of age); V–25 (five-year follow-up); and V–26 (ten-year follow-up). It also played a role in Table III–5 (male juvenile delinquents in correctional schools at seventeen through twenty-one years of age).

* * *

By way of emphasis of some points previously made regarding the promise of the predictive instrument in the management of criminal justice, we present, in conclusion to this chapter, a passage from *Five Hundred Delinquent Women* (long since out of print):

> If the discipline of Criminology ever reaches a point where it can accurately foretell the behavior of various types of offenders, it will enter on a new and far-reaching era of development. The first steps toward such an evolution have

---

[11] See Chapter V, Tables 2, 4, 6, 7, 8, 12, 15, 18, 19, 20, 22, 28, 29, and 30.

been taken in recent years by the creation of several types of prognostic devices to be used by parole boards and, as the authors have urged, by sentencing authorities. Without the employment of such devices the definite effects of treatment applied by correctional agencies can never be put to a test; the types of offenders who require prolonged or permanent custodial care cannot be differentiated; the length of extramural supervision needed by different classes of offenders cannot definitely be determined. Correctional and parole officials, as well as judges sentencing offenders, are still working more or less in the dark. . . .

It is often argued that the "practical experience" and "wisdom" of the sentencing, correctional, and paroling authorities is adequate to the task of choosing the particular form of treatment required in the individual case; of determining when and if to release any offender on parole, and which offenders to incarcerate permanently. But even the most intelligent officials work blindly as long as they do not consider each case which comes before them in the light of past outcomes in hundreds of similar cases. They cannot rely on their memories of what happened to various types of offenders whom they previously sentenced, or released on parole. A systematic study of the results of different forms of penal treatment is certainly essential if the disposition of cases is to be guided scientifically on the basis of previous experience. The present research is an effort in that direction.

The staff of the Massachusetts Reformatory for Women is particularly intelligent and forward-looking. The superintendent[12] and her aids made certain recommendations and prognoses in many of our cases. In not a few instances their prognoses were wrong and might have worked great havoc because of the very circumstance that these cases had not been considered in the light of a scientific analysis of experience with hundreds of similar cases. Actually, of seventy-eight cases in which they made a prognosis, subsequent outcomes revealed that they had grossly erred in at least two fifths of their prognoses.

Consider these illustrations: In one instance the staff recommended that a woman be placed in permanent custody. Examination into the behavior of this woman during the five-year period following the expiration of her sentence revealed that she had in fact made a very satisfactory adjustment in freedom. Had the Reformatory officials utilized predictive tables based on a study of the post-institutional adjustment of hundreds of women, they would have seen that this inmate had more than an even chance of adjustment if released on parole, a fact borne out by her subsequent reformation. The Reformatory officials prognosticated that another inmate would "revert to shiftlessness," and averred that "she is of the kind who does not profit much by experience or counsel." It happened, however, that this woman married and settled down nicely. Her home is neat and clean; she takes good care of her children and is no longer delinquent. Again, had the officials consulted

[12] This refers to the late Jessie D. Hodder.

prognostic tables which objectively embodied experience with similar cases, they would hardly have fallen into such a marked error of judgment, for the factors in the make-up and career of the woman indicated in advance that her rehabilitation was very probable. In still another case the Reformatory staff was of the conviction that there is "nothing about her which is at all hopeful for the future." Here again the woman in question was completely rehabilitated, and use of predictive instruments would have shown a great likelihood of this eventuality. One more case may be cited, showing that "common sense" must be supported by scientific method if true progress is to be achieved in dealing with the criminal classes. In this case the Reformatory officials recommended to the parole board that the offender, who was a mental defective, be committed to a school for the feeble-minded. The family of the offender, on the other hand, urged that the authorities "give her a chance in the community first on parole." She was paroled only because there was no room for her in the school for the feeble-minded. The ultimate outcome proved that the family was far wiser in its suggestion for treatment than the Reformatory officials; for the woman, who has been watched closely by her relatives, is leading a decent life. All of which illustrates the fact that the Reformatory officials cannot really develop expertness in gauging the future conduct of inmates without checking their prognoses in numerous cases. The "common sense" approach may supplement, but it certainly cannot replace, the less impressionistic approach offered in the predictive tables. . . .[13]

[13] *Five Hundred Delinquent Women*, pp. 284–286.

VIII

Illustration of Application of Prediction Tables

Introduction

We have presented prediction tables indicating the probable behavior of juvenile delinquents during each form of peno-correctional treatment, and tables indicating their probable behavior five to fifteen years after completion of their first sentence by a juvenile court. We have also presented a series of tables to be applied to adult offenders. It is our aim in this chapter to illustrate the use of these tables as an aid to the sentencing and paroling of offenders.

A judge, whether of a juvenile or an adult court, in deciding which, among several alternatives presented to him by the law governing disposition of the cases of delinquents, does not have many alternatives: probation (with or without suspended sentence to an institution and with or without a requirement of restitution or reparation), commitment to one of two or three institutions, and, very occasionally, a fine. However, even in the selection of the most promising disposition among these relatively few alternatives, the judge has a most difficult choice to make. He can either operate by some mechanical rule[1] or bring to bear his wisdom and experience. But even the latter, unaided by some device for focusing on each case the organized and meaningful precipitate of experience with similar cases, is not likely to be very successful. In some courts, the judge has little to go on except the facts of the offense and perhaps the prior criminal record; in many, nowadays, he has a more elaborate investigation report made by a probation officer; in a few, he has the aid of

---

[1] "Disposition is a function of clinical judgment, of which treatment is the consequence. Notwithstanding, in many courts (how many, it would be difficult to document), probation and institutionalization are mechanically and impatiently applied with little or no thought, induced through careful study, given to human needs. . . ." F. W. Killian, "The Juvenile Court as an Institution," 261 *Annals* (1949), p. 97.

a guidance clinic[2] staffed by psychiatrists and psychologists. But even with the best of such resources he must still make the choice among alternative methods of treatment. The probation officer's investigation report and even the recommendations of a clinic can only suggest what might be done; they do not indicate the relative weights to be assigned to the various factors as determined by the relationship of such data to behavior. It is in the process of choosing the most promising alternative among the several at his command for dealing with the particular case before him, that the judge might find prediction tables helpful.

Obviously, if a judge is shown that, in the light of systematized experience with other cases, an offender characterized by a certain pattern of traits and background factors tends to behave more satisfactorily under one form of peno-correctional treatment than under another, he might welcome such devices. This does not mean that he would necessarily follow the indication of prediction tables in the instant case; for it may be that other considerations would have a greater bearing on his decision.

We have already cautioned that prediction tables cannot replace the wisdom and experience of a judge but rather that they are meant to serve as an aid to trained intuition and judgment. It is in this spirit that we present a few cases illustrating the use of prediction tables in the administration of justice.

Prediction Profiles of Juvenile Offenders

We shall illustrate the application of the tables to juvenile delinquents, preferably (though not necessarily) those appearing in juvenile court for the first time; for it is at this early stage in the officially-coped-with career of a young offender that society's major effort has to be expended toward making the wisest disposition of a case not only in the light of the delinquent's probable response to a particular form of treatment but of his ultimate adjustment as well.

At the outset we examine four cases of juvenile offenders to note the variations in the likelihood of adjustment of different offenders during and following the completion of the first correctional treatment (omitting fines)

[2] For a functional analysis showing the relationship of a clinic to a juvenile court, the extent to which the court followed the recommendations of the clinic and the differential results of the various dispositions where the judge followed or did not follow the clinical recommendations, see S. and E. T. Glueck, *One Thousand Juvenile Delinquents*, Cambridge, Mass., Harvard University Press, 1934, especially Chapters VII–XI.

that a juvenile court can prescribe. It should be pointed out that these illustrative profiles represent only three of seven different treatment profiles found among the delinquents of *Unraveling Juvenile Delinquency*. See Appendix C, Table 18.

Frank, twelve years of age, is before a juvenile court for the first time, arrested for the commission of a crime against property.

To understand how a juvenile court judge would apply the summary prediction tables presented in Chapter III, and in greater detail in Appendix B, the reader is asked to examine the case of Frank. Once the presentation becomes clear, there should be no difficulty either in preparing or using similar case charts whether they involve juvenile offenders or adult offenders (male or female). The method is the same, even though the age spans, the treatments, and the sex of the offenders differ. Once the data comprising a sample illustrative prediction chart are clearly understood, we can forego the details set forth in the case of Frank and confine ourselves to an indication of the relative chances that a particular offender has of adapting to various kinds of peno-correctional treatment and continuing or discontinuing his criminal behavior after the completion of sentence.

Prediction Profile of Frank

Since it is our hope that prediction tables, such as those presented in Chapter III, will be used in making decisions regarding offenders on their first appearance in court (on the assumption that the usefulness of the tables is at a peak near the initial stage of a criminal career), we have limited this illustration to six of the ten tables presented in Chapter III: namely, those dealing with behavior during straight probation, during probation with suspended sentence, in correctional schools, and on parole, and those dealing with the likelihood of ultimate social adjustment of a juvenile delinquent (five years and fifteen years) after the end of the correctional treatment first prescribed by a court.

In Frank's prediction profile which follows (Exhibit H) is indicated his status on each of the fifteen factors that enter into scoring him on the six relevant tables. First, it will be seen, for example, that Frank's father and mother had been in the United States for six years; that at the time of his appearance in juvenile court, Frank was one of eight children; that his father was an erratic disciplinarian; and so on. The reader will readily comprehend the remaining factors listed in Section A of the Profile.

Consultation of Appendix B, Table III–1, which deals with the prediction

Exhibit H. Prediction Profile of Frank at Twelve Years of Age
Section A

Predictive Factors*	Classification
Birthplace of Father	Ireland
Birthplace of Mother	Ireland
Time Parents Were in United States	Six years
Religion of Parents	Both Catholic
Number of Children in Family of Offender	Eight
Moral Standards of Home	Poor
Discipline by Father	Erratic
Discipline by Mother	Firm but kindly
Conjugal Relations of Parents	Fair
Affection of Father for Offender	Warm
Bad Habits in Childhood	Some
Age at Onset of Antisocial Behavior	Five years
School Retardation	Two years
School Misconduct	Truancy and other
Time Between Onset of Antisocial Behavior and First Arrest	Seven years

* For definitions of factors, see Appendix B, pp. 245–255.

Section B
Prediction Scores for Each Treatment or Post-Treatment Period

Type of Treatment (or Period) and Classification	Scores
STRAIGHT PROBATION	
Birthplace of Father: Ireland	53.7
Discipline by Father: Erratic	45.5
Discipline by Mother: Firm but kindly	15.4
School Retardation: Two years	62.7
School Misconduct: Truancy and other	62.1
Total	239.4
PROBATION WITH SUSPENDED SENTENCE	
Birthplace of Father: Ireland	78.4
Discipline by Father: Erratic	55.8
Discipline by Mother: Firm but kindly	33.3
Affection of Father for Offender: Warm	64.1
School Misconduct: Truancy and other	73.9
Total	305.5

Exhibit H.   Prediction Profile of Frank at Twelve Years of Age (Continued)
Section B

CORRECTIONAL SCHOOL	
Number of Children in Family of Offender: Eight	41.9
Moral Standards of Home: Poor	42.3
Conjugal Relations of Parents: Fair	48.1
Bad Habits in Childhood: Some	45.7
Time Between Onset of Antisocial Behavior and First Arrest:	
Seven years	43.2
Total	221.2
PAROLE	
Birthplace of Father: Ireland	89.7
Birthplace of Mother: Ireland	86.7
Discipline by Father: Erratic	63.9
Discipline by Mother: Firm but kindly	50.0
School Misconduct: Truancy and other	72.2
Total	362.5
FIVE YEARS AFTER COMPLETION OF FIRST JUVENILE COURT SENTENCE	
Discipline by Father: Erratic	83.6
Discipline by Mother: Firm but kindly	68.4
Age at Onset of Antisocial Behavior: Five years	92.0
School Retardation: Two years	88.1
School Misconduct: Truancy and other	91.3
Time Between Onset of Antisocial Behavior and First Arrest:	
Seven years	90.8
Total	514.2
FIFTEEN YEARS AFTER COMPLETION OF FIRST JUVENILE COURT SENTENCE	
Birthplace of Father: Ireland	25.2
Birthplace of Mother: Ireland	25.8
Time Parents Were in United States: Six Years	22.9
Religion of Parents: Both Catholic	30.0
Age at Onset of Antisocial Behavior: Five years	35.3
Total	139.2

Section C
Summary of Frank's Prediction Profile

Type of Treatment or Period		Score	Rate of Good Adjustment
Straight Probation	(III–1)	239.4	64.0 (More than even chance)
Probation with Suspended Sentence	(III–2)	305.5	37.8 (Less than even chance)
Correctional School	(III–3)	221.2	34.5 (Less than even chance)
Parole	(III–6)	362.5	15.4 (Less than even chance)
Five Years after Completion of First Sentence	(III–7)	514.2	16.9 (Less than even chance)
Fifteen Years after Completion of First Sentence	(III–8)	139.2	72.8 (More than even chance)

Note: Numbers in parentheses to right of type of treatment or period refer to table numbers in Appendix B; definitions of the predictive factors and the scores for the respective subcategories will also be found in Appendix B.

103

of behavior of juvenile offenders on straight probation, will explain the scores assigned, in Section B of the case, to each subcategory of the factors encompassing this particular form of sentence and treatment. Since Frank's father was born in Ireland, Frank is assigned the score of 53.7; as his father is an erratic disciplinarian (i.e., vacillating between laxity and overstrictness with the boy), the boy is given the score of 45.5. But note that Frank's mother is firm and kindly in managing the boy; and this gives him a score of 15.4. He is two years behind grade for his age at the time of his first juvenile court appearance, which yields a score of 62.7. Inquiry into his behavior in school reveals him to have been a truant and to have been misbehaving himself in other ways, giving him a score of 62.1. Thus, the *total* of Frank's scores on these five factors is 239.4.

There is no need to go beyond this in illustrating the scoring of Frank on the other five tables, predicting his behavior under probation with suspended sentence, in a correctional school, on parole, and five years and fifteen years after the completion of the first disposition made by the juvenile court.

If the reader will again consult Appendix B, Table III–1 (behavior of juvenile delinquents on straight probation), he will see that Frank's score of 239.4 places him in the category in which he has less than an even chance (36 in 100) of violating probation and more than an even chance (64 in 100) of not doing so.

In Section C of Frank's Profile in which are presented his chances of good adjustment during each type of peno-correctional treatment, and his probable adjustment by the end of five and of fifteen years after the completion of first sentence, it will be noted that Frank's chances of good adjustment during straight probation are 64 in 100, i.e., *more than even*; examination of his scores under suspended sentence and in a correctional school indicate that the chances are less than even that he will behave acceptably under a suspended sentence or in a correctional school; and he appears to have less than an even chance of behaving acceptably on parole. The probability of his making a good adjustment during the five years following the completion of the sentence imposed by the juvenile court is also low. Taking the longer view of his behavior by the end of fifteen years, the probability that he will continue to be a problem to legal authorities is very slight.

We are now ready to proceed to a consideration of how a juvenile court judge might utilize the data in Frank's prediction profile. Frank is, at twelve years of age, appearing in juvenile court for the first time, charged with breaking and entering.

The judge might reason that since Frank has a greater likelihood of responding satisfactorily to straight probation than to probation under a suspended sentence, and has clearly a better chance of acceptable behavior during probation than in a correctional school, he would be justified in placing him on probation, providing the officer to whom Frank is assigned would supervise him closely. Frank does not appear to be too "good a risk" for other forms of peno-correctional treatment ordinarily given a juvenile offender. Although the likelihood that he would "reform" during the first five years after the end of probation is slight, the probability that he would make a good adjustment by the end of fifteen years is considerable.

(It should be stated that the particular judge before whom Frank actually did appear following his first arrest gave him *a suspended sentence*; the sentence was shortly invoked, and Frank was sent to a correctional school. If the judge had had Frank's prediction profile before him he would readily have noted that in this instance straight probation was more desirable for Frank than a suspended sentence with its continuing threat of incarceration.

What further happened to Frank is not the subject of this chapter. He is among the 500 delinquent boys, initially studied in *Unraveling Juvenile Delinquency*,[3] whom we have followed from the onset of their criminal careers until age twenty-three, through all the vicissitudes of their peno-correctional experiences. For each of them a prediction chart was prepared at the time they were selected for inclusion in that inquiry, and laid aside pending completion of the follow-up study into their behavior during all the peno-correctional treatments given them from the onset of their delinquent careers until age twenty-three, in order to determine the extent of agreement between their predicted and their actual behavior. A resumé of the findings of this inquiry has already been presented in Chapter IV.)

Comparison of Prediction Profiles of
Four Juvenile Offenders

In Exhibit I are presented, in juxtaposition, the chances that Frank, James, John, and Robert, will make a good adjustment during each form of peno-correctional treatment (straight probation, probation with

[3] S. and E. T. Glueck, New York, The Commonwealth Fund, 1950.

suspended sentence, correctional school, and parole) and the likelihood of acceptable behavior five years and fifteen years after the end of the first sentence prescribed by the juvenile court.

Exhibit I.   Sample Prediction Profiles of Frank, James, John, and Robert

(Offense: Breaking and Entering)

Type of Treatment or Period		Rate of Good Adjustment			
		FRANK (Age 12)	JAMES (Age 8)	JOHN (Age 7)	ROBERT (Age 10)
Straight Probation	(III–1)	64%*	14%	14%	14%
Probation with Suspended Sentence	(III–2)	38	13	13	13
Correctional School	(III–3)	35	55*	55*	37
Parole	(III–6)	15	10	10	10
Five Years after Completion of First Sentence	(III–7)	17	17	17	17
Fifteen Years after Completion of First Sentence	(III–8)	73*	73*	43	43

* More than even chance of good adjustment; all others, less than even chance of adjustment.

Note: Numbers in parentheses to right of type of treatment or period refer to table numbers in Appendix B; definitions of the predictive factors and the scores for the respective subcategories will also be found in Appendix B.

The four prediction profiles, showing the probabilities of non-delinquent conduct during and following the end of sentence by the juvenile court and its associated agencies and institutions, do not by any means represent the many types of cases that come before a juvenile court, which has to act on minor or casual (pseudo) as well as true offenders. The cases in *Juvenile Delinquents Grown Up*[4] and *Unraveling Juvenile Delinquency*,[5] from which these illustrations are drawn, are of the latter type, a large proportion of whom are likely to continue in delinquent careers and not likely to get on too well during extramural, and even during intramural, treatment.

A comparison of the prediction profiles of Frank and James shows that, unlike Frank, James is not a good risk on straight probation; but he has more than an even chance of adapting himself in a correctional school.

[4] S. and E. T. Glueck, New York, The Commonwealth Fund, 1940.
[5] For the definition of delinquency, see Chapter II, footnote 6, of the present volume.

Like Frank, he has little chance of doing well on parole, and he is quite likely to recidivate during the next five years; but both boys have a considerable likelihood of being non-offenders at the end of fifteen years.

James was eight years old when he first appeared in a juvenile court. The judge probably would, because of the boy's youth (if for no other reason), be inclined to "give him a chance on probation." However, commitment to a correctional school is indicated by his prediction profile—and for a *longer* rather than a shorter period because he is such a poor risk not only for probation but for parole.

(Actually, the judge did place James on probation for a year. During this period, the boy committed many larcenies and at nine years of age he was given a suspended sentence to a correctional school. He continued to steal and, less than two years later, landed in the institution. There, except for poor work in the classroom, James got on well—so well, in fact, that he was paroled after eight months. However, his chances of good behavior on parole were very low; within five months, his conduct was so bad—breaking and entering, larceny—that he was returned to the correctional school. He had some slight difficulty in readjusting, which expressed itself in "talking out of turn" and some cheating in class, but he was quickly "in the groove," and after a year was once more paroled. Again he got into serious difficulties with his "gang," committing larcenies and other depredations.

There is no need to go on with the tale of James. It seems clear that, considering the quality of correctional alternatives available to the court, the boy should have been committed to a correctional school on his first court appearance and not released on parole for some years until he had sufficiently matured, bearing in mind that although his chances of early reformation were low, the likelihood that he would, in the long run, *continue* to be a *serious* offender was slight.)

We now turn to John, who made his first court appearance when seven years old. In his case, it is noteworthy that he is much like James in his prediction profile, with the difference, however, that there is more than an even chance that he will continue to be a serious offender even fifteen years hence. With this in mind, a judge might well commit John to a correctional school, indicating to the authorities that he not be released on parole for some time to come. This does not mean that John should not be paroled from the correctional school, but it does suggest that if a boy of this type is to succeed he would need very close supervision and attention from a parole officer; and failing that, a plan for longer institutionalization would have to be worked out.

(John was committed, on his first court appearance, to a correctional school. He must have been looked upon as "a bad actor" for it is unusual that probation not be attempted first. Although John broke minor rules in the institution, he did respond well to firmness and to reprimand. After eight months he was paroled and soon began to commit burglaries. After twenty-one very unsatisfactory months on parole, he was again returned to the correctional school where his good conduct warranted early release on parole. Soon thereafter, a kind fate took him into the Army where he made a remarkable adjustment, became a corporal in the U.S.A.F. assigned to the payroll division, and was in due course honorably discharged. We did not follow him subsequently, so cannot report what he is doing now.)

We now turn to Robert, a boy of ten, whose prediction profile shows him to be even more of a treatment problem than John because, although he, too, appears to be a poor risk for straight probation, suspended sentence, and parole, and is likely to continue for the next fifteen years to be a serious offender, the probability that he would adjust in a correctional school is not as good as John's.

(The follow-up investigation of Robert shows that he failed all along the line, in the correctional school and on parole. The judge, in whose court he made his first appearance, did actually commit him to a correctional school. Here he stole, fought, and "carried on." After eleven months, he was paroled and soon became so unmanageable that he was returned to the institution. This time, in addition to his other depredations, he committed sex offenses; but, again, after a stay of ten months, he was paroled to a foster home in the hope no doubt that removal from his own family would be beneficial. But he stole from his foster parents, was generally difficult to handle, and finally ran away. Again he was returned to the correctional school.

History continued to repeat itself and until Robert was eighteen he experienced four more releases on parole and four more returns to the correctional school; and finally, at the age of twenty-three, he was sent to an institution for defective delinquents. Here in the very strict, almost military type of regime, he is getting along.)

In order to reduce the investigation of the factors entering into the prediction tables, it is suggested that if the likelihood of adaptation to probationary supervision is found to be high, there is hardly any need to ascertain the chances of adaptation in an institutional setting. However, an examination of the total prediction profile of an offender has its merit.

Before turning to the application of prediction tables to adult offenders, it should be mentioned that we have been able to construct treatment profiles for 479 of the 500 young offenders in *Unraveling Juvenile Delinquency*, indicating their probable response to the usual forms of correctional treatment—probation, with or without suspended sentence, commitment to correctional school, and parole (see Chapter IV and Appendix C, Table 18).

A boy was considered treatable if he was predicted as having *more than one and a half* in ten chances of behaving acceptably during probation or probation with suspended sentence, or as having *more than one* chance in ten of behaving on parole and/or as having *more than three and a half* chances in ten of being manageable in an institution. A juvenile offender who did not meet these conservative criteria was labeled "untreatable."

In order to develop a prediction table to make it possible for juvenile court judges to determine in advance of sentence how treatable[6] an offender is by the usual peno-correctional methods, we related 151 items (74 traits drawn from the psychologic, psychiatric, and Rorschach tests, and 77 sociocultural factors) of *Unraveling Juvenile Delinquency* to the prediction profiles of the delinquents.

Of the seventy-four traits, only one was found to bear a significant relationship to the untreatability of the delinquents, namely, *Conflict in Relationship of Boy and Father*. But of the seventy-seven sociocultural factors, thirty-six were found to differentiate significantly between the treatable and the untreatable offenders.[7] It is of especial significance

[6] From Appendix C, Table 18, it will be seen that the delinquents labeled "untreatable" are those with Profile A. All the others are "treatable" delinquents.

[7] The thirty-six factors are listed in the following table:

Factors*	Treatable Offenders		Untreatable Offenders		Differ-ence
	No.	%	No.	%	%
Cleanliness and Neatness of Home (VIII–8)	124	89.9	274	76.3	13.6
One or Both Parents Foreign-Born (IX–2)	94	74.6	186	52.1	22.5
Delinquency of Father (IX–10)	63	45.7	268	74.0	−28.3
Alcoholism of Father (IX–10)	68	49.3	246	68.0	−18.7
Emotional Disturbance in Mother (IX–10)	48	34.8	172	47.5	−12.7
Delinquency of Mother (IX–10)	47	34.1	177	48.9	−14.8
Alcoholism of Mother (IX–10)	20	14.5	95	26.2	−11.7
Financial Dependence of Family (IX–14)	37	26.8	144	39.8	−13.0
Poor Work Habits of Father (IX–18)	58	45.0	226	69.3	−24.3

that four of the highly related factors are the same as those already serving as the basis for our Social Prediction Table—*Supervision of Boy by Mother, Discipline of Boy by Father, Affection of Father for Boy*, and *Cohesiveness of Family.*

The resulting table for identifying treatable juvenile delinquents by the usual methods at the disposal of a juvenile court appears in Appendix B, XI–4. Similarity between four of the five factors identifying potential delinquents in a school population (see Chapter IX and Appendix B, Tables IX–1 and IX–1a) and factors discriminating between already delinquent youngsters predicted as untreatable by the usual juvenile court prescriptions is of the utmost significance. This important finding, resulting from the testing of our juvenile court prediction tables (constructed from the cases of 1,000 boys studied in *One Thousand Juvenile Delinquents* and followed up in *Juvenile Delinquents Grown Up*) on the delinquents encompassed in *Unraveling Juvenile Delinquency*, has yielded a predictive cluster almost identical with that derived in *Unraveling* for the purpose of identifying *potential* delinquents. There is an implication in these findings that the juvenile offenders who are very probably "untreatable" by the usual methods used by juvenile courts are the same youngsters who are identifiable by our Social Prediction Table (Appendix B, Table

Poor Management of Family Income (X–1)	70	51.1	259	72.1	−21.0
Careless Household Routine (X–2)	89	65.0	283	79.7	−14.7
Lack of Cultural Refinement in Home (X–3)	115	83.3	338	94.9	−11.6
Self-Respect of Family Lacking (X–4)	38	27.5	178	49.2	−21.7
Ambition of Parents Lacking (X–5)	114	82.6	332	92.0	− 9.4
Low Conduct Standards of Home (X–6)	112	81.2	340	93.9	−12.7
Incompatibility of Parents (X–7)	62	45.3	250	70.0	−24.7
Unsuitable Supervision by Mother (X–10)	69	50.0	249	69.2	−19.2
Family Group Recreations Lacking (X–11)	72	52.9	261	72.9	−20.0
Lack of Family Cohesiveness (X–14)	92	66.7	327	90.6	−23.9
Broken Home (XI–8)	62	44.9	241	66.6	−21.7
Rearing by Parent Substitute (XI–12)	50	36.2	180	49.7	−13.5
Father's Lack of Affection for Boy (XI–13)	57	41.6	237	66.8	−25.2
Father Unacceptable to Boy for Emulation (XI–16)	24	20.3	100	34.9	−14.6
Mother's Lack of Concern for Boy's Welfare (XI–19)	65	65.7	208	82.2	−16.5
Father's Lack of Concern for Boy's Welfare (XI–19)	66	68.0	192	86.1	−18.1
Unsuitable Discipline by Father (XI–22)	108	80.6	325	100.0	−19.4
Unsuitable Discipline by Mother (XI–22)	117	84.8	359	100.0	−15.2
Frequent Moves (XIII–2)	51	37.0	217	60.0	−23.0
Less than 8 Years of Age at Onset of Misbehavior (IV–1)	54	39.1	188	51.9	−12.8
No or 1 Year of Retardation (XII–5)	101	73.2	194	53.6	19.6
Poor Scholarship (XII–10)	42	30.4	165	45.6	−15.2
Truanted (XII–26)	120	87.0	354	97.8	−10.8
Less than 11 Years of Age at Start of Truancy (XII–27)	62	45.3	237	65.5	−20.2
No Household Duties (XIII–10)	49	35.8	175	49.4	−13.6
Ran Away from Home (XIII–13)	65	47.1	230	63.5	−16.4
Irregular Church Attendance (XIII–21)	64	46.7	234	65.9	−19.2

* The table numbers following each factor are cross-references to chapters and tables in *Unraveling Juvenile Delinquency* in which the particular factors are presented.

110

IX–1) as having nine in ten chances of developing into serious persistent offenders. *This may well explain the recalcitrance to treatment of certain types of offenders.*

Application of Prediction Tables to Adult Offenders

The principles underlying the application of predictive devices to adult offenders are the same as those pertaining to juvenile delinquents. As is true in the case of juveniles, if a battery of such tables is to be of maximum use they should, ideally, be applied at the time of the first adult court appearance of an offender, in order that a soundly based course of peno-correctional treatment can be initiated as early as possible. This does not imply that the prediction tables would not be helpful at any stage in the offender's career; but it should already be evident that peno-correctional treatment based on an isolated event in a criminal's history is likely to be nullified by the next court that takes hold of the case. It is just this piecemeal, instead of planned and consistent, processing of cases that must be avoided if we are to make even a little progress toward integrating the management of delinquents and criminals.[8]

Judges who are inclined to experiment with the prediction tables for adult offenders are asked to remember that they were constructed from a group of 510 young men who were committed to the Massachusetts Reformatory. Consultation of the volume, *500 Criminal Careers*,[9] in which the background of these offenders is described, indicates that the great majority of them were persistent offenders[10] and that three-fourths of them had been juvenile delinquents.[11]

As already stated in Chapter V, only one in the series of tables pertaining to adult male offenders has yet been checked, i.e., applied to cases other than those in the group on which the tables were constructed (Appendix B, Table V–28, Civilian Delinquents in Armed Forces). In the illustration of prediction profiles of juvenile offenders, we were able to relate the predictions in each case to what actually happened to four boys, by comparing their predicted behavior with their conduct during various forms of peno-correctional treatment. We cannot do this in regard to adult offenders since we have not yet applied the prediction tables constructed

---

[8] See "Report of the Unpaid Special Commission Relative to Prisoners," House No. 2198, January, 1953, The Commonwealth of Massachusetts.

[9] S. and E. T. Glueck, New York, Knopf, 1930.

[10] *Ibid.*, p. 140.

[11] *Ibid.*, p. 143.

on the cases of *500 Criminal Careers* and *Criminal Careers in Retrospect*[12] to another sample of cases. Such a study is reserved for the future.

Although we should like to present cases of adult offenders whose behavior during various forms of peno-correctional treatment is actually contained in our case histories, the lack of prediction scores and profiles for any of our adult offenders makes this impossible.

We can only suggest that, given a prediction profile of an adult offender, a judge would have an aid to his choice among alternative sentences, based on objectified experience involving the response of offenders already subjected to one or another type of peno-correctional treatment. To show how much more significant, in the sentencing process, are these indications as compared to those which frequently determine the sentence, we quote a relevant passage from *500 Criminal Careers*:

> . . . The relationship between the total-failure score on the factors embraced in the preceding prognostic instruments, and post-parole criminal conduct was found to be very high. The coefficients expressing that fact ranged from .44 to .68. . . .[13] It was, however, established that the coefficient expressing the relation between the type of offense committed—that is, whether it was a burglary, larceny, robbery, or sexually motivated crime—and post-parole criminal status is but .12. This coefficient is so low as to indicate only a negligible relationship between the nature of the offense and post-parole conduct. Again, the coefficient of contingency between the seriousness of the offense for which the men were sentenced to the Reformatory and their post-parole criminal record but was .05—that is, practically nil. *But the modern disposition of cases is fundamentally based on these factors. In other words, legislative prescription of penalties, and judicial sentencing, are founded upon considerations almost wholly irrelevant to whether or not a criminal will thereunder ultimately be a success, a partial failure, or a total failure.*[14]

* * *

We have briefly illustrated how the analysis of the prediction tables might be of value to courts and parole boards making treatment and release decisions. It is well to point to a value, apart from immediate sentencing

[12] S. and E. T. Glueck, New York, The Commonwealth Fund, 1943.

[13] The greatest possible value of Professor Karl Pearson's "mean square contingency coefficient" is "only unity if the number of classes be infinitely great; for any finite number of classes the limiting value of C is the smaller the smaller the number of classes. In a twofold table, C cannot exceed .71; in a threefold, .82, etc." G. Udny Yule, *An Introduction to the Theory of Statistics*, 1922, pp. 65–66.

[14] *500 Criminal Careers*, p. 295.

and releasing practices, to be derived from a battery of prediction tables covering all forms of existing peno-correctional treatment:

> ... A deplorable proportion of criminals never reform. The reason for this may be our very imperfect technique. But at any rate, with the methods thus far tried by civilized society, *there has always been a considerable residue of persons who do not respond to any known form of correctional or punitive treatment.* Social facilities are limited, and emphasis must therefore be placed on the most promising human material. The great social need is to evolve, through experimentation, more efficient methods of analyzing and remaking the human personality. But that is a task of colossal proportions.[15]

By isolating the offenders who fail under *all* existing forms of peno-correctional treatment, and noting the factors that distinguish them from others, a start can be made in designing new peno-correctional experiments to cope with the presently irreformable malefactors.

[15] *Ibid.*, p. 316.

IX

Identification of Potential Delinquents

Introduction

In the field of medicine or of fire control, the aim is to prevent disease or conflagration from starting. In the field of criminology the ideal, likewise, ought to be to prevent the *origin* of delinquent careers. This means early detection of incipient antisocial attitudes and tendencies which may not necessarily have as yet expressed themselves in any, or in only minor, peccadilloes.

We have seen how permeative is the influence of age at onset of delinquency. In virtually every form of peno-correctional treatment explored, *the earlier the signs of maladjustment, the more likely is maladaptation to continue unless suitable therapeutic intervention occurs.* Of further relevance is the fact that, in *One Thousand Juvenile Delinquents*,[1] boys whose antisocial behavior did not begin until relatively late had a better subsequent record than early delinquents. So, also, the youngsters who had shown no early antisocial behavior manifestations prior to their officially determined delinquency had a better behavioral record after contact with the juvenile court than did the other boys.[2] Moreover, it was found that in the cases in which the court had carried out recommendations made by a child guidance clinic, there was an appreciably better behavioral result than in other cases of like background.[3] This would appear to mean that early detection of antisocial tendencies followed by fulfilled clinical prescription is of real importance.

It was further found in *Unraveling Juvenile Delinquency*[4] that in a sample of 500 persistent delinquents from the underprivileged areas of Boston, the average age at onset of maladapted behavior was somewhat

[1] S. and E. T. Glueck, Cambridge, Mass., Harvard University Press, 1934, p. 180.
[2] *Ibid.*, p. 180.
[3] *Ibid.*, pp. 188–189.
[4] S. and E. T. Glueck, New York, The Commonwealth Fund, 1950, p. 28.

over eight years, with almost half the group showing clear signs of antisociality at seven or younger, and nine-tenths at ten or younger; among
juvenile offenders investigated by us some twenty years before the research
in *Unraveling* (i.e., in *One Thousand Juvenile Delinquents*), the average
age at onset of delinquency was found to be nine and a half years, with
some two-thirds of the 643 boys seriously misbehaving at the age of ten
or younger.[5]

All such evidence points to the crucial need of a "preventive medicine"
of delinquency, a system of prophylaxis in the field of childhood maladjustment. Early treatment of *potential* delinquents gives promise of preventing
the development of criminal careers with its attendant damage, waste,
and heartache. But early prevention requires early *identification* of the
children whose rearing or temperamental distortions are prodromal of
ultimate delinquency. Such identification is not easy; for, on the one hand,
it cannot wait on overt misbehavior, and, on the other, even patent
misbehavior may be but a transient occurrence rather than indicative of
a tendency to persistent delinquency.

We have attempted to design discriminatory tables which may serve as
an instrument for identifying delinquency-prone children at an early age.
In the next chapter we give the evidence that exists thus far of the validity
of such devices.

Before presenting the tables, a brief description of the research on
which they are based is in order. In *Unraveling Juvenile Delinquency* we
give the detailed results of a multidisciplinary research based on a sample
of 500 true (i.e., persistent) delinquents and 500 proven non-delinquents.
As a basis for the detailed examinations and investigations of these 1,000
boys, the delinquents and the control group of non-delinquents were
first matched, case by case, by age, general intelligence, ethnic derivation,
and residence in economically and culturally underprivileged urban
areas. Detailed investigation of the two groups was then made by a
specially trained staff, consisting of a physician-psychiatrist, two physical
anthropologists, eight psychologists (two of them outstanding experts
on the Rorschach "ink-blot" test of personality), and ten social investigators. In Chapters II through VIII of *Unraveling Juvenile Delinquency*, full
account of the method of the enquiry is rendered; but one point might be
stressed here: namely, that the various participants were not shown the
findings of the other staff members, so that when we finally collated the

[5] *One Thousand Juvenile Delinquents*, p. 95.

data deriving from several disciplines, we would be assured of insulation against "reading in" and circular reasoning.

Comparison of the delinquents and the non-delinquents in respect to some 400 biologic, psychologic, psychiatric, and sociocultural factors enabled us to determine in what respects the two groups differed.[6] It seemed reasonable to assume that among factors most markedly distinguishing true delinquents from true non-delinquents were some that were operative *prior* to the time of school entrance, i.e., before six years of age; and that predictive devices based on such factors might make it possible to determine in advance of the actual onset of clearly defined antisocial behavior those children who are or who are not in danger of developing into delinquents.

Four prediction tables were constructed from among the factors of most marked difference between the 500 delinquents and 500 non-delinquents, one of which—based on psychologic data from the Wechsler-Bellevue intelligence test and the Stanford achievement test—was not published in *Unraveling Juvenile Delinquency*, and appears here for the first time.[7]

Table IX–1, which is the only one thus far experimented with, is based on five factors in the early family history as derived from the social investigations; Table IX–2, on five traits of basic character structure as derived from the Rorschach test; Table IX–3, on five personality traits as determined by psychiatric interview; and Table IX–4, as already

[6] The extent of the enterprise may be judged from the fact that the medical schedule comprised 30 factors; the physique schedule, 55; the psychological, 56; the Rorschach, 57; the psychiatric examination, 55; and the social investigation, 149; making a total of 402 factors, all carefully defined, gathered, and verified, on which the 500 persistent delinquents and the 500 non-delinquents were ultimately compared, factor by factor. It took a considerable and highly trained staff of social investigators eight years to compile and verify these 1,000 social case histories.

[7] In constructing a table out of the data gathered in the psychologic study of the boys in *Unraveling*, we recognized that the resulting prediction table would not be as sharply differentiative of true delinquents and true non-delinquents as the three tables already published, for the reason that the boys were originally matched on the basis of the resemblance of the delinquents and the non-delinquents in terms of general or global intelligence as measured by the Wechsler-Bellevue full-scale intelligence quotient. Nevertheless, analysis of the components of general intelligence and of the school achievement tests in reading and arithmetic have revealed differences which, though not as great as those emerging from other portions of the research and embodied in the three tables discussed above, are nevertheless statistically significant.

It is to be remembered, however, that, as Wechsler has pointed out, the Wechsler-Bellevue test is not applicable to children under ten years of age. Therefore, Table IX–4 cannot safely be used at the point of a boy's school entrance.

Four Tables Identifying Potential Delinquents

Summary Table IX–A.   Identification of Potential Juvenile Delinquents

Prediction Base	Less than Even Chance of Delinquency		More than Even Chance of Delinquency	
	Score Class	(Rate)	Score Class	(Rate)
Based on Five Social Factors[1] (IX–1)	Less than 250	(16.0%)	250 or Over	(79.1%)
Based on Five Traits of Character Structure[2] (IX–2)	Less than 255	(28.9)	255 or Over	(81.6)
Based on Five Personality Traits[3] (IX–3)	Less than 245	(21.6)	245 or Over	(82.8)
Based on Five Psychological Test Factors[4] (IX–4)	Less than 230	(36.1)	230 or Over	(62.0)

[1] Predictive Factors: Discipline of Boy by Father; Supervision of Boy by Mother; Affection of Father for Boy; Affection of Mother for Boy; Cohesiveness of Family.

[2] Predictive Traits: Social Assertiveness; Defiance; Suspiciousness; Destructiveness; Emotional Lability.

[3] Predictive Traits: Adventurousness; Extroverted in Action; Suggestibility; Stubbornness; Emotional Instability.

[4] Predictive Factors: Information Weighted Score; Deviation of Digit Symbol Weighted Score from Mean Performance Weighted Score; Reading Quotient; Arithmetic Quotient; Arithmetic Computation Age Score in Months.

Note: Numbers in parentheses to right of prediction base refer to table numbers in Appendix B; definitions of the predictive factors and the scores for the respective subcategories will also be found in Appendix B.

indicated, on five intelligence scores derived from the Wechsler-Bellevue and the Stanford achievement tests.

We hope that opportunities will occur to test the other three tables. Meanwhile, it should be pointed out that it has already been established that the Social Prediction Table bears a high relationship to Tables IX–2 and IX–3[8] (its relationship to Table IX–4 has not been tested). It is

[8] S. and E. T. Glueck, "Early Detection of Future Delinquents," 47 *J. Crim. L., Crimin. & Police Science* (1956), pp. 174–182. This study establishes not only that the Social Prediction Table would do as good a job of prediction as either of the other two tables, but also as any combination of the fifteen factors which make up all three tables.

Each prediction table standing alone does not predict correctly in all instances. In an analysis made in *Unraveling Juvenile Delinquency* of the predictive capacity of the three tables, it was ascertained that in all but 2.4% of the cases (10 out of 424), for whom each of the three clusters of five predictive factors was known, at least one of the three tables, if not all three, correctly identified a boy as a delinquent or as a non-delinquent (see *Unraveling*, Tables XX–15 and XX–16, pp. 267–268). It is important, therefore, to learn more than we know about why all the boys are not correctly identified as delinquents or non-delinquents by each of the three tables in order to throw further light not only on prediction but also on the etiology of delinquency.

Although the most promising method of reaching this goal is through intensive case study, a preliminary statistical inquiry comparing the traits and characteristics of those

especially desirable that experimentation go forward with the newly-presented table based on psychological test factors (Appendix B, Table IX–4).

Social Prediction Table

Focusing, then, on the Social Prediction Table (IX–1), it will be observed that a youngster scoring under 250 in the five intrafamily factors has less than an even chance of developing into a delinquent; conversely, a boy scoring 250 or over has more than an even probability of becoming a delinquent. An examination of Appendix B, Table IX–1, shows that it is the group scoring 250 to 300 which requires special attention; for youngsters in this group have a little more than an even chance of becoming delinquent (six in ten). Early detection of such cases followed by preventive measures should aid in reducing the ranks of delinquents. Youngsters with a greater likelihood of delinquency may be more difficult to rehabilitate. (See Chapter VIII, footnote 7 and text, pp. 109–111.)

Perhaps at this point it would be helpful to illustrate the method of scoring a youngster with reference to the likelihood of his becoming a delinquent (see the scores assigned to each subcategory of the five factors entering into this table—Appendix B, p. 233). If, for example, Johnny is always harshly disciplined by his father, he would be scored 72.5 on this factor. If the mother generally leaves him to his own devices, letting him run around the streets and not knowing what he does or where he goes, her supervision would be rated "unsuitable" and the score on this factor would be 83.2. If it is learned, further, that the father dislikes the boy, Johnny would be scored 75.9 on this factor. If the mother is shown to be indifferent to her son, expressing little warmth of feeling for him, or if she is downright hostile to him, the score on this item would be 86.2. Finally, if it is found that the family is unintegrated because, for example, the mother spends most of the day away from home, giving little if any thought to the doings of the children, and the father, a heavy drinker, spends most of his leisure in bars and cafes, ignoring his family, the score

---

incorrectly predicted by one or another of the tables with those correctly predicted would appear to be necessary. Since the data from *Unraveling* make this possible to a limited extent, we have carried out a series of correlations, the result of which the interested reader will find in Appendix D. It is hoped that the findings presented will act as a stimulus to further research into the merits and limitations of our prediction devices as well as into the etiology of delinquency.

on this factor would be 96.9. Addition of these scores results in a total of 414.7. Consultation of the prediction table (Appendix B, Table IX–1) makes it evident that a boy of this type, *whether or not he has as yet overtly manifested any antisocial behavior*, is in grave danger of becoming a delinquent, for he is in the score class that gives him a nine in ten chance of delinquency.[9]

Nature of Social Predictive Factors

Let us now examine the factors of the Social Prediction Table from the point of view of their resemblance to those appearing in the other prediction tables presented in prior chapters.

The first factor in Table IX–1, *Discipline of Boy by Father*, was also found to be predictive in several of the tables in Chapter III dealing with the prediction of behavior of boys already delinquent. It was there included in Table III–1 (straight probation); Table III–2 (probation with suspended sentence); Table III–6 (parole); Table III–7 (five-year follow-up period); and Table III–10 (prisons).

The second factor in Table IX–1 of the present series, *Supervision of Boy by Mother*, did not appear in prior tables. However, it is analogous to *Discipline by Mother*, which was found to be one of the predictors in Tables III–1, III–2, III–6, and III–7 of the series dealing with juvenile delinquents.

The third factor predictive of delinquency, *Affection of Father for Boy*, had also been found predictive in Table III–2 (behavior on probation with suspended sentence) and Table III–10 (behavior of former juvenile delinquents in prison), in the series dealing with boys already delinquent. *Affection of Mother for Boy*, the fourth factor in the present series dealing with the prediction of delinquency, had not been previously employed as a predictor, because other factors were found to be more differen-

---

[9] A practical issue that has developed in connection with checking the Social Prediction Table against other samples of cases is the difficulty sometimes encountered even by the most skilled social investigators in securing the needed data on all five factors of the Table. This has raised the question whether it is possible to get as good or almost as good a discriminatory instrument with fewer than five factors. A case-by-case correlation of the results arrived at with the five-factor table and that reached with four, three, and two factors has resulted in competent predictive devices. (See Appendix B, Table IX–1, and Tables IX–1a through IX–1e.)

Abbreviated devices have been developed also for the table based on five traits of character structure, as well as for the table based on five psychological test factors. (See Appendix B, Tables IX–2, IX–2a through IX–2d, IX–4, and IX–4a and 4b.)

tiative of successes and failures after contact with the juvenile court.[10] *Cohesiveness of Family,* the fifth and last factor in the Social Prediction Table designed to forecast delinquency in young boys, has also not been used previously, although other factors reflecting the family situation have been employed in some of the tables in Chapter III dealing with behavior after contact with the juvenile court.

The traits of character structure as derived by the Rorschach test in Table IX–2 have not been used previously in tables dealing either with already-confirmed juvenile delinquents or adult offenders; but the reason for this is the simple one that Rorschach test data were obtained only for the cases in *Unraveling Juvenile Delinquency,* on which the present tables are based.

As to the traits of temperament in Table IX–3, obtained as the result of psychiatric interviews with the boys, they differ from any psychiatrically-oriented data contained in our prior studies, where only gross diagnoses of mental disease and marked distortion were available. On the other hand, the psychiatric interviews for *Unraveling* included such specific traits of temperament as *Adventurousness, Extroversion in Action, Suggestibility, Stubbornness, Emotional Instability* (the five traits employed in Table IX–3 of the series in this chapter), and others of like tenor.

The factors in Table IX–4, based as they are on Wechsler-Bellevue and Stanford achievement tests, have also not been previously included in our researches.

Social Prediction Table as a Guide to Treatment

An instrumentality for identifying potential delinquents can be of little value if it does not furnish some clue to treatment needs. The specific program of treatment to be applied, of course, depends ultimately on the individual case; but it depends initially, in large measure, also on the characteristics of many similar cases, that is, on a typology; and one of the great values of prediction tables is that they *focus attention on the factors most relevant* to behavioral expectations. The differentiative subcategories of the five areas of *interpersonal family relations* encompassed

---

[10] The reader is also reminded that, occasionally, for practical reasons, such as the relative difficulty of gathering certain classes of data, we have used, in prediction tables, a factor of somewhat lower predictive power than one that might have been used. The interested reader might compare the list of "Categories of Family and Personal Factors in which Reformation is Highest," Table XXXV, pp. 179–180, and "Rate of Recidivism in Sub-classes of Six Significant Factors," Table XXXVIII, p. 187, of *One Thousand Juvenile Delinquents.*

in the Social Prediction Table are quite sharply defined. The preventive social worker is thus given specific targets toward which to direct therapeutic efforts in various types of cases. It may be that lack of family cohesiveness, for example, can be remedied by proper social work, financial aid, or intervention of a family guidance counsellor or clergyman. *Why* a parent lacks affection for his son, or a mother fails properly to supervise him, or parental discipline is defective—these are matters that may well vary in individual cases; but the definition by the prediction table of the areas of family life that have proven to be crucial to the formation or malformation of character is a considerable step forward in any preventive program. More intensive study should reveal the various patterns and mechanisms which make for friction in parent–child relationships and for family disintegration;[11] but the prediction table is of great value even before this information has been obtained in detail.

One of the encouraging features of such an approach to prevention is that the worker knows that by eliminating, as it were, even two of the five highly divisive factors in the family life, the probabilities of delinquency are substantially reduced, provided the new constructive influence persists. Thus, for example, if the efforts of the social worker were to change the father's typical discipline of the boy from "overstrict or erratic" to "firm but kindly," and the mother's supervision from "unsuitable" to "suitable," the resultant delinquency score would be reduced from 414.7 to 278.2 (i.e., from 89/100 to 64/100). Although this is, to be sure, a still hazardous situation, it is much more promising than heretofore. This illustration may give the impression of a rather mechanical operation of cause and effect. This is not the intention. The illustration is given to make more vivid the fact that however crude or subtle are the "causal" influences, the fewer the pressures toward antisocial behavior, the lower the chances of its occurring. Moreover, these factors of family life are to some extent interrelated; and any breach on the front of these five crucial factors should be helpful in weakening the other divisive influences at play on a youngster.

Similarly, the factors governing the traits of character structure, temperament, and intelligence as revealed by the other three prediction tables are of value in outlining the basic targets of effort, even though more intensive psychologic penetration may reveal deeper-lying mechanisms of character malformation. The only fundamental difference between

[11] The Thom Clinic for Child Guidance in Boston is engaged in such studies.

121

what might be called our *crucial target approach* to preventive socio-psychiatric effort in the Social Prediction Table and in the tables dealing with traits ascertained by the Rorschach test and psychiatric and psychological examination, is that in these latter the point of departure is the individual being tested for potential delinquency, while in the former it is the family matrix.

Because of the nature of the factors included in the Social Prediction Table, it can be applied at any age level ranging from six to sixteen years. The question it is designed to answer is simply: *Is a youngster not yet manifesting behavioral difficulties likely to become a delinquent; or if already evidencing symptoms of antisociality, is he a true delinquent?* Such checks of the Table as have been made to date (see Chapter X) would appear to suggest its efficacy for the latter purpose. Its efficacy when applied *before* the onset of overt evidence of maladapted behavior is in process of determination in an experiment being conducted by the New York City Youth Board in several public schools in New York City.[12] True, it is somewhat more difficult to arrive at the exact delinquency score in the case of a child of six because, for example, although there is evidence of a trend toward the disintegration of a family, the parents may still be living together and some semblance of unity is being maintained. Such a case would have to be categorized as showing some elements of cohesion; while later, evidence of lack of cohesiveness might be clear. However, since all the factors refer to the entire period from birth of the child up to the

---

[12] See pp. 133–136. See, also, "Prediction," by Edwin Bidwell Wilson, in a "Symposium on *Unraveling Juvenile Delinquency*," 64 *Harvard Law Review* (1951), p. 1041. ". . . A tool for distinguishing confirmed delinquents from nondelinquents may or may not be serviceable in distinguishing within a group of nondelinquents those who are potential delinquents from those who are not.

"One may argue about the probable serviceability of the tables for this suggested use. If one holds that the personality of an individual in respect to liability to delinquency is largely determined genetically or at any rate almost wholly determined genetically and environmentally prior to entrance to school, and that the syndrome of delinquency attributes can be observed as determinately in the earlier predelinquent age as later when delinquency has become confirmed, then one might also hold that the prediction tables would work pretty well—and one might fear that the preventive treatment might not easily be successful. If, however, one holds that personality or behavior is extremely labile and that delinquency arises not from genetic constitution nor even from pre-school conditioning but from associations and conditions surrounding the individual during his school years, then one might hold that the prediction tables would work badly, but he could entertain the hope for good success with preventive treatment if only he knew to whom to apply it.

"A priori argument will not get far, howsoever it be extended. What one needs is trial and observation. . . ."

point at which the prediction table is actually applied, it is the *usual*, or the most prevalent condition with which we are concerned and not with a small segment of it.

Varied Uses for Social Prediction Table

As regards uses of the Social Prediction Table once signs of maladapted behavior are clear, the reader's attention is directed to a study made by Richard E. Thompson[13] and briefly described in Chapter X, pp. 128–129. The boys he reports on were all "behavior problems" to their teachers; but the Table correctly distinguished (as established by subsequent follow-up) 90% of those who were true delinquents from those who were only pseudodelinquents. This means that if a pupil is showing signs of what *appears* to a teacher, or social worker, or police officer, to be evidence of *true* predelinquency, the Table would be helpful in arriving at a decision in the matter.

Moreover, at the clinical level it has its uses in distinguishing, from among a group of children referred for a wide variety of behavioral difficulties, those who are likely to "act out" their tensions in overt antisocial behavior. We have had more than gleanings of this, not only from the findings of Thompson's study, but also from the experience of the Thom Clinic for Child Guidance in Boston, as well as from other sources (see Chapter X).

What of the uses of the Social Prediction Table in a juvenile court? The tables in Chapter III are designed to predict the behavior of children adjudicated delinquent; but not all children with some prior record of offenses are necessarily headed for persistent careers of delinquency. And some children, though labeled "minor offenders," may actually be serious delinquents. The Social Prediction Table applied here would serve as an aid to juvenile court judges and probation officers in separating minor from serious offenders. It could be especially important in one of the most difficult and puzzling aspects of juvenile court procedure, "intake policy."[14]

Much more could be said about the possible uses of the Table in juvenile courts and elsewhere. Only its further experimental application

[13] "A Validation of the Glueck Social Prediction Scale for Proneness to Delinquency," 43 *J. Crim. L., Crimin. & Police Science* (1952), pp. 451–470.

[14] How a delinquent or endangered child comes to the attention of a juvenile court, and the policy decisions that must be made once he gets there, comprise the problem of "intake." Police departments and juvenile aid bureaus have a basic "sifting" function

will reveal its full potential. Of even more importance, however, than the practical task of determining how and where the Social Prediction Table works, is the dissection of the factors comprising the Table, in order to determine what their meaning is in the dynamics of delinquency. Such research is already going forward in the Thom Clinic for Child Guidance in Boston.

We have already stressed the fact that prediction tables are not to be applied mechanically, as a substitute for clinical or judicial judgment. Such tables, however, should help the teacher, the social worker, the clinician, the juvenile court judge, the intake officer, and the probation officer to evaluate a particular child in the perspective of organized experience with hundreds of other children who, in many crucial respects, are like the one in question. Used properly, this instrumentality can open the way for dealing more directly with the root causes of delinquent behavior than has thus far been possible. If validated, we can forsee its application as a screening device in public health programs for the prevention and treatment of delinquency.

It will not be amiss, at this point, to repeat our observations in *Unraveling Juvenile Delinquency* on the use of these tables:

> Our concern at this stage is not so much in expressing caution in the use of these predictive devices—obviously they must be in the hands of highly experienced persons, and the necessary prediction scores must be derived from absolutely accurate data—as in suggesting to those who may use the tables that if two or three of them are applied in an individual case, the likelihood of placing a boy in his proper predictive category is thereby increased.
>
> It has occurred to us that if a boy has a high chance of potential delinquency as determined by the factors of his social background, but a low chance as derived from the factors of his basic character structure (Rorschach) or the dynamics of his personality (psychiatric), this would indicate that the chances of early preventive treatment are excellent, if the necessary attention is directed

---

in deciding which of numerous complaints of neighbors, storekeepers, railway guards, and others can best be disposed of without taking the children to court. On the police function with juveniles, see *Police Services for Juveniles*, Children's Bureau, U.S. Department of Health, Education and Welfare, Washington, D. C., 1954; "Intake," in *Standards for Specialized Courts Dealing with Children*, Children's Bureau, U.S. Govt. Printing Office, 1954, pp. 36–43.

Once a child gets into court, there are further policy problems involving the sifting of cases. In a number of courts, many cases are handled "informally," i.e., without prior official adjudication of a delinquency status. At both these stages, relevant prediction tables should be very helpful. See S. Glueck (Editor), *The Problem of Delinquency*, Houghton Mifflin, 1959, Chapter 19, "Intake, Detention, Clinical Examination and Hearing."

toward improving the conditions revealed by the social data (family inter-relations). It would seem, in such a situation, that we are dealing essentially with an environmental offender, and that the environmental stimuli to delinquency have been so recent or superficial that their impact has not reflected itself in basic personality or character structure. If the opposite is true, namely, that the boy's chances of delinquency are low in accordance with the social prediction table, but high in accordance with either or both the Rorschach and psychiatric prediction tables, it should indicate to the therapist that he may be dealing with a very recalcitrant individual, the prevention of whose delinquent career might be extremely difficult and involve nothing short of a basic reorganization of his character structure and tempera-mental constitution. Here it is probable that the difficulties are deeply rooted, perhaps genetically, perhaps in the very first few years of the parent-child emotional interchange.

A matter requiring further exploration is whether it is possible to use other psychological tests in place of the Rorschach Test, which is not only very time-consuming but requires exceptional skill in administration and inter-pretation, in order to derive more readily the factors in the basic character structure that have been shown to be sharply differentiating between delin-quents and non-delinquents. If a simpler and less time-consuming test could be developed to bring out the presence or absence of the particular Rorschach traits shown to be most differentiative of potential delinquents from non-delinquents, it would be a powerful aid to those clinics, schools, courts, and institutions that do not have the trained personnel or cannot take the time to administer and interpret the entire test. Of course, there is the danger of such a procedure degenerating into a mechanical routine imitation of the true testing and interpreting processes. However, a beginning in the direction of simplifying the administration of the Rorschach Test has already been made by giving it to groups, through projection of the Rorschach cards onto a screen, or to individuals who can administer it themselves.

The same question arises in connection with the personality characteristics that form the basis of the psychiatric prediction table. Psychiatric services are both expensive and difficult to obtain. If psychiatric social workers and psychologists could derive the necessary data by simpler methods with acceptable skill, the application of the psychiatric prediction table could then be extended.

As for the use of the social factors, certainly trained case workers could readily gather and interpret the materials. From a practical point of view, the five factors in the social background can be more easily and widely obtained than the factors of the other two prediction tables, simply because there are many more persons skilled in gathering social data than there are in securing and interpreting Rorschach and psychiatric data.

In this [chapter] we have not gone beyond the development of prediction tables that can be applied at or soon after school entrance [except for Table

IX–4]. It would be possible to construct some additional tables from the social data in *Unraveling Juvenile Delinquency* which, though not applicable at the point of school entrance, could be used at later stages in the school career.

School systems will not be able and ready to use these predictive instrumentalities on all children. It is suggested that a beginning might be made in cases in which maladaptive behavior is already present and school authorities wish to determine whether or not the boy in question is really a potential delinquent. In an enlightened educational system, the school could function as the litmus paper of personality maladaptation, reflecting the acid test of the child's success or failure in his first attempts to cope with the problems of life posed by a restrictive, impersonal society and code. In such a system the best psychiatric, psychologic, social, medical, and other facilities would be focused to cope with problems of personality distortion and maladaptive behavior at a critical point in the development of the child.[15]

* * *

In the next chapter we present a summary of the experimental checks that have thus far been made of the Social Prediction Table, all of which appear to indicate that this may develop into a promising instrument for early identification of true delinquents.

[15] *Unraveling Juvenile Delinquency*, pp. 268–269.

126

X

Checkings of Table Identifying Potential Delinquents

Introduction

It has already been pointed out that until a table designed to forecast behavior is applied to samples of cases other than the one on which it was constructed, there is insufficient evidence that it will have adequate prognostic efficacy. It is well, therefore, at the pretest stage, to refer to such an instrument as an *experience* table rather than a predictive device.

It need hardly be stressed that it is no easy matter to carry out validation experiments. In the first place, it must be made certain that the information is adequate on the subcategories of the factors included in the experience table, so that judgments derived from the instant facts are soundly based. In the second place, one must be sure that the checkup on the behavior under scrutiny is equally complete and thorough, so that the systematic correlation between the factors and the conduct will be reliable.

It is gratifying to report that the Social Prediction Table, derived from five significant factors involving family life and parent–child relationships, an instrument originally set out in *Unraveling Juvenile Delinquency*,[1] has been and is being subjected to testing on several and varied samples of cases both retrospectively (i.e., involving cases already delinquent) and prospectively (i.e., involving very young children not yet showing signs of delinquency).

Since most of these experiments have already been reported in published articles, only brief reference to them need be made.

Testing Social Prediction Table on Juveniles Already Delinquent

(a) The first retrospective study—made by Bertram J. Black and Selma J. Glick of the Jewish Board of Guardians in New York City—

[1] S. and E. T. Glueck, New York, The Commonwealth Fund, 1950.

appeared in the spring of 1952.[2] The Table was applied to a group of 100 Jewish delinquent boys confined in the Hawthorne-Cedar Knolls School in New York State, with a view to determining the extent to which it would have been possible, years earlier, to have identified them accurately as potential delinquents. Black and Glick ascertained that, by early application of the Social Prediction Table at the source, 91% of the group would have been correctly identified. It is especially significant that although the Table was compiled on the basis of underprivileged Boston boys, largely of English, Italian, and Irish descent and of Protestant and Catholic religions, it was found to operate so satisfactorily on a sample of New York Jewish boys.

(b) Another study, by Richard E. Thompson,[3] established the Social Prediction Table as an effective instrument for distinguishing from among children already showing some behavioral difficulties in and out of school, those who are true delinquents and those whose maladapted behavior is probably temporary. It was found that in a group of 100 boys, included originally in a research in Massachusetts known as the Cambridge-Somerville Youth Study,[4] it would have been possible (as in the study by the Jewish Board of Guardians) to discriminate correctly between potential delinquents and true non-delinquents in 91% of all the cases. The discriminative potential of the Table was found to be considerably greater than that of three experienced clinicians (psychiatrist, psychologist, and criminologist) who had been initially charged with selecting the boys for the Cambridge-Somerville Youth Study; for, in contrast, subsequent follow-ups proved that they correctly identified the predelinquents and the non-delinquents in only 65% of the cases.[5] It should be borne in mind, incidentally, that the clinicians had at their disposal a variety of case history data on each boy, including the judgment of school teachers who had had an opportunity to observe them, and that not infrequently, they devoted several clinical sessions to discussing a boy's potential.

In this experiment, as in that made by the Jewish Board of Guardians,

---

[2] "Predicted vs. Actual Outcome for Delinquent Boys," New York, Jewish Board of Guardians, 1952.

[3] "A Validation of the Glueck Social Prediction Scale for Proneness to Delinquency," 43 *J. Crim. L., Crimin. & Police Science* (1952), pp. 451–478.

[4] E. Powers and H. Witmer, *An Experiment in the Prevention of Delinquency*, New York, Columbia University Press, 1951.

[5] See pp. 464 *et seq.* of Thompson's article.

the Table reveals a capacity for usefulness on boys whose status and background differ from those of the boys on whom it was originally constructed, for its power was maintained among the Cambridge-Somerville boys who were younger than those in *Unraveling Juvenile Delinquency*, on those who were of different ethnic origin, on those who were of higher intelligence, on those of better economic status, and on those who grew up in neighborhoods that were not as disadvantaged as the ones in which the boys in *Unraveling Juvenile Delinquency* had been reared.[6]

(c) Another check on the Social Prediction Table was published in April, 1955. This is a study made by the New Jersey Department of Institutions and Agencies in which the Table was applied to fifty-one delinquent boys who were on parole. "It will be observed," says the report, "that the closeness of the findings on the basis of the New Jersey data with the original findings in the study of *Unraveling Juvenile Delinquency* is rather noteworthy, since the New Jersey boys were selected at random, and no attempt was made to match the individual characteristics of the New Jersey delinquent boys with the delinquent boys included in the Harvard Law School Study."[7]

(d) Thompson, in a recently published study,[8] reports on the application of the Social Prediction Table to fifty boys appearing before the Boston Juvenile Court in 1950 who averaged 13.1 years of age (compared with an average age of 14.6 years of the boys in *Unraveling Juvenile Delinquency*) and also to fifty girls. He found that had the Table been applied when the boys were six years old it would have been possible to determine that, barring effective therapeutic intervention, 92% would become delinquents. These boys also differed in some ways from the original sample of cases on which the Table was constructed: not only were they younger, but half of them had no prior court appearances. (All the delinquent boys in *Unraveling Juvenile Delinquency* had been in court before.) The religious distribution of these boys was also different: a higher proportion being Protestants than in the group studied in *Unraveling Juvenile Delinquency*; they were less retarded in school; in a higher percentage of cases both of the parents were native-born; and,

[6] *Ibid.*, pp. 466–469.

[7] "Predicting Juvenile Delinquency," *Research Bulletin* No. 124, April 1955, published by the State Department of Institutions and Agencies, Trenton, N. J.

[8] R. E. Thompson, "Further Validation of the Glueck Social Prediction Table for Identifying Potential Delinquents," 48 *J. Crim. L., Crimin. & Police Science* (1957), pp. 175–184.

in a far higher proportion, one or both parents had attended high school.

In applying the Table to girl offenders, Thompson found that all of the fifty girls would have been correctly identified as potential delinquents. This is a finding which we can explain only by the fact that Thompson's analysis indicates that there is much more family pathology in the background of girls who are actually brought to court than in that of the boys to whom the Table has thus far been applied. This is clearly reflected in the categorization of this group of girl offenders on the five social factors that comprise the Prediction Table, as compared with the boys of *Unraveling Juvenile Delinquency*, on whom the Table was constructed. For example, as regards laxity of discipline by their fathers, this was found for 75.6% of the girls as contrasted with 26.6% of the boys in *Unraveling Juvenile Delinquency*; the fathers were indifferent or hostile to 87.5% of the girls, as compared with 59.8% of the boys. In the matter of the affectional relation of the mother to the girl, the mother was indifferent or hostile to the daughter in 80.6% of the cases, as compared with 27.9% of the boys. The families of 76.0% of the girls were not cohesive, as contrasted with 24.7% of the families of the boys. It is, to our minds, this greater social pathology reflected in the family life which accounts for the 100% result in the application of the Social Prediction Table to the fifty girl offenders.

Although the rate of agreement between predicted and actual behavior would probably not always be so high, this checkup reveals that the same cluster of factors associated with the delinquency of boys is also potent in predicting delinquency among girls.

Incidentally, testing of the Table on girl delinquents is the second such attempt, the first having been made by Selma Glick and Catherine Donnell of the Jewish Board of Guardians in 1953 on 150 unmarried mothers, in which it was found that 81% of the girls would have been identified as potential delinquents had the Table been applied to them at the age of six.[9]

(e) Another opportunity to test the Social Prediction Table came in 1954 when the Douglas A. Thom Clinic for Children in Boston (a psycho-analytically-oriented agency) applied the Table to fifty-seven boys, ranging in age from six to twelve years, who had been treated for aggressive, destructive, antisocial behavior. The scorings made by the clinic

[9] This study has not yet been published.

130

psychologist indicated that 82.3% of these boys would have been clearly identified by the Table at the age of six as potential delinquents.[10]

(f) An application of the Social Prediction Table to 150 delinquent boys in upper income families ($7,500 and thereabouts) by Selma Glick of the Jewish Board of Guardians has not been completed. At the time of this writing, the Table has been applied to 81 boys and it has been reported informally that the Social Prediction Table would accurately have identified 89% of these boys as delinquents. It is to be noted, of course, that the income level of the families of the boys in *Unraveling Juvenile Delinquency* was much lower, and that the group studied by the Jewish Board of Guardians was far different in ethnic distribution—the current sample being entirely Jewish.

In addition to the checkups made in the United States, there are two which have been carried out in foreign countries—one in Japan and one in France—about which we are able to report briefly just as this volume goes to press.

(g) In Japan the Social Prediction Table has been applied to thirty juvenile delinquent boys, who appeared before the Juvenile Court in Morioka, Japan, and to a control group of thirty non-delinquent boys from a Middle School in Morioka, with the result that the future behavior of 89% could have been correctly predicted in early childhood. This research, carried out by Mr. Tokuhiro Tatezawa, Probation Officer of the Yokohama Family Court, entitled *A Study of Prediction of Juvenile Delinquency*, was published by the Japanese Ministry of Justice in 1957 and revised and reissued in 1958.

We quote briefly from Mr. Tatezawa's report:

> This prediction study revealed that the factors used in the Gluecks' prediction table show rather high predictive power when applied to the Japanese juvenile cases which have their own cultural and social background. It also suggests that it is worthwhile to construct prediction tables by modifying the Gluecks' tables according to the Japanese social and cultural background. It should be noted that in Japan 'nature of employment of father' is a factor of larger significance than as noticed by the Gluecks. We also found that there are some other significant factors which were not regarded as important factors in the Gluecks' study. This finding has not only etiological significance, but also practical value for the improvement of prediction tables. For instance, if we substitute this factor for the fourth social factor, i.e., 'affection of mother

[10] E. N. Rexford, M. Schleifer, and S. T. Van Amerongen, "A Follow-Up of a Psychiatric Study of 57 Antisocial Young Children," *Mental Hygiene* (April, 1956), pp. 196–214.

for boy,' and reconstruct a prediction table on the new set of five social factors, it will be quite likely for us to get a more reliable prediction table which will be more suitable to the Japanese social conditions. After all this study may be considerably encouraging for those who are trying to develop the prediction studies in Japan. . . .

This, incidentally, is the first study to make possible adequate comparison of American and non-American delinquents because the author examined his cases not only for the presence of the five social prediction factors, but for 120 factors of family and personal background, comparable to those used in *Unraveling Juvenile Delinquency*, and he indicates by adequate statistical techniques in which of these factors the Japanese delinquents and non-delinquents resemble and in which they differ from the delinquents and non-delinquents of *Unraveling Juvenile Delinquency*.

(h) More recently, a study under way for about a year in Strasbourg, France, on a population of French juvenile offenders has also provided encouraging evidence of the usefulness of the Social Prediction Table. It is hoped that a more elaborate research following the completion of the initial experiment can be carried out by staff members of the Institut de Sciences Criminelles et Pénitentiaires of the Faculty of Law of the University of Strasbourg.

The results of the pilot project on forty-six cases of persistent juvenile offenders selected at the Centre d'Observation pour Garçons in Strasbourg, as informally reported by Professor Jacques Léauté and his associates, indicate that in 91.2% of the cases the boys would have been correctly identified as true juvenile offenders had the Social Prediction Table been applied to them at the age of six.[11] It is anticipated that a report of these findings will be available in the form of an article.

In view of the variety of samples of cases to which the Social Prediction Table has been retrospectively applied at different times, in different places, and by different workers, it would seem reasonable to conclude that the results cannot be entirely attributed to "the long arm of coincidence." However, even those readers who consider that the evidence is far from conclusive, will grant that the findings can at least be accepted as "straws in the wind" that are blowing in the right direction.

[11] This work is being carried out under the direction of Professor Léauté and his associates—Professor Didier Anzieu, Director of the Institut de Psychologie, University of Strasbourg, Dr. R. Durand de Bousing, Laboratoire de Psychologie Clinique Psychométrique, Hôpital Civil, Strasbourg, and Dr. Réné Oberlé, Centre d'Observation pour Garçons de Strasbourg-Bischheim.

Testing Social Prediction Table on Young School Children

It would appear to be a reasonable assumption that if delinquents are found to resemble each other in their interpersonal family relations, as evidenced by the checking of the Social Prediction Table on groups of juvenile offenders differing in one way or another from the 500 delinquents of *Unraveling Juvenile Delinquency*, such factors appearing in the background of children not yet delinquent are danger signals of budding criminal careers. However, this must be put to a rigid test by applying the Social Prediction Table to a sufficient group of children, preferably in a public school setting, when they enter first grade, and following them over a period of several years, in order to determine whether the predicted results actually occur. One such study is in progress in New York City. This experiment is being carried out by the New York City Youth Board,[12] which has applied the Table to some 260 boys in the first grade of two public schools in high delinquency areas in the Bronx. This experiment has been in progress since 1953. The boys' behavior in school, home, and community is being followed up. Although it will be several years before the results are definitive, the New York City Youth Board has recently published an interim report[13] covering the first four years of the project. Thus far, the results show a clear trend in the direction of the ability of the Social Prediction Table to identify, at the time of the first contact of organized society (namely, at school entrance), those children, not yet showing overt signs of delinquent behavior, who are in danger of becoming delinquent unless suitable therapeutic intervention changes the predicted course.

The Social Prediction Table was initially applied to 224 boys, comprising the entire first grade population in two public schools in highly under-privileged areas of New York City in the school year 1952–53. These children ranged in age from five and a half to six years. Of these 224 boys, 53 were white (mostly Jewish); 131, Negro; and 40, Puerto Rican. (The reader is reminded that the cases on which the Social Prediction Table was developed in *Unraveling Juvenile Delinquency* did not include any Negroes or Puerto Ricans and very few Jewish boys.) It was clear at the

[12] R. W. Whelan, "An Experiment in Predicting Delinquency," 45 *J. Crim. L., Crimin. & Police Science* (1954), pp. 432–441.

[13] "An Experiment in the Validation of the Glueck Prediction Scale," *Progress Report from November, 1952 to December, 1956*, New York City Youth Board, Research Department, July, 1957.

outset of the Youth Board Study that because of the marked difference between the sample of cases to which the Social Prediction Table was being experimentally applied and the cases in *Unraveling Juvenile Delinquency*, the Table is being subjected to the most rigid kind of a test. Although later in the study the research group engaged in this project decided to equalize the number of white and Negro boys by having approximately 130 of each, the interim report is based on the application of the Social Prediction Table to the original sample of 220 of the 224 boys.

The reader is probably interested in two basic questions: (a) What proportion of the boys were identified by the Table as non-delinquents and what proportion as delinquents? (b) To what extent have these predictions thus far eventuated?

(a) Details will be found in the New York City Youth Board Report; but, briefly, of the 220 boys to whom the Table was applied, 69.6% were predicted as probable non-delinquents and 30.4% were designated as having more than an even chance of becoming delinquent. (So high a delinquency rate is most atypical; but it should be pointed out that the two schools from which the children were drawn are located in the highest delinquency areas of New York City. The selection of such regions was deliberately made by the Youth Board Research Staff in order to assure a sufficient number of potential delinquents for study purposes; and it might incidentally be mentioned that the principals and teachers of the two schools involved had expressed the opinion to the Youth Board that in their experience in these schools approximately one-third of the children develop into delinquents. The distribution of the cases, therefore, on the basis of their prediction scores on the five factors involved in the Table does not appear to be out of line with experience.)

(b) What, now, of how these boys actually turned out during the subsequent four years?

There is but one definitive test of the validity of the predicted scores; and that is an intensive follow-up of these children preferably until they are seventeen. Before stating the outcome of the follow-up, it should be emphasized that the results to date, as determined up to the time these boys were nine and a half to ten years old, are based not only on a checkup of their behavior within the school setting (a cumulative record of their school conduct being kept), but also on their conduct as reflected in information secured systematically from social agencies and from the

134

Juvenile Aid Bureau of the New York City Police Department. Full details of the follow-up procedures and the classification of the 220 boys into the appropriate categories of behavior are presented in the Progress Report.[14]

Here, however, is the crux of the Youth Board's interim report:

> Data covering behavior for the four-year period since the study was begun were classified into an eight category behavior classification according to their current involvement or non-involvement in delinquent or pre-delinquent behavior. This report relates the behavior of 220 of the 224 boys to the scores assigned to them four years ago. These boys are now between $9\frac{1}{2}$–$10\frac{1}{2}$ years of age. *The findings at this point reveal that the majority of the boys are behaving in accordance with the prediction made when they entered school. The majority of those who were rated with a low probability of becoming delinquent are currently presenting no serious community problem. The majority of those who are already showing delinquent or pre-delinquent tendencies were assigned a high probability of becoming delinquent.*[15]

Table XI[16] of the Report indicates that the proportion of all children behaving as the Table had predicted was found to be 88.9%; and a breakdown by ethnic groups (see Table X)[17] indicates that of the sample of white boys, 90% are conducting themselves as the Table had forecast; of the Negroes, 85%; and of the Puerto Ricans, 91%.

Although, as already stated, these findings cannot yet be accepted as definitive, the most conservative estimate is that they legitimately encourage the belief that the Social Prediction Table will prove to be a useful instrument in identifying true potential delinquents at a sufficiently early stage in life to make therapeutic intervention at least promising.

No one can say with assurance that the trend indicated so far will continue as these children grow older. But all the evidence set forth in these pages strongly suggests this to be so. In his Foreword to the Youth Board's Report, Mayor Robert F. Wagner of New York City says:

[14] As some indication of the great difficulty of carrying out this study, it should be pointed out that the boys initially selected from the two schools were, at the time of the preparation of the New York City Youth Board's Progress Report (1957), scattered over no fewer than eighty-nine schools, a fact which of course greatly complicated the follow-up of these cases.

[15] "An Experiment in the Validation of the Glueck Prediction Scale," Youth Board's Report, p. 35.

[16] *Ibid.*, p. 32.

[17] *Ibid.*, p. 31.

Should the trend noted in this progress report continue, it would constitute a significant contribution both for the preventive and treatment aspects of this important social problem. Screening methods based on this research and utilized by trained personnel at the point of school registration could quickly select those children in need of various types of help. Such an instrument could be applied to large segments of the school population and we would thus have for use a social "Geiger counter" for detecting potential delinquents at an early age where help would be most effective.[18]

Should the Social Prediction Table continue to prove efficacious in the early detection of endangered children, not only schools, but clinics, police, and juvenile courts would have a very important practical aid.[19] Doubtless, some parents would have to be educated to appreciate the value of this early detection of danger signals; to realize that the issue is not one of stigmatizing the child but, as in the case of physical and mental illness, of recognizing the need of timely aid and offering services to deflect a course of behavior that so often leads to the juvenile and criminal court. With the use of the Table, if its efficiency continues to be demonstrated:

> Referrals could then be made to those public and private agencies which would assume responsibility for the various treatment aspects of a delinquency program. This would permit the pinpointing of services of the delinquency-oriented groups to the high risk children and their families. It would also conserve the time of much professional personnel whose services are now dispersed in many directions.[20]

[18] *Ibid.*, p. 3.
[19] The fact that the checkings of the Social Prediction Table are so consistently encouraging should dispel doubt as to the soundness of the sample of true delinquents and true non-delinquents in *Unraveling Juvenile Delinquency*, on which the Table is based. (It might be mentioned that a recently completed follow-up of the non-delinquents studied in *Unraveling* has demonstrated that with few exceptions these boys were indeed not, and at twenty-five are still not, delinquents.) The checkings of the Table should also counter the suggestion of some critics that the Table was not properly constructed on the ground that delinquents comprise but a small segment of the total boy population while our Table was derived from a matched sample (500 delinquents, 500 non-delinquents). The evidence proves that the factual outcomes of application of the Table to a wide variety of samples are very similar to the Table as originally constructed. The critics are in error theoretically as well as practically in that they confuse the necessity for similarly-sized *samples* of cases with the existence of similarly-sized universes from which samples are drawn. Thereby, they beg the question in assuming that the difference in ratio of non-delinquents to delinquents in general seriously influences the operation of the predictive table, which must therefore be adjusted to take account of this ratio.
[20] Youth Board's Report, pp. 3–4.

XI

Identification of Juvenile Delinquents and Neurotics*

Introduction

The prediction method gives promise not only of distinguishing potential delinquents from potential non-delinquents at an early stage in life but also of distinguishing neurotic *delinquents* from both non-neurotic delinquents and neurotic non-delinquents, as well as neurotic non-delinquents from emotionally sound non-delinquents.

In this chapter we present three tables designed to bring out the distinctions in question. Because there were relatively few delinquent or non-delinquent boys in *Unraveling Juvenile Delinquency* who were either prepsychotic or frankly psychotic, we excluded them from consideration entirely.[1] For present purposes we also eliminated those who were diagnosed as psychopathic or "asocial" because—although they were considerable among the delinquents, there were relatively few of them among the non-delinquents. It should be possible at a later time, however, to construct a table that would discriminate emotionally healthy youngsters not only from neurotics but also from those who are psychopathic or asocial.

It is to be hoped that similar devices for the early identification, or early diagnosis, not only of delinquent but of emotionally disturbed non-delinquent children will be developed by others, notably by psychiatrists and psychologists, who have access to intensive and extensive case materials.

The reader is invited to consult *Unraveling Juvenile Delinquency* regarding the diagnostic procedures that led to a determination of neuroticism

* This chapter is based largely on "Identifying Juvenile Delinquents and Neurotics," by E. T. Glueck, 40 *Mental Hygiene* (1956), pp. 24–43.
[1] S. and E. T. Glueck, *Unraveling Juvenile Delinquency*, New York, The Commonwealth Fund, 1950, Table XVIII–43, Mental Pathology, p. 239.

137

(including marked and mild neurotics and those with neurotic trends).[2] Briefly, a comparison of diagnostic findings arrived at independently, by the Rorschach experts[3] and the psychiatrist who examined the boys,[4] was made, and differences in diagnostic classification were resolved by them in those few instances in which the diagnoses were conflicting.[5]

Before proceeding to the construction of a table distinguishing neurotic from non-neurotic delinquents, it should be pointed out that we did not design the research, which eventuated in *Unraveling Juvenile Delinquency*, to encompass the development of the tables that form the subject of this chapter. Had this been among our objectives, we would in the initial selection of delinquents and matched non-delinquents have deliberately included a greater number of neurotics as well as youngsters with other forms of mental pathology. The use of the data for the present purpose is purely a by-product of the larger work and should be accepted only as illustrative of the kind of instruments that mental hygienists might well develop to aid (by large-scale early identification) in the prophylaxis of emotional disturbance in the hope of preventing or intercepting the development of personality distortions.

For the present purpose, analysis was made of forty-seven social factors, forty-two traits of character structure (obtained from the Rorschach test), and eighteen traits of temperament (derived through psychiatric examination). Although in *Unraveling Juvenile Delinquency* we found, when comparing delinquents as a group with their non-delinquent controls, that they differed markedly in the factors reflecting what we have chosen to call the *under-the-roof culture*, this did not prove to be significantly so in differentiating neurotic from non-neurotic delinquents, neurotic delinquents from neurotic non-delinquents, and neurotic non-delinquents from emotionally stable non-delinquents. It may well be that there were more subtle aspects in the early rearing of these children which would have reflected marked differences between the two groups, but in this inquiry, at least, they were not revealed.

Examination of the factors studied disclosed the most significant differences to be in traits of basic character structure (derived from the

[2] See Chapters XVIII and XIX.
[3] Ernest G. Schachtel and the late Anna Hartoch Schachtel.
[4] Dr. Bryant E. Moulton, who was for twelve years associated with the Judge Baker Guidance Center.
[5] *Unraveling Juvenile Delinquency*, pp. 242–243, note 8.

Rorschach test), i.e., in the deposits in the personality of *intrapsychic tension or conflict.*[6]

Utilizing markedly differentiating traits of basic character structure, three tables were developed—one distinguishing neurotic from non-neurotic juvenile delinquents; another distinguishing neurotic delinquents from neurotic non-delinquents; and a third distinguishing neurotic non-delinquents from non-neurotic non-delinquents. These tables are summarized in Table XI–A. The more detailed tables and definitions will be found in Appendix B, Tables XI–1, XI–2, and XI–3.

Distinguishing Neurotic from Emotionally Healthy Juvenile Delinquents

The first screening table developed, XI–1 (which, like our other tables, of course, requires testing against other samples of cases) has to do with

Summary Table XI–A. Identification of Juvenile Delinquents and Neurotics

Prediction Base		Less than Even Chance of Neuroticism or Delinquency		More than Even Chance of Neuroticism or Delinquency	
		Score Class	(Rate)	Score Class	(Rate)
Neuroticism among Juvenile Delinquents[1]	(XI–1)	300 or Over	(14.8%)	Less than 300	(84.9%)
Delinquency among Neurotic Juveniles[2]	(XI–2)	Less than 200	(20.7)	200 or Over	(73.9)
Neuroticism among Juvenile Non-Delinquents[3]	(XI–3)	Less than 250	(15.6)	250 or Over	(86.7)

[1] Predictive Traits: Common Sense; Enhanced Feeling of Insecurity and/or Anxiety; Feeling of Helplessness and Powerlessness; Fear of Failure and Defeat; Defensive Attitude.

[2] Predictive Traits: Enhanced Feeling of Insecurity and/or Anxiety; Suspiciousness; Masochistic Trends; Self-Control; Compulsory Trends.

[3] Predictive Traits: Enhanced Feeling of Insecurity and/or Anxiety; Fear of Failure and Defeat; Feeling of Resentment; Defensive Attitude; Compulsory Trends.

Note: Numbers in parentheses to right of prediction base refer to table numbers in Appendix B; definitions of the predictive factors and the scores for the respective subcategories will also be found in Appendix B.

[6] In order to develop suitable diagnostic instruments it was necessary to limit the initial selection of basic character traits (from among which five were to be chosen) to those not only significantly differentiating the neurotic delinquents from the neurotic non-delinquents, but at the same time differentiating the neurotic non-delinquents from the non-delinquents who were emotionally healthy. Otherwise, we would, in effect, be making a comparison of delinquents as a group with non-delinquents as a group (already accomplished in *Unraveling Juvenile Delinquency*, p. 264).

differentiating, in a group of true delinquents (excluding for the present those who are prepsychotic, psychotic, psychopathic, or asocial), between those who are neurotics and those who are emotionally healthy. As already indicated, sufficient differences were not disclosed in the *social* background of neurotic and non-neurotic delinquents to make possible the construction of a diagnostic table utilizing social factors. But among the traits of basic character structure (derived from the Rorschach test) there are eighteen (out of a total of forty-two) from among which we could make a choice of five as a basis for the screening or diagnostic table.

In selecting five traits from among eighteen possibilities, we were guided by considerations largely related to (a) the number of known cases, and (b) the size of the differences between the incidence of a trait among the emotionally healthy delinquents, on the one hand, and the neurotic delinquents, on the other. The five traits chosen, and their weighted scores, are presented in Appendix B, Table XI–1.

Assuming its validation, Table XI–1 indicates that if a boy scores less than 300 on the five traits, there is more than an even chance that he is neurotic; it would appear to be a certainty that he is, if he scores under 200 (see detailed table in Appendix B, XI–1). If he scores 300 or over, there is more than an even chance that he is emotionally sound; this becomes almost a certainty if he scores 400 or over.

Distinguishing Neurotic Delinquents from Neurotic Non-Delinquents

The second screening device made possible by our materials (Table XI–2) is designed to distinguish neurotics who are likely to *act out* their aggressive impulses from those who "bottle up" their aggressiveness or turn it inward against themselves. Such a differentiation ought to be of assistance to clinicians who are charged with the psychotherapy of neurotics.

Of a total of forty-two traits, there were twelve which sufficiently differentiated the two groups to be utilized in a screening table.[7] A final selection of five traits was again guided essentially by considerations relating to (a) the number of known cases, and (b) significant differences between the incidence of a trait among the neurotic delinquents and the neurotic non-delinquents. These considerations resulted in utilizing the five traits, which are listed in Table XI–2.

Summation of the highest possible weighted score and of the lowest

[7] See E. T. Glueck, "Identifying Juvenile Delinquents and Neurotics," pp. 24–43.

that can be achieved by an individual in order to establish his status on the five traits yields the extremes of 269.6 and 156.2, respectively. Within these limits, the neurotic delinquents and the neurotic non-delinquents were distributed into score classes in each of the two groups separately. Thus from Table XI–2, it is determined (assuming its validation on other samples of cases) that among a group of neurotics a boy scoring under 200 is not likely to act out his aggressive impulses in terms of delinquent behavior; one scoring 200 or over, very probably will do so.

Distinguishing Neurotic Non-Delinquents from Emotionally Healthy Non-Delinquents

Although our primary focus of interest is in the development of instruments for the early detection of juvenile offenders, the control group of non-delinquents in *Unraveling Juvenile Delinquency* makes it possible for us to step out of the area of distinguishing between those among delinquents or potential delinquents who are neurotic and non-neurotic and to consider the screening of non-delinquents as neurotics or non-neurotics. Although we are hesitant to go beyond the limits of our special field of inquiry, we permit ourselves to do so because there is significance, as will be seen below, in the fact that three of the five traits markedly distinguishing neurotic delinquents from non-neurotic delinquents also differentiate neurotic non-delinquents from emotionally sound non-delinquents. Since two of the traits are different, however, there would appear to be evidence that delinquency may be conceived of as an entity different in some respects from other forms of affective disturbance. Apart from this, those who are concerned with the early recognition and treatment of emotional illness may find this third table suggestive and worthy of testing on other samples of cases.

Applying the same considerations as in the two prior tables to the selection of factors on which to construct a screening device, we have utilized the five traits presented in Table XI–3 from which it is determined (assuming its validation on other samples of cases) that if a boy scores under 250, there is only a slight chance that he is a neurotic; if he scores 250 or over, it is very likely that he is a neurotic.

* * *

The value of such discriminative instruments will be determined only by experimental applications. The problem of skillful administration

141

and interpretation of Rorschach test findings may limit the usefulness of such devices. It may be, however, that simpler projective tests can be developed which would elicit the data needed. Perhaps, as suggested in Chapter IX, a group Rorschach test could be devised which would focus on the particular traits of basic character structure that appear to be significant in differentiating between neurotic delinquents and neurotic non-delinquents, between neurotic delinquents and non-neurotic delinquents, and between neurotic and emotionally stable non-delinquents.

A beginning must be made in utilizing tables such as the three presented here in order to determine how well they apply to other samples of cases. Some such syndromization of traits or symptoms makes possible the arrival at diagnoses by methods other than purely psychiatric, and by persons other than psychiatrists. From the trend of evidence in the checks that have thus far been made of the Social Prediction Table developed in *Unraveling Juvenile Delinquency*, we are encouraged to think that we have in these three new diagnostic instrumentalities additional means for early recognition of neuroticism in delinquents and non-delinquents. We envisage the use of these three discriminative tables as a supplement to the Social Prediction Table in order that, following the spotting of potential delinquents, a further step can be taken in distinguishing the emotionally healthy delinquents and non-delinquents from the neurotics, and also in sorting out from among the neurotics those who are likely to give vent to their aggressive impulses in delinquent behavior. If, in addition, a table can be designed to identify those who are psychopathic or asocial, the mass screening of children (through group projective tests), at the point of school entrance, would be closer to realization, making possible a concerted attack not only on the prevention of delinquency but of emotional disturbance.

XII

Some Objections to Predictive Devices

Introduction

In the foregoing pages we have presented a series of prediction tables growing out of our various researches, and have discussed their application to some fundamental problems of practical criminal justice and preventive effort. We believe that such devices will influence judges, parole authorities, and clinicians to reflect fruitfully upon the results of day-to-day decisions they make in exercising discretion and in making prognoses. Cautious employment of predictive devices should act as a spur to general improvement in sentencing, treatment, and releasing practices and to a search for more promising devices.

Whether the application of more appropriate treatment in various types of cases will tend to shorten delinquent careers, or result in rehabilitating a greater proportion of offenders, remains for future research to determine. It must be borne in mind in this connection, that the skill and dedication of those who administer justice at various stages are important elements in the total situation. But it seems reasonable to suppose that, at least during treatment, the better selection of appropriate sentences should lead to a more reflective and therefore more effective and more economical administration of justice. It should therefore ultimately bring about a better safeguarding of the public which, as much as the offender himself, is the victim of inefficiency in the administration of the sentencing and paroling functions.

Moreover, the considered use of predictive devices in the screening of *potential* delinquents should spearhead the improvement of existing preventive-therapeutic programs and the experimental development of new techniques. It may well be, also, that further reflection on the traits and factors which occur most frequently in prediction tables will yield fruitful clues to the most potent and most permeative causes of delinquency.

Objections

But despite these apparent advantages of the prognostic approach, certain objections have been raised to the employment of prediction tables that deserve consideration[1]:

(1) Underlying predictive techniques, it is said, is the assumption of a deterministic, indeed a fatalistic, sequence of cause and effect in human affairs; and this, supposedly, does violence to the nobler conception of human action as the result of the exercise of a "free will."

This objection can be met as follows: Nobody, in the long history of philosophic speculation, has been able to find the definitive answer to the puzzling problem of freedom or determinism. But apart from the philosophic issue, the factor of free will cannot, practicably, be used in a prediction table since it is impossible to measure the degree of freedom which distinguishes recidivists from non-recidivists, or potential delinquents from actual delinquents. Since other factors, which can be assessed, do bear a considerable relationship to subsequent conduct, they may usefully be employed in a prognostic instrument without necessarily taking any final position in respect to any particular view of the mainsprings of human behavior. In every walk of life, including law and medicine, causal sequences are expected and accepted as practical realities that have to be coped with in the management of human affairs. So, in regard to the use of prediction tables.

(2) It has been urged that prediction tables fail to take account of the important reality of change in personal and social conditions; that they are built on the assumption that personal traits and environmental factors will remain as they were when the tables were constructed.

As to this objection, it is true that predictive devices will have to be modified from time to time to take account of changing conditions; but this does not prevent their effective use during lengthy spans when conditions remain relatively stable. The methods of treatment by probation, commitment to industrial schools, incarceration in reformatories and prisons, and parole do not radically change in most jurisdictions over long periods. For example, in Chapter IV, it was shown that a prediction table founded on one set of delinquents was effective in forecasting the behavior of another group many years later.

[1] Thoughtful discussions of some of these objections were submitted by Ohlin, Overbeek, and others to the Third International Congress of Criminology, London, September, 1955. See S. Glueck, *Prognosis of Recidivism*, General Report Section IV, London, 1955, pp. 15–19.

(3) Another objection raised involves the point that while human conduct is the outcome of the dynamic interplay of many and complex influences of person and environment, prediction tables can at best employ only a small number of them.

Regarding this criticism, experience has shown that devices limited to few factors do, in fact, provide a significantly high degree of predictability. Indeed, it is one of the merits of predictive devices that they narrow the field of basic interest in decision-making and therapy to the relatively few items found to be *most relevant to outcomes.* Investigation reports in the better probation and parole offices and clinics contain a wide variety of detailed data. It is time that every item in such reports, which has been routinely included for a number of years, be, as it were, required to produce its passport, to prove its relevancy to expectable conduct. By use of the prediction table, based on the preliminary intercorrelation of many factors with varieties of behavioral outcome, the case historian would have a means of determining which, of the numerous factors now included, do in fact bear a substantial relationship to outcomes and may therefore be regarded, if only indirectly, as causally involved and relevant to therapeutic endeavor. Each predictive factor represents, in a general way, many subtle interpersonal dynamisms. The deeper exploration of such mechanisms leading to misconduct must be left to psychiatrists, psychologists, and psychiatric social workers. But the relevant targets of such further exploration—the crucial starting points—are furnished by the predictive factors. Thus the predictive approach, far from ignoring the multiplicity of etiologic factors and the complexity of causation, can serve as a disciplinary device on loose thinking regarding cause, cure, and prophylaxis.

(4) It is said also that since prediction tables deal with individuals as statistical types, they cannot truly "individualize;" for by considering the problem in the mass, those who use the tables will perforce lose sight of the uniqueness of the individual case, especially in respect to the more subtle and unmeasurable features of the personality observed in the "clinical situation."

This criticism springs from the misconception that judges, parole board members, and clinicians, by use of predictive devices, should and will make their decisions mechanically, that is, exclusively on the odds presented by the prediction tables. However, as has been frequently stressed in the foregoing pages, the aim is not to substitute statistical

145

tables for judicial or other experience in the sentencing or release of individual offenders. It is rather to supply the judge and administrator with an instrument of prime importance in putting a solid foundation beneath the process of individualizing justice. Neither a judge nor a parole board member nor a clinician should follow such tables blindly. They are designed to help in viewing the individual offender in the perspective of organized experience with many other offenders whom he resembles in certain crucial respects. As to some traits, each offender, of course, remains a unique personality. The dimensions of the special problem presented by a particular offender can be much more accurately assessed by the judge or administrator if the particular delinquent is compared with a group of other offenders than if reliance is placed exclusively on the presentence or clinical investigation report, or on unsystematized "experience" or "hunch."

The use of predictive devices as an aid to decision is not intended nor likely to lead to a form of what Pound calls "mechanical jurisprudence." While the opponents of parole prediction methods feared that the use of prediction tables would result in mechanical parole selection, this has in fact not been the experience in Illinois (the only state which thus far employs predictive devices). On the contrary, "the net result of the use of the tables has been to challenge the application of mechanical formulas at every point and to force more detailed examination of the unique merits of the individual case."[2]

(5) The opposite criticism to a mechanical use of predictive devices has also been advanced. It has been suggested that judges would dispose of cases just as erratically with the use of prediction tables as they do at present.[3]

This is not likely. A basic purpose of such tables is to help the judge to marshal his experience more effectively in the light of systematized correlations between types of offenders and behavioral outcomes. While, as has been emphasized, a judge should not follow such tables blindly or mechanically, he is, by consulting them, bound to evolve a set of principles and practices based, not on hunch or guess, or on what can be and often is a mistaken conception of the kind of behavior to be expected from the particular person involved, but on objectified experience with many

[2] L. E. Ohlin, quoted in S. Glueck, "Prognosis of Recidivism," note 14, p. 19.
[3] See S. Rubin, "Sentencing Goals: Real and Ideal," 21 *Federal Probation* (1957), pp. 51–56; and S. Glueck, "Further Comments on the Sentencing Problem," *ibid.*, pp. 47–54.

similar cases. And the dispositions he makes in the light of the systematized experience as reflected in the tables, when focused on the presentence reports, should tend to be not only more appropriate to the individual case but more consistent with the general run of cases than those under the present *ad hoc* method.

(6) It has been suggested that although our prediction tables do distinguish between offenders who are and those who are not likely to behave well *during* treatment, they do not indicate what form of treatment is most likely to result in an offender's ultimate reform.

Some of our tables do, of course, indicate what the likelihood is of rehabilitation following incarceration in a reformatory and its associated parole system; and among our tables are several that indicate the behavior of both juvenile and adult offenders five to fifteen years after the completion of the first sentence in a juvenile court and the first sentence in an adult court without, however, specifying whether the first sentence was probation, a suspended sentence, or an institutional commitment.

However, even when a prediction table focuses only on the probabilities of antisocial or non-criminal behavior *during* a sentence, much is gained. First of all, if the information provided by a prediction profile (see Chapter VIII) were used by a judge, public security would be protected by releasing into the community only those offenders who have a good likelihood of non-recidivism.

Apart from this, the American system of criminal justice is at least partially based on the assumption that there is a substantial relationship between the type of person who successfully or unsuccessfully responds well to one or another kind of peno-correctional treatment and his ultimate reform or recidivism. If this were not so, legislatures would not have provided a variety of alternative types of sentence. Probation, for example, is intended for the most promising and least dangerous offenders and not merely for those who would do well only while on probationary oversight.

(7) It has also been said that to the extent that retribution and deterrence, or the general educative effect of the criminal law on the people, are involved in the sentencing decision, the prediction tables contain no relevant material of use to a judge.

But who can supply the yardsticks that will measure the relatively exact quantum of the retributive or deterrent or educative elements that should be included in any sentence, and predict its probable relationship to the subsequent behavior of the particular offender or any class of prospective offenders? This is inherently impossible. It is the merit of the system expounded in these pages that, at least in the central task of determining the relationship of traits and factors in personality and environment to variations in expectable behavioral response of offenders to different types of sentence and treatment and during reasonable periods beyond, there is presented a method of relative precision based on organized experience. An island of relatively solid fact is blocked out in a sea of speculation, guesswork, and hunch in which it is impossible to measure the elements of retribution and deterrence. It is to be noted, however, that any judge who, taking account of the indications of the prediction tables, still believes that the particular case requires special emphasis upon the ingredients of retribution and/or deterrence, however unmeasurable these may be, is of course free, as he is at present, to bring them into the total situation in making his sentencing decision.

(8) Finally, as to prediction tables designed to spot predelinquent children in school before they overtly misbehave (or to determine whether childhood mischief is or is not truly prodromal of delinquency), it has been urged that their use would result in an unfair "labeling" or even stigmatization of innocent children as fated delinquents.

This objection can be countered with the question whether it is better to allow delinquency-inducing influences to take their toll of youngsters (and of society) in overt and persistent delinquency, than it is to detect these dangerous influences sufficiently early in life to permit doing something constructive to deflect them. As in the health field, some education of parents in the advantages of early detection of delinquent tendencies would undoubtedly help to allay apprehensions regarding the application of the tables. It goes without saying that in the administration of a device such as a prediction table, intelligent, trained, and tactful social investigators are needed. In the long run and in the final analysis, it is far better that endangered children be identified early in life than be permitted to stumble on until arrested by the police, brought into court, and sent to institutions. The best available opinion of psychiatrists and criminologists would seem to indicate that the early discovery and treatment of aberrant affective or behavioral tendencies would make the rehabilitative task easier. Finally, it should be borne in mind that it is not suggested that examination of youngsters from the point of view of potential delinquency be compulsory. Parents and schools must decide whether or not such services are desirable, through considering the advantages and disadvantages in the light of reports by clinicians and other informed persons.

Improvements in Predictive Devices[4]

Prediction tables need to be tested from time to time with a view to their improvement. Methods for enhancing the scientific soundness and practical utility of such prognostic devices might be considered under the headings of (a) improvement of the raw materials entering into construction of the tables; (b) further checking of the tables to convert them, where possible, from "experience tables" into true prediction tables; and (c) refinement of the tables.

(a) A basic reason for the considerable variation in traits and factors among our tables and in other studies is the great divergence in the reliability of the raw data which originally entered into the researches from which the predictive factors were drawn. Studies in the United States and in a number of European countries (see Appendix A) suggest that the variety in the factors found most significant for purposes of prognostication is probably in large measure due to this fundamental difference in the building blocks of the respective predictive structures. Neat tables and sophisticated mathematico-statistical devices cannot transform unverified raw data regarding personality, character, and sociocultural conditions into adequate information. This applies, likewise, to the checkup on recidivism.

(b) As regards further checking of the tables, there is great need for this. Judges of both juvenile and adult courts can do much to contribute to such testing by comparing the outcomes of their present disposition of cases with the predicted results based on the tables. We personally hope to have the opportunity to validate some of our adult prediction tables and to apply the already once-checked juvenile court tables to other samples of cases.

(c) There has, in recent years, been interest in researches which use more sophisticated mathematical techniques than those employed by us. These are intended to attack fundamental theoretical problems of prediction. They involve such matters, among others, as determination of the relative accuracy of different syndromes of factors as indices of the total set of forces affecting behavior on parole; determination of how various existing tables differ in the degree of "predictive efficiency," that is to say,

[4] This discussion is derived from *Prognosis of Recidivism, op. cit.*

in the extent to which they improve prognostication over choices made simply on the knowledge of an over-all actual rate of recidivism;[5] the problem, emphasized in the work of Mannheim and Wilkins,[6] of enhancing the accuracy of forecasting the behavior of borderline risk groups; the problem of maintaining the "predictive stability" of experience tables when applied to other samples of cases at successive times; the problem of reducing "overlap" between factors; the original selection of predictive factors for a table in accordance with some pre-existent theory of criminal causation or of recidivism.

Much could be said on all of these problems; and it is gratifying to note that competent research on them is in process in the United States and abroad. In the meantime, it remains for the proponents of more sophisticated predictive devices to demonstrate pragmatically that the application of various refinements does in fact markedly improve the practical utility of predictive instruments. In the long run, the issue will be determined not so much by mathematical sophistication or theoretical speculation as by "the proof of the pudding."[7] In the meantime, however, we think this book yields enough evidence of the promise of the simple predictive devices it describes to justify their experimental application in identifying true predelinquents and in the various stages of the administration of criminal justice which entail the exercise of informed discretion.

* * *

In our judgment, the time has arrived in the history of criminology when it can be said, on the basis of already existing evidence, that the predictive approach opens up a promising path through the dense forest of guesswork, hunch, and vague speculation concerning theories of criminal behavior. It gives hope of the ultimate transformation of criminology into a discipline approaching scientific stature.

[5] "Analysis of published results shows that the predictive efficiency of the experience tables in follow-up samples varies from an efficiency of 25 per cent to a loss of 41 per cent in efficiency over what could be achieved with a simple prediction of success for all cases," a "notable exception to these modest prediction results" being the predictive efficiency of the Glueck Social Prediction Scale from *Unraveling Juvenile Delinquency* which has been computed by Ohlin as 55 per cent. Report by L. E. Ohlin to Third International Congress of Criminology, London, 1955.

[6] H. Mannheim and L. T. Wilkins, *Prediction Methods in Relation to Borstal Training*, London, H. M. Stationery Office, 1955.

[7] See "Prediction," by Edwin Bidwell Wilson, in "A Symposium on *Unraveling Juvenile Delinquency*," 64 *Harvard Law Review* (1951), pp. 1039–1041.

APPENDIXES

Appendix A

"Historical Survey of Prediction Studies in the Field of Criminology"*

I.1 The bulk of existing prediction studies in Criminology has been produced in the United States. The most important American studies will be discussed in Part I of this chapter, whereas Part II will deal with the work done in Europe.

PART I
AMERICAN PREDICTION STUDIES

I.2 These studies cover approximately 30 years and have been largely concerned with prediction of the future conduct of adult prisoners for the use of Boards of Parole, occasionally also with the future conduct of juvenile offenders discharged from Reformatories, and in a few cases with that of probationers.

I.3 It should be understood that, as a rule, only studies in which an attempt is made, by means of prediction tables, to predict future conduct, not mere follow-up studies without prediction tables,[1] are included in this survey.[2]

THE PRE-GLUECK PERIOD

I.4 Professor S. B. Warner's study,[3] made at the invitation of Mr. Sanford Bates, then Commissioner of Correction of the State of Massachusetts, is usually regarded as the first of its kind. His paper, published in 1923, is interesting not on account of its positive findings, which were negligible, but because of the thought-provoking effect it had on subsequent workers. He selected 680 prisoners of the Massachusetts State Reformatory, 300 of them parole successes, another 300 parole violators and 80 not paroled, who had appeared before the Board of Parole mostly between 1912 and 1920,

* Comprising Chapter I of *Prediction Methods in Relation to Borstal Training*, by Dr. Hermann Mannheim and Leslie T. Wilkins, London, Her Majesty's Stationery Office, 1955. The authors wish to acknowledge with thanks the permission of Dr. Mannheim and Mr. Wilkins, as well as of the Controller of Her Britannic Majesty's Stationery Office, to reproduce this chapter.

153

collected the information available in their files under 64 headings and compared his three groups with regard to these factors.   He further considered the criteria used by the Board of Parole for determining whether or not to grant parole, namely: 1. whether a man had profited by his stay in the institution and so far reformed as to be unlikely to commit another offence; 2. his conduct in the institution; 3. whether suitable employment was awaiting him upon release; 4. whether he had a home or other proper surroundings to which to go; 5. a man's ability to tell the exact truth when interviewed by the Board; 6. the seriousness of his offence and the circumstances surrounding it; 7. his previous record in Court or otherwise; 8. the appearance which a man makes before the Board in applying for his parole; 9. behaviour on former parole.

I.5   As the next step, Warner tried to demonstrate that for most of the criteria used by the Board there appeared to be no foundation in the light of his comparative figures for parole violators and non-violators.   The Board regarded, for example, the commission of a sexual crime as militating against release on parole (criterion 6), whereas actually two-thirds of paroled sex offenders proved successes against an overall success rate of only one half.   On the other hand, prisoners committed for larceny and breaking, who were most readily paroled, had a violation rate of 57%. Another of Warner's criticisms referred to the fact that for most of the information on family background, nationality, residence, education, habits and circumstances at time of crime, i.e. approximately one half of the factors, the Board relied exclusively on the answers obtained from the prisoners themselves.   In short, Warner concluded that none of the 64 factors on which information was available, with the only exception of the psychiatric report, showed any significance as a criterion of success or failure and that no considerable improvement was possible in this respect "without a complete change both in the methods of obtaining information for the Board and in the nature of the information obtained".   The blame for the Board's failure to obtain better criteria for parole had, he thought, to be placed "upon the present undeveloped state of the science of criminology rather than upon either the Board of Parole or the Department of Correction".

I.6   Warner's conclusions were immediately attacked by Hornell Hart[4] as merely due to his failure to apply accurate statistical tests.   He maintained that the Massachusetts Board of Parole "could greatly improve its parole results by proper utilisation of the information already at its disposal". Applying to Warner's figures the formulæ and tables developed by Yule and Davenport, he showed that for at least 15 items "the contrast between violators and non-violators was greater than would be exceeded by chance once in one hundred times"; it was, therefore, statistically significant. For another 20 items the contrast, while not clearly established, was "very probably significant". These contrasts were found mainly with regard to home environment, character of the prisoner himself and his physical conditions, "all consistent with other findings in criminology". Presenting a table of these factors where the probability that the observed contrast was due to chance was less than about one in 100, he showed that there was a considerable number of factors where prisoners falling in the favourable sub-class of the factor would have a very high chance of success on parole. Of equal importance was Hart's suggestion that all the significant factors should be combined into a prognostic score for each prisoner. "To devise such a scoring system, the intercorrelation between the various items tabulated by Professor Warner, as well as their correlations with parole violations, would have to be studied, so as to work out the best possible weighting system for scoring the pertinent facts." Such a system, he argued, would not only enable the Board of Parole to make reliable forecasts as to the probability of parole violations, but could also be used by the Courts to determine the kind and length of the penalty.

I.7 It is a weakness of Hart's paper that he accepted the prisoners' own story when it suited him, but rejected it when it seemed to conflict with previous criminological findings. Moreover, he merely indicated the possibility of devising a weighted scoring system, but did not construct one.

I.8 The stage was now set for the first important prediction study, that of Professor Ernest W. Burgess of the University of Chicago. In the course of an investigation into "The Workings of the Indeterminate-Sentence Law and the Parole System in Illinois",[5] made jointly with Judge Andrew A. Bruce and Dean Albert J. Harno, he studied the factors making for success or failure on parole. On 21 such factors information was extracted for three groups of 1000 men each, paroled at least $2\frac{1}{2}$ years previously from (a) the Illinois State Reformatory at Pontiac, (b) the Illinois Penitentiary at Joliet, and (c) the South Illinois Penitentiary at Menard, altogether for 3000 men. Each factor was divided into a number of categories, for example, type of offence into larceny, robbery, burglary, fraud and forgery, sex offences, murder and manslaughter, and all other offences. When the general rate of parole violation was compared with the rate for each of the factors, it was found that for certain categories the rate was higher and for others lower than the general rate. For example, while in the Joliet group the general rate of parole violation was 28·4%, it was 42·4% for offenders convicted of fraud or forgery, but for those convicted of murder or manslaughter only 9%; for those with no previous work record it was 44·4%, but for those with a record of regular work only 12·2%, and so on. "Do not these striking differences", asked Burgess, "which correspond with what we already know about the conditions that mould the life of the person, suggest that they be taken more seriously and objectively into account than previously? These factors have, of course, been considered, but in a common-sense way so that some one or two of them have been emphasised out of all proportion to their significance."[6]

I.9 The question now arose of how to make the differences in the rate of violation found for the various categories of each of the 21 factors usable for practical purposes. Burgess solved this problem by attributing to each factor an arbitrary weight of one point, so that a parolee whose violation rate for, say, 12 factors was found to be below the general rate for his institution was given 12 favourable points, whereas the factors for which his violation rate was above the general rate of violation were ignored. The individual cases were then scored and a table of "Expectancy Rates of Parole Violation and Non-Violation" was constructed for the various score classes which showed the Expectancy Rate of Violation for men having, for example, 16 to 21 favourable points to be 1·5%, for men with only 2 to 4 favourable points, however, 76·0%.[7] Burgess cautiously regarded this table as merely "illustrative of the possibilities of the method and not in any sense as in a form adapted for immediate use". "Indeed", he wrote, "the method needs to be still further refined and then applied to from 3000 to 5000 cases for each institution in order to obtain an adequate statistical basis for the accurate working of satisfactory expectancy tables." He also uttered the warning—repeated by every serious research worker after him—that, although statistical prediction had now become feasible, no exclusive reliance should be placed on it at the expense of the more intensive study of the individual case.

I.10 As will be shown below, the Burgess method has since become one of the two most widely used techniques in criminological prediction. It has, however, also been criticised on the following grounds, conveniently summarised by Vold.[8]

(a) Only the material contained in official records was used.

(b) Only conduct during the official period of parole was considered.

(c) Some of the categories used to differentiate between violators and non-violators were overlapping and too subjective. This applies in particular to Burgess's category "social type" which was divided into subclasses such as "hobo", "ne'er-do-well", "mean citizen", "gangster", etc.

(d) There was no check upon the reliability or consistency of the findings by reclassification or similar tests.

(e) A system of scoring was used that assigned equal weight to every one of the 21 factors, whereas it was evident from the tables produced that certain factors were more strongly correlated to success or failure than others.

I.11 Different weight has to be given to these various criticisms. Whereas those under (a) and (b) question the completeness and reliability of the factual material used as the basis of the statistical work, the others are criticisms of the statistical techniques employed.

THE GLUECK STUDIES

I.12 (a) Almost simultaneously with the Burgess study, the first large-scale piece of follow-up and prediction research in the long series of the Glueck studies was completed: "500 Criminal Careers."[9] As Monachesi writes,[10] in this book "is found answers to some of the questions raised by the work of Burgess". In view of the unique place which it occupies in the history of prediction research a full analysis of its contents and achievements seems to be appropriate. Such an analysis is also needed on account of certain important differences between the case material from the Concord Reformatory, Massachusetts, used for the Glueck research and the case material of the present study. It should be understood that the present survey is concerned with the prediction techniques rather than with the follow-up methods used by the Gluecks.

I.13 The Glueck study is based "upon a careful investigation into the life histories of all prisoners released from the Massachusetts Reformatory whose sentences expired in 1921 and 1922. There were 510 such men".[11]*
This yielded a follow-up period of at least 5 years between the expiration of their sentences and the beginning of the investigation in 1927.[11a] The period between discharge from the Reformatory and the beginning of the Investigation was in most cases longer, however, as many men had left the institution already before the expiration of their sentences, namely 51·3% of them in 1917 and 1918 and another 17% in 1919 and 1920.[12] In 85·3% of the cases the sentences imposed on the men were of indeterminate length, mostly with a maximum of 5 years, and in the remaining cases usually of 2 years. The fixed sentences ranged from 3 months to 6 years. The average period actually spent in the Reformatory was 21 months, the most typical period being 12 to 15 months.[13] 310 of the men had been committed to the Reformatory during the years 1916 and 1917, 86 between 1910 and 1915, and the rest between 1918 and 1921. The theoretical length of supervision after discharge, i.e. the difference between the time actually served and the maximum limit of the sentence, varied from nil to 50 or

* It should be noted already at this stage that in most of the tables in "500 Criminal Careers" the number of cases is smaller than 510.

more months, with an average of 39·8 months; the actual periods were much shorter, however, with an average length of 18 months.[14]   While the average age of the men at committal was 20·19 years, with a few of only 15 or less and 15·4% of 17 or less, there were, on the other hand, 33·1% between 21 and 27 and 6·6% even between 28 and 36.

I.14   Without going into details concerning institutional treatment and similar matters, some of the principal differences between the system at Concord and the Borstal system may be summed up as follows: the age range of the Concord cases was wider than that for Borstal cases, and the average age was higher than that of the cases used in the present study (20·19 years against 18·0 years).   Some of the sentences received were longer than a Borstal sentence, up to 6 years.   The average period of stay in the institution was 21 months as against 17·7 months for the present cases.   The theoretical period of supervision after discharge was longer than in Borstal, whereas the actual period may have been not much different.   The follow-up period after discharge from the institution, in many cases not much less than 10 years, was considerably longer than that for the Borstal cases. Another difference is that, whereas the cases used for the present study are a sample of the male population of English Borstal Institutions as a whole, the Glueck material covers only a single Reformatory.   In their discussion of the "typicality" of their findings, the Gluecks express the view that their cases are representative not only of the general "run of the mill" of the Massachusetts Reformatory, but also of the population of Reformatories in other American states, although in the latter respect they regard this as a strong impression rather than as an established fact.   The same applies in their view to the regime at Concord.[15]   A very detailed description is given of the latter, whereas, as pointed out in Chapter II below in the present study, the general features of the English Borstal system have been taken as generally known and attention has been paid almost exclusively to certain special features prevailing at the time from which the cases are taken.   With regard to the question of typicality, it should be added that, as in a high proportion of Concord cases the men had committed their offences and/or had been sent to the Reformatory during the first World War, wartime conditions may have affected the typical character of the sample.

I.15   While a comparison of the principal findings of the Gluecks with those of the present study will be given below in Chapter VI their technique of investigation may here be contrasted with that of Burgess.   The following differences should be noted:

In view of the unreliability and incompleteness of much of the information contained in the official files, the material was carefully checked and supplemented from many other sources. The finger-print files of the Department of Correction were consulted to verify the identity of the men. Moreover—and this has been regarded as one of the greatest advances made in this field of research—in a considerable proportion, 73% of the cases, the ex-prisoners or their near relatives were interviewed by an experienced field investigator to check and supplement the material and to obtain a truthful picture of the adjustment made.[16]   As a result, there were finally only 27 cases out of 510 on which no subsequent information whatsoever was available.   The whole investigation, which had lasted for three academic years, and the methods used were described in the greatest detail. Every aspect of the various stages in the lives of the 510 men was scrutinised: their families, their personal and social background, criminal experience before committed to the Reformatory, their condition, conduct, occupation, etc., within the institution, and its effect on them; finally their parole and post-parole histories.   In two other chapters the data thus collected were related to the criteria of success, partial failure and total failure as defined on the strength of the criminal records.[17]   (Of the 422 men whose post-parole conduct could be ascertained, $21 \cdot 1\%$ were successes, $16 \cdot 8\%$ partial and $61 \cdot 1\%$ total failures.)   First, the relation of the pre-Reformatory factors and, after that, the relation of Reformatory, parole, and post-parole factors, altogether of over 50 factors, to post-parole criminality were analysed, using the statistical technique of the mean square contingency coefficient—a feature absent in Burgess's study. There were, however, deficiencies in their weighting system which will be discussed later.   It was rightly stressed by the Gluecks that the correlations established in this way were not to be taken as indicating causes of criminal behaviour or recidivism; that some of the factors having a low correlation with recidivism might, nevertheless, have been responsible for initial delinquency and that these factors should, therefore, be carefully studied and recorded in the files.[18]   The factors examined were classified as (a) those having a coefficient of correlation of under $\cdot 20$ and, therefore, only slightly or not at all related to the criterion of success or failure; (b) those having a coefficient of from $\cdot 20$ to $\cdot 40$ and, therefore, appreciably related to the criterion; (c) those having a coefficient of $\cdot 40$ to $\cdot 60$ and, therefore, considerably related to the criterion.[19]   Among pre-Reformatory factors of the first category were, for example, the type of crime for which the men had been sentenced to the Reformatory and their intelligence; in the second category there were, among others, their age at first delinquency, their physical condition on entering the Reformatory, and their psychiatric condition; in the third category was, in particular, the factor pre-Reformatory work habits.   Among the post-commitment factors, in the lowest category were, for example, their working record in the Reformatory, and their length of stay in it; in the second category were the frequency and seriousness of their offences in the institution; in the highest category were their post-parole working habits and family relations.

I.16   The next step was to construct prognostic tables, using the 6 most important pre-Reformatory factors, i.e. pre-Reformatory work habits (C = ·42), seriousness and frequency of pre-Reformatory crime (C = ·36), arrest for crimes preceding the offence for which sentenced to Reformatory (C = ·29), penal experience preceding Reformatory incarceration (C = ·29), economic responsibility preceding sentence to Reformatory (C = ·27), and mental abnormality on entrance to Reformatory (C = ·26).   It should be noted, however, that the total score yielded a correlation of ·45, which is only very slightly above that of ·42 for the single factor pre-Reformatory work habits.   Whereas these 6 factors formed the basis for the construction of prognostic tables for the use of judges, the corresponding tables for Boards of Parole in deciding on release on parole or further supervision and similar matters included, in addition, the following factors: frequency of the offences in the Reformatory (C = ·33) and criminal conduct during parole (C = ·47).   For the use of judges dealing with recidivists who had already been through the Reformatory and parole stages 5 post parole factors were added.   Factors with a coefficient of less than ·20 were excluded from consideration.   The scoring was done by adding up the highest and the lowest percentages of total failures which an offender could have and by adding two more score-classes between these two extremes. Finally, each individual offender was classified within these score-classes, and nine illustrative cases not used for the construction of the tables were presented to show the failure rates of men in the various score classes.

I.17   "Later Criminal Careers"[21] is a follow-up study to "500 Criminal Careers," undertaken some years after the publication of the first investigation.   Of the original group of 510 men, 56 had meanwhile died.   The remaining 454 were followed up over a second 5-year period after the expiration of their sentences, with the primary object of examining the biological, psychological and social changes and the changes in criminal behaviour brought about by the passage of time.   As we are not concerned here with these aspects there is no need to discuss the answers presented by the investigators.   In the chapter dealing with prediction, the range of predictability is extended from the original 5-year span to a period of 10 years after expiration of sentence.   In all, 63 factors were examined.   Of the 26 factors showing a considerable relationship to criminal conduct over these 10 years the 5 which bore the highest relationship, correlations ranging from ·23 (age at first delinquency) to ·43 (mental condition), were used for the construction of the prognostic table. On the whole, it was found that the same factors as in the first study were again prominently related to success or failure, though the coefficient of correlation was now lower than before for the factor "work habits" and considerably higher for the factor "mental condition". In other chapters of the book, emphasis is placed upon mental abnormality as the strongest impediment to reformation,[22] whereas "the benign process of maturation" emerged as the principal factor producing success.[23]

I.18   No attempt was made in this study to check the validity of the tables produced in "500 Criminal Careers."

I.19   In the third work of this series, "Criminal Careers in Retrospect",[24] the same group of ex-prisoners was followed up for another 5-year period, i.e. for altogether 15 years after expiration of their sentences, and prediction tables were constructed to enable a judge to select the particular form of peno-correctional treatment best suited to the individual offender with special reference to his age at any particular stage of the whole period. Again no general validation of the tables was attempted, but the question of validation was discussed in general terms, and the 9 cases whose histories were presented in "500 Criminal Careers" were used to show their failure scores over the whole 15-year period and how they might have been dealt with by the authorities if the prediction tables had been available.[25]

I.20   In their second series the Gluecks are concerned with juvenile delinquents. The principal object of the first of the two studies in this series, "One Thousand Juvenile Delinquents",[26] was to examine the procedure followed by, and the co-operation between, the Boston Juvenile Court and the Child Guidance Clinic of the Judge Baker Foundation in Boston (now Judge Baker Guidance Center), as illustrated by a follow-up study of 1000 boys referred to the Clinic by the Court for clinical examination between 1917 and 1922. Did the carrying out of the recommendations of the Clinic have any influence on the after-conduct of these boys? Finding that the after-histories of those cases where the recommendations of the Clinic had been carried out by the Court were only slightly more favourable than the after-histories of the other boys (C = ·12), the authors had to consider the possibility that in the first group factors other than the carrying out of those recommendations might have been responsible for the more favourable result. The relations of sixty-odd factors to success or failure were studied by means of two different statistical methods, the "factor method" and the "failure-score method". Including even factors where the correlation of the most favourable sub-class to reformation was very slight (factor method), the authors found that regardless of the carrying out of the Clinic recommendations that correlation was ·28. For the cases where the recommendations had been carried out the correlation was ·39, which proved that this factor had some favourable effect independent of other favourable factors. For the construction of the prediction tables, however, which are presented in Chapter XI of the book, only the 6 factors bearing the highest correlations with success are used: discipline of juvenile by father (·233), discipline of juvenile by mother (·161), school retardation (·151), school misconduct (·206), age at first-known behaviour disorder (·187), length of time between onset of delinquency and examination of child by the Clinic (·161). It will be noted that the correlations are only moderately high and that the last-mentioned factor applies exclusively to a group of cases all of whom were examined by a Child Guidance Clinic. The correlation of all 6 factors to the criterion was ·28, whereas if the computation was confined to those cases where the Clinic recommendation had been carried out it was ·45.

I.21   The second study in this series, "Juvenile Delinquents Grown Up",[27] is a follow-up study, over a further period of 10 years, of the original boys. These boys, at the end of the first follow-up period of an average age of 18½ years, were now of an average age of about 29 years.   60 of them had in the meantime died, but all but 47 of the remaining 940 could be traced and in 591 cases the men or members of their families were personally interviewed.[28] While we are not concerned with the results of this study as far as it shows the changes in the circumstances and conduct of this group, it may be mentioned that one of the major findings was the improvement in conduct with advancing age. Published 3 years before "Criminal Careers in Retrospect", it was the first study covering a period of 15 years and relating conduct to age and treatment.   Conduct was studied not only, as in the previous investigations, for the period after the completion of the various forms of peno-correctional treatment, but also for the treatment period itself, and an attempt was made to distinguish different "conduct types" and "treatment types".[29]   Prediction tables were then constructed in the usual way by selecting, out of a total of some 60 factors examined, the 5 factors showing the highest correlations with success or failure, i.e. birthplace of father (·26), birthplace of mother (·22) time parents were in United States (·20), religion of parents (·20), age of offender at first misbehaviour (·22).   With regard to the first 3 of these factors it might be of interest to note that the incidence of serious criminality was considerably higher in the case of those whose parents were born in U.S.A. and resident there for life. Moreover, it should be noted that these 3 factors are specifically related to American conditions, and also that the highest correlation reached by any single factors was ·26. The general prediction table was then supplemented by 8 others showing the likelihood of success, failure, early failure and later success, or erratic behaviour during various forms of treatment such as probation, probation under suspended sentence, Reformatory, prison and also in the Army and Navy. The practical application of these tables to a small number of cases was demonstrated, but no general validation was attempted.

I.22 "Five Hundred Delinquent Women",[30] published in the same year as "One Thousand Juvenile Delinquents", is unique in so far as it is the only one of the Glueck studies dealing with females and that it is not part of a series. 500 cases of women were selected in consecutive order whose parole from the Women's Reformatory at Framingham, Massachusetts, expired between 1921 and 1925. Their average age at the end of their 5-year post-parole was 32·6 years. After a full description of the Framingham Reformatory and a detailed account of 11 life histories, the usual pains-taking study was made of these 500 women, their characteristics and development after discharge. If anything, the investigation was even more detailed and more difficult than in "500 Criminal Careers".[31] 285 factors were examined, of which 60 or 70 had to be discarded because of lack of adequate information. For the tracing and interviewing of the women one male and one female field worker were employed, and special attention was paid to the differences between follow-up studies of male and of female offenders.[32] With regard to the "typicality" of their findings, the authors took the same view as in "500 Criminal Careers" that, although no absolutely conclusive answer was possible, "the frequent incidence among female offenders in other Reformatories of many of the characteristics of our women" could be reasonably assumed.[33]

I.23 In constructing their prediction tables the authors tried to simplify the technique adopted in "500 Criminal Careers". Instead of using the "somewhat involved computation of mean square contingency", the degree of association between any particular factor and non-recidivism was established by the "determination of the maximum percentage difference between any sub-class of a particular factor and the expectancy of recidivism for the entire group of cases involved".[34] As, for example, the total rate of non-recidivism for the group was 23·5 and that for those with regular church attendance 28·4, for those with irregular church attendance 14·9 and for those with no attendance 40·0, the degree of association was taken to be $40·0 - 23·5 = 16·5$. Of the 15 factors bearing the highest association to non-recidivism the 5 which seemed to be most suitable were used for the construction of the tables, i.e. retardation in school, neighbourhood influences within a year of commitment, steadiness of employment, economic responsibility, mental abnormality. No validation of the tables was attempted, but the common-sense prognoses made in 78 of these cases by

163

the staff of the Reformatory, described as "particularly intelligent and forward-looking", were compared with the actual outcome, with the result that at least two-fifths of these prognoses had to be regarded as grossly erroneous.[35]

I.24   The 6 Glueck studies so far described may be presented in a diagram as follows:

5 years	5 years	5 years	= 15 years
			follow-up
500 Criminal Careers	Later Criminal Careers	Criminal Careers in Retrospect	
1000 Juvenile Delinquents	Juvenile Delinquents grown up		
500 Delinquent Women			

I.25   While "After-conduct of Discharged Offenders"[36] contains mainly a brief recapitulation of the main aspects of the earlier Glueck studies, "Unraveling Juvenile Delinquency"[37] bears a different character.   It is primarily a control-group study of 500 delinquent boys committed to State Correctional Schools in Massachusetts and 500 non-delinquent boys from ordinary State schools in Boston.   Their average age when selected for study was over 14 years.   There was no follow-up work connected with this study, which covered altogether 402 factors, but some of the differences between the two groups discovered in its course were used to construct tables designed to predict the future conduct of children at school entrance, i.e. aged six or seven.   While the differences in physique and health and those emerging from certain psychological tests (Wechsler-Bellevue and Stanford Achievement Tests) were not regarded as suitable for the purpose, 3 tables were constructed based respectively on (a) traits of character structure derived from Rorschach Test, (b) personality traits derived from psychiatric interview, and (c) social background.   In accordance with the technique used in previous studies, each table was made up of 5 factors, i.e. for the first table: assertiveness, defiance, suspiciousness, destructiveness and emotional lability; for the second table: adventurousness, extroversion in action, suggestibility, stubbornness and emotional instability; for the third table: discipline of the child by the father, supervision of the child by the mother, affection of the father for the child, affection of the mother for the child and cohesiveness of the family group.   The authors explain that, as it was the object of these tables to identify potential delinquents already at school entrance age, the predictive factors had to be selected from those operative in boys of that age. The tables were then constructed by comparing the incidence of three sub-classes of each factor for the delinquent and the non-delinquent groups and by establishing score classes. It was pointed out that the total score retained its quality as a predictor regardless of variations of its component parts. Comparisons of the results of the three tables showed that there was agreement between the social and the psychiatric tables in 67·9 % and between the psychiatric and Rorschach tables in 69·8 %. In 49 % all three tables placed a boy in the predictive category to which he properly belonged in view of his conduct, and in another 37·8 % at least two of the three tables succeeded in doing so. Only 2·4 % of the boys were incorrectly identified as delinquents or non-delinquents. In explanation of disagreements between the tables the authors pointed out that a high failure score had a different meaning in different tables, the Rorschach table referring to basic character structure, the psychiatric table to the dynamics of the personality, and the social table to family inter-relations.

I.26 "Unraveling Juvenile Delinquency" differs from most other prediction studies in trying to predict future delinquency in boys not yet delinquent and in trying to utilise their characteristics at the age of fourteen to predict future delinquency of children aged six or seven.

I.27 While an assessment of the various aspects of the Glueck technique will be made in the appropriate sections of subsequent chapters, a few observations of a general nature may be not out of place already at this stage:

I.28 A certain amount of overlapping will have been noticed between some of the factors used for the construction of the Glueck tables. Although, for example, the factors "industrial habits preceding sentence to Reformatory" and "economic responsibility preceding sentence to Reformatory" cover to some extent the same ground,[37a] both factors are included in the prediction tables in "500 Criminal Careers" and "Later Criminal Careers". The authors have been aware of the problem and discuss it in some of their later books. While in "After-conduct of discharged Offenders"[38] overlapping factors are regarded as "largely dead-wood in the prognostic process", in "Criminal Careers in Retrospect",[39] where the matter is more fully treated, the authors take the view that the use of 5 partially inter-related factors might be preferable to that of 3 independent factors as in the former case errors in classification on the part of those charged with the collection of the data would have less serious results. In a special statistical examination of the factors used, which the Gluecks arranged for one of their tables, only a very small degree of overlap was actually discovered. Nevertheless, the authors express themselves in favour of avoiding unnecessary interrelations.

I.29 Another important point made by the Gluecks concerning the selection of predictive factors is that, for practical reasons, objective factors on which information is easily obtainable and easily verifiable by the Courts should be preferred to factors involving difficult subjective evaluations such as, for example, "mental condition".[40]

I.30 The question of what number of factors is most profitably employed for the construction of the tables leads to a discussion of several other American studies made after the publication of Burgess's investigation and of "500 Criminal Careers".

OTHER AMERICAN STUDIES

I.31 Professor George B. Vold of the University of Minnesota has made several important contributions to the subject. In his book "Prediction Methods and Parole"[41] he used the records of 542 men discharged from the Minnesota State Prison and of 650 men discharged from the Minnesota State Reformatory during the period 1922 to 1927. The number of factors on which information was collected from the records was 49 (34 of them pre-parole factors). Using the coefficient of mean square contingency, the correlations were worked out, for the combined prison and reformatory groups, between 44 factors and outcome on parole. The highest correlation, that for previous work record, was 0·283; the two lowest were age at conviction (·060) and aid given to dependants while the inmate was in prison (·050). The author concluded that, while no single factor appeared to be of outstanding importance, few, if any, appeared to be without any significance. In one respect his figures were at variance with the findings of most other investigators before and after him: parole violations showed no tendency to be most frequent in the earlier part of the parole period, but occurred fairly uniformly throughout the whole year. This seemed to be a strong argument against the practice then prevailing in Minnesota to limit the period of parole to one year.[42] As in previous studies, in a considerable number of the cases information was not available on some of the factors.[43] Whereas no use had been made of this category in the Burgess and Glueck studies, Vold paid special attention to the various possibilities of dealing with it (see below).

I.32 An interesting feature of Vold's study is his comparison of the efficiency of the Burgess technique of using all available factors without weighting them with the Glueck technique of using only the most significant factors. Both techniques were tried out in combination; for example, only the highest 17 factors, all of them with C values above ·100, were used

166

together with the Burgess method of crediting each man with one point for every favourable category. In addition, prediction tables were also constructed from the lowest 17 pre-parole factors and from selected 25 pre-parole factors on which information was nearly complete. Very little difference was found between the results obtained by the two first-mentioned techniques, and in view of the greater laboriousness of the Glueck method of scoring no further use was made of it. [44] The most satisfactory results, i.e. those producing the sharpest differentiation between parole violators and non-violators, were obtained from tables based on the selected 25 factors, whereas the least satisfactory, but, nevertheless, by no means negligible, differentiation was obtained from the 17 factors showing the lowest contingency values. Actually, the difference in predictive value between tables using only high contingency and those using only low contingency values was comparatively small. [45] Other noteworthy features of this study are Vold's attempt to validate his tables by dividing his material into two randomly selected halves in order to use the one group as the "operating" and the other as the "control" group, and his use of another investigator to make an independent assessment of some of the cases. In a later study [46] Vold compared, for a group of 282 Minnesota prisoners, (a) the correlation between predicted and actual outcome, which was about ·4, (b) the correlation between the estimate of a parole officer and the actual outcome, which was not quite ·3. In this connection Vold rightly emphasised that such comparisons between predicted and actual outcome refer only to the number of cases in the various categories without giving any information regarding the correctness of the prediction for individuals.

I.33 A year after Vold, Professor Elio D. Monachesi, also of the University of Minnesota, published his book "Prediction Factors in Probation", the first prediction study using probation material. [47] A total of 1515 probation cases, adults and juveniles, handled by a Probation Office in the State of Minnesota during the years 1923 to 1925, were examined. The information found in the records was reduced to 50 factors for the juvenile and 34 for the adult group. Following Vold's technique, the classification of certain "highly conceptual" items, such as "social type" (Burgess), was rechecked for a small sample of the cases and the agreement between the first and second entries checked by means of three statistical measures of reliability. Also in conformity with Vold, the group of "no-information" cases was treated in the same way as the rest and comparisons were made between prediction according to the Burgess and the Glueck techniques. It was again found that the two techniques furnished approximately the same results.

I.34 Simultaneously with Vold and Monachesi, Clark Tibbitts published two articles incorporating the results of a study of 3000 youths paroled within the 7-year period 1921–7 from the Illinois State Reformatory at Pontiac.[48] The object of his study was to validate Burgess's findings by applying his technique to a larger sample taken from one institution. With regard to his definition of "success", it is worth noting that, as in the experience of the author most violations of parole other than purely technical ones occurred within the first 12 months, subsequent violations were not counted. The technique employed was essentially the same as that of Burgess, i.e. a comparison of violation rates for each of the sub-classes of a number of factors. Most of the factors employed by Burgess, including "Social Type", were retained, but the total number was increased to 23. No Pearsonian coefficient of correlation was used, but to some extent a tetrachoric "r" was calculated. The highest correlation thus reached was ·179 for type of offender (first offender or recidivist). With regard to the predictive value of the type of offence for which the parolee had been committed, Tibbitts's figures confirm Burgess's finding that "those guilty of the crimes that shock society are the least likely to violate parole". The type of neighbourhood where the offender lived at the time of the offence and his work record were found to be even more predictive than in Burgess's study. Whereas offenders of low intelligence fared less favourably than in the previous investigation, "emotionally unstable" individuals showed in both cases the lowest violation rates.

I.35 A prediction scheme not based upon follow-up studies was published in 1935 by Walter Webster Argow.[49] He devised a "Criminal-Liability Index" (CLI) by analysing 37 factors in a group of 563 inmates of Connecticut jails, contrasting the percentage of first offenders and of recidivists from each factor. If, for example, the percentage of first offenders among men between 36 and 40 years of age was 8 and that of recidivists 14, the ratio between the two groups, using the recidivist figure as base, was ·57 or, translated to the scale of 10, it was 6. In this way, each individual's score was established by adding the values for 31 factors, dividing the total by the number of factors and by the mean for the group. The result was called the CLI.

I.36 In the same year, Dr. Norman Fenton published his book "The Delinquent Boy and the Correctional School",[50] an account of the work of the Whittier School in California. It contains a comparison with regard to 200 factors of the after-histories of 400 Whittier boys over a period of 3 to 5 years after admission, i.e. mainly for the first 2 years of their post-institutional history. The statistical method used was to work out the differences between those who were regarded as adjusted and those who had failed to adjust according to a "critical ratio" of significance. A critical ratio of 3·0 was regarded as significant, one of 2·0 to 2·9 as probably significant. For a number of factors the critical ratio was over 3·0 or even over 4·0 (Tables 44 and 45), particularly for factors relating to conduct at Whittier, and the author concludes that "some general rating of social adjustment at the institution and of school spirit may offer valuable data as to the probabilities of the boys' future adjustment". He also stresses the importance of the first 2 years after discharge.[51]

I.37 The much discussed technique used by Ferris F. Laune[52] differed from that of previous investigators in that he placed the emphasis on a study of the prisoner's attitudes which he tried to explore, in the first instance, by using the subjective "hunches" of particularly well qualified fellow-prisoners regarding the parolability of the inmate. Discussions between the prisoner-investigators produced a number of commonly agreed factors which had, apparently, formed the basis of the original hunches.

I.38 H. Ashley Weeks's[53] comparison of 420 delinquent and 421 non-delinquent boys, picked at random from secondary schools of the city of Spokane, is another example of a prediction study not based upon follow-up research.

I.38a In 1939 the United States Department of Justice published as part of the Attorney-General's comprehensive "Survey of Release Procedures"[53a] an analysis, based on the case histories of approximately 100,000 felons, of "some factors associated with parole selection and outcome". This analysis showed that, while with the criteria so far employed those prisoners who had a better chance of being paroled were in general those who turned out to be "better risks", the results did not seem to imply that the methods of parole selection were in fact adequate. A second analysis was, therefore, made of the case histories of 22,593 persons released from Federal institutions between 1930–5, of whom 17,049 had been paroled while 5554 had been given conditional release. The object was to ascertain whether the construction and use of prediction tables would materially improve the "common-sense" selection made by the Federal Parole Board. Even this second study is not a prediction study in the strict sense of the term as no prediction tables were actually constructed. The association of 82 factors to outcome was shown, not by way of coefficients of contingency, but in percentages of agreement, and there was no weighting of the individual factors. To test the reliability of the official records used, consistency tests were made by having the information on 113 factors which had been abstracted by one group of survey recorders from 500 cases histories recorded by a second group of workers. The results indicated that the extent of consistency in the recording of the data was as high as, if not higher than that found in previous studies by Vold, Monachesi and Tibbitts.

In view of the considerable variations of violation rates in the various Federal institutions it was not regarded as appropriate to present figures based upon combined violation rates, and data were shown separately for the three largest institutions: Leavenworth, Atlanta and Chillicothe. The factors studied were divided into 5 groups: parental, social, criminal, institutional and post-institutional history, with special emphasis on the last-mentioned category. Some of the factors used were highly subjective, as for example, "Congeniality of parents", which included "frequent bickerings", "abandonment of home for short or long periods" and other "indications of strained relations"; "congeniality of marriage"; "congeniality with parents"; "habits", which included, among others, the subcategories "nomadic" and "sexual promiscuity". As the results are shown without any weighting and for each institution separately, no summary can conveniently be given. The final conclusion of the authors of the study is that, while it would have been possible to construct prediction tables using 39 of the 82 factors, there was no evidence that the use of such tables would produce any substantial improvement in the Federal parole practice. It was admitted, however, that, parole prediction still being relatively new, with more information and reliable official records and more refined statistical techniques the possibility of more accurate predictions could not be excluded.

I.39 Dr. Ohlin's book "Selection for Parole"[54] deserves special attention not only because of its scientific value but also in view of the author's official position as the research sociologist of the Division of Correction of the State of Illinois, where a routine prediction system for parolees was established as early as in 1933.[55] Dr. Ohlin's technique is largely derived from Burgess's pioneer study, also carried out on Illinois parolees. The following are the principal stages in the construction of Ohlin's prediction or, as he prefers to call them, experience tables:

I.40 First, a sample of at least 1000 cases had to be selected having behind them a period after discharge long enough for the outcome of their parole to become final, which in Illinois means a period of 5 years. The selection of predictive items was made from factors likely to be significant in view of the results of previous researches. For the construction of the table currently used in Illinois and based on material from 4941 parolees, the following 12 factors, out of 27 on which information had been collected, were retained: type of offence, sentence, type of offender, home status, family interest, social type, work record, community, parole job, number of associates, personality, psychiatric prognosis.[56] Each factor was broken down in subclasses, numbering from 2 to 7, and the violation rate was obtained for each of these subclasses by dividing the number of violators by the total of persons in the subclass. For the factor "family interest", for example, the violation rates ranged from 5% in the subclass "very active" to 40% in the subclass "none", compared with an overall rate of 28% for the total of 4941 cases. Accordingly each subclass was marked as a favourable, neutral or unfavourable predictive item; for example, under "type of offence" homicide and sex offences were rated as favourable, burglary as unfavourable, items. Each parolee was given one favourable point for every favourable subclass in which he fell, one unfavourable point for every unfavourable and one zero for every neutral subclass. His final score was obtained by subtracting the number of unfavourable from that of favourable points, whereas the neutral subclasses were ignored as having no predictive value. As a result of a series of tests designed to measure the statistical significance, association with outcome, reliability and stability of the value of the subclasses some of the latter were omitted. The experience table was then constructed showing a range in violation rates from 3% for persons with 5 to 10 favourable points to 75% for those with 5 to 6 unfavourable points. Dr. Ohlin does not believe in highly complicated scoring and weighting procedures which, in his view, add very little to the value of the table. Nor does he regard the individual interview technique of the Gluecks as practicable in view of its high cost. On the other hand, he stresses the need for field investigations to supplement the classification and prediction reports; the need for constant checks of the reliability of the classifications; and for routine adjustments of an experience table to keep it abreast of the changes incessantly occurring in the parole situation. Further technical suggestions for the organisation of a routine prediction system are made in the Appendixes, and it is stated that experience in Illinois has shown up to 36% increase in accuracy of prediction through close adherence to the prediction table.

I.41 Ohlin follows Burgess not only as far as the absence of a weighting system is concerned, but also in his adoption of such factors as "social type" with the same or similar subclasses (see above under I.10), which he regards as one of the most useful predictive items. Even for highly subjective subclasses reclassification, according to Ohlin, showed a remarkable degree of agreement. Some of the other factors used by Ohlin are also highly subjective, in particular "personality" and "psychiatric prognosis". In their Introduction to Ohlin's book, Burgess and Sellin suggest that data obtained by personality tests and interviews, and also the ratings of the inmate by members of the staff, should be used in conjunction with statistical prediction.

I.42 The principal difference between Ohlin and Burgess is that the former, in so far following the Gluecks, is in favour of using only a small number of highly predictive factors for his table, and that in other respects, too, his statistical technique bears evidence of the improvements in methods of research brought about in the past 20 years.

I.43   Nearly 20 years after Monachesi, Professor Morris G. Caldwell of the University of Alabama published the preliminary results of another large-scale follow-up study of probationers.[57]   His material consisted of 1862 Federal probationers whose probation terminated between 1st July, 1937, and 31st December, 1942.   The 5 factors most significantly related to outcome were: Age at beginning of Probation (C = ·152), occupational status (·162), number of criminal offences (·290), number of commitments to correctional institutions (·240) and length of probationary supervision (·520).   With regard to the latter factor, the author concluded that the turning point towards greater success seemed to occur between $2\frac{1}{2}$ and 3 years on probation.   On the other hand, probation violation occurred most frequently during the first 2 years.   No prediction tables were published by Caldwell.

I.44   Albert L. Reiss, Jr.,[58] developed prognostic instruments to predict the recidivism of a sample of 736 juvenile delinquents placed on probation in the years 1943 and 1944 by the Juvenile Court of Cook County, Illinois. A follow-up sample of 374 cases was used to test the validity of the prediction instruments.   Starting from the hypothesis that a small number of stable predictors is likely to yield the greatest accuracy and efficiency in prediction, he selected, out of a total of 20 unfavourable factors found to be significant, the following 5 as stable predictors: (a) economic status of family: dependent; (b) truancy: usually truant; (c) deportment record in school: poor or very poor; (d) adequacy of personality controls: relatively inadequate ego and super-ego controls; (e) recommendations for treatment: place delinquent in adequate community environment or closed institution or psychotherapy.

I.45   These items were classified as stable predictors because they were not only significantly correlated with the criterion but had also shown the same direction of association in at least two previous prediction studies undertaken at different times.   Prediction based upon these items was found to be more accurate than prediction based upon five unstable items.   Generally speaking, it was found that stable predictors were those with relatively higher associations with the criterion than unstable predictors.   Attention was also drawn to the fact that predictions are likely to be more efficient for socially homogeneous samples than for a heterogeneous population, such as one including Negroes and Whites.   This is in accordance with an observation made by Vold with regard to a sample consisting of inmates of prisons and reformatories.

I.46   It has to be noted that the fourth of these items contains strong subjective elements and may be defined differently by different observers.   No definition of "adequacy of personality control" is given by the author.   In a second paper[59] the author explains, however, that data on this item were obtained "from the judgments of the social work staff at the juvenile court and the reports of the psychiatrists at the Institute for Juvenile Research (in Chicago)".   This item was, in fact, found to be the most efficient single predictor and only slightly less efficient than prediction from a battery of four items.

I.47   In the "Cambridge-Somerville Youth Study",[60] the social development of 650 boys aged between 6 and 12 years and resident in these two cities of the State of Massachusets, some of them regarded as "pre-delinquent", others as "normal" or doubtful, was studied over a considerable period of time under experimental conditions, i.e. 325 of them were given the benefit of the services of specially selected counsellors, whereas the other 325 were left to the ordinary social services existing in their localities.   The practical side of the research, which was commenced in 1935, came to an end in 1945, though for reasons mainly connected with the war many boys had lost touch with the study already some years earlier. As each of the boys had in the years 1937 to 1938 been given a careful prognosis as to his likely future delinquency by a Selection Committee consisting of a psychiatrist and two penal administrators of wide experience in dealing with young offenders, it was only natural that some of the material collected by the Study should be used to check the accuracy of their prognoses in the light of subsequent actual developments.[61]   For the purpose, 100 T-boys, i.e. boys belonging to the group which had been provided with counsellors, and 100 C-boys, i.e. those who had received no such assistance, were selected.   69% of them had originally been labelled as probably future delinquents, 25% as likely non-delinquents, and 6% as doubtful.   These predictions were based upon information regarding the mental and physical condition of the boys, progress in school, family conditions and the boys' adjustment to them and to their environment in general.   Little information was available on the boys' heredity and the first few years of their lives, nor had the predictors been able to interview them in person.   It was found that the factors regarded by the predictors as important could be arranged under 52 headings, of which 21 seemed to be of particular importance. When, approximately 10 years later, these 200 cases were reassessed by two judges, the result was as follows: In 22 of the hundred T-boys and 16 of the hundred C-boys there was perfect agreement between predictors and judges.   Of 70 T-boys and 68 C-boys regarded as pre-delinquents by the predictors only 23 and 27 respectively had actually become delinquents.

Of 23 T-boys and 27 C-boys regarded as not pre-delinquent 20 and 24 respectively were later judged "seldom or least delinquent". Delinquency had been accurately predicted for most cases in which it subsequently occurred, but it had also been predicted in many cases in which it failed to occur. The correlation between prediction and outcome was ·44 for the T-boys and ·54 for the C-boys; for both groups together it was ·49. The difference between ·44 and ·54—a difference which had to be expected in view of the special treatment received by the T-boys—was not regarded as statistically significant.

I.48 Two other attempts were made by the Study to check the predictive value of prognostic techniques: Teachers were asked to make a prognosis, and a Behaviour Rating Scale (Haggerty-Olsen-Wickman) was also used. In the case of the teachers, the correlation between their predictions and the outcome was ·35 for the T-group and ·59 for the C-group, and for both groups together ·48. Here the difference between the two groups was regarded as a slight indication of the effectiveness of the special treatment received by the T-boys. With regard to the predictive value of the Rating Schedule, the result seemed to show that the Schedule was able to differentiate the "most delinquent" from the "least delinquent" cases.

VALIDATION STUDIES

I.49 In the Social Science Research Council's Bulletin on "The Prediction of Personal Adjustment", published in 1941, the principal author, Paul Horst, made the well-founded criticism that "most 'prediction studies' end without ever attempting to predict".[62] It was not enough, he added, to show that a prediction formula worked well when applied to the original sample; its applicability to other cases had to be demonstrated. In the field of penology, he was able to quote only three such attempts to validate a previously established formula: those by Tibbitts (above paragraph 34), Vold (above paragraph 32) and an inconclusive study by Sanders. Since Horst's survey was published, there have been several further attempts to validate some of the Glueck tables:*

I.50 The first of these validation studies was made during the last war by Schneider and La Grone with the co-operation of Professor and Mrs. Glueck.[63] They applied some of the prediction tables in "Criminal Careers in Retrospect" to a sample of 200 soldiers who had been delinquents in civilian life and were at the time of the inquiry in confinement for military offences. The sample was chosen from a group of 500 by selecting those files which contained the most adequate data on the 5 factors of the prediction table. The investigator, Mrs. Glueck, was given information

* German validation studies will be mentioned below under Part II.

only with regard to these 5 factors (education of parents, intelligence of offender, age at first delinquency, age began work, industrial skill). The object of the study was to find out in how many of these 200 cases it would have been possible, without any additional information, merely by applying the prediction table to foresee and predict that they would cause trouble in the Army. The result was that 47·5% of the men had only a 3 in 10 chance of becoming successful soldiers and another 37% had a chance of $3\frac{1}{2}$ in 10, whereas 10% had a 50:50 chance. In other words nearly 85% of them might reasonably have been rejected forthwith if the table had been applied. This is, however, an incomplete test since all cases were failures.

I.51   Another attempt to validate some of the Glueck tables was made by the staff of the Hawthorne-Cedar Knolls School at Hawthorne, New York.[64] This school, which is maintained by the Jewish Board of Guardians for children with behaviour disorders and personality problems, provides a combination of the usual environmental techniques with the services of a fully equipped psychiatric clinic. The tables used for the study were taken from "One Thousand Juvenile Delinquents" and from "Unraveling Juvenile Delinquency" (only the Social Prediction Table was used). After a pilot study of 50 boys committed to Hawthorne in 1932–5, the tables were applied to a group of 100 boys admitted as delinquents between 1940 and 1942. These boys differed in many respects from the boys in "One Thousand Juvenile Delinquents". As these differences, however, did not, or only slightly, refer to any of the 6 factors used for the construction of the prediction table, they were, in particular in the light of previous experience, regarded as immaterial. The application of the earlier Glueck table showed the following results: 64 of 100 boys had 92.6 out of 100 chances of recidivism, 19 had 83·1 chances, 9 had 67 and 8 had 50 chances. The application of the table from "Unraveling Juvenile Delinquency" had only slightly more favourable results. Actually, the follow-up of the 100 boys made in 1950 showed that many more, namely 70 of them, had been successes, and the explanation of the considerable difference between prognosis and real outcome was found in the intensive psychotherapy provided at Hawthorne.

I.52   Richard E. Thompson tried to validate the Glueck Social Prediction Table, published in "Unraveling Juvenile Delinquency", by applying it to some of the case material of the Cambridge-Somerville Youth Study.[65]   A sample of 100 boys, pre-delinquents and others, was selected for whom sufficient information was available in the files on all 5 factors used for the construction of the Glueck Social Prediction Table, i.e. discipline of boy by father, supervision of boy by mother, affection of father for boy, affection of mother for boy, cohesiveness of family. These 100 cases were then scored by Dr. Eleanor T. Glueck, who was given no other information than that relating to the 5 predictive factors. When her prognoses were compared with those of the three members of the Selection Committee (see above) it was found that, whereas the latter had made accurate predictions in 61·5 to 65·3%, Mrs Glueck had been correct in 91%. There was a difference in accuracy between the predictions for those boys who became delinquents and for those who did not. Of the 20 boys who actually became delinquents 18 were accurately predicted by the Selection Committee and by Mrs. Glueck. Of the 80 who remained non-delinquent 91·3% were accurately predicted by Mrs. Glueck, but only 53·5% to 58·7% by members of the Committee.

I.53 The author stresses that the Glueck Social Prediction Table can be applied not only to boys of 11 to 17, but also to younger ones, and that it works regardless of racial origin, intelligence and social status.

PART II

EUROPEAN PREDICTION STUDIES

I.54 Prediction research in Germany was initiated by the late Professor Franz Exner of the University of Munich as a fruit of his visit to the United States some years after the publication of the first Glueck studies.[66] One of his students, Robert Schiedt,[67] examined in 1935 the records of an un-selected sample of 500 offenders discharged from Bavarian prisons in 1931. The prognoses made for these men by the prison doctors on discharge had been favourable in 38%, unfavourable in 29% and doubtful in 33%. Four years later it was found by Schiedt that the favourable prognoses were wrong in 26% and the unfavourable prognoses in 28%. Not considering the cases, numbering one-third of the total, in which the doctors had been unable to express any definite views, their prognoses had been mistaken in 26·5%, a proportion which was regarded as unduly high in view of the detailed examinations of prisoners by the crimino-biological service established in German prisons. When Schiedt made a statistical analysis of a number of characteristics of these 500 ex-prisoners he found that individuals showing one of the following 15 factors had a rate of recidivism considerably above the average of 49%: 1. bad heredity; 2. serious criminality of ascendants; 3. unfavourable educational conditions; 4. bad scholastic attainment and school conduct; 5. premature breaking off of an apprenticeship; 6. irregular working habits; 7. beginning of criminal activities before the age of eighteen; 8. more than four previous convictions; 9. particularly short intervals between discharge from a penal institution and subsequent conviction; 10. criminality extending over the areas of several district courts; 11. psychopathy; 12. drunken habits; 13. bad general conduct in prison; 14. discharge from prison before the age of 36; 15. bad social and family conditions after discharge.

I.55   In accordance with the Burgess technique, Schiedt allotted to each case one "bad point" for each of these 15 factors.   Offenders with nil to 3 bad points he regarded as "corrigible", those with 10 or more as "incorrigible", and those with 4 to 9 as "doubtful".   Of 131 corrigibles, only $16 = 12 \cdot 2\%$ were failures, whereas of 288 doubtful ones $52 \cdot 9\%$ and of 81 incorrigibles $78 = 96 \cdot 3\%$ failed.   For some of the factors, i.e. 9, 10 and 15, the percentage of recidivism exceeded 80 or even 90%, against the general rate of recidivism of 49% for the whole sample.

I.56   Schiedt's point system was criticised by Trunk and Gerecke. Trunk[68] applied it in 1937 to a sample of 100 convicts with sentences of not more than 3 years, discharged from the prison at Straubing, Bavaria, not later than at the end of the year 1932, and for whom he had made prognoses before discharge in his capacity as the prison medical officer.   He had regarded 38 of the prisoners as corrigible, 45 as incorrigible and 17 as doubtful, and when checking his prognoses he found that 71% of them had been correct, whereas under Schiedt's point system only 51% of them would have been correctly predicted.   His criticisms of Schiedt's system are in part concerned with technical details such as definitions and overlapping of factors, in particular 11 and 12; with the absence of any weighting of factors; and with the high rate, 57%, of "doubtful" cases.   In part, however, his objections are directed against the point system as such, which he regards as inferior to the intuitive prognosis of the total personality of each individual.

I.57   Gerecke,[69] who also criticised the absence of any weighting of factors, tried to improve the point system by substituting different factors for some of those used by Schiedt; by attaching different point values to the factors (e.g. age of first conviction: point value 9; bad environment: point value 2); and by multiplying each point value by 1 to 4 according to the intensity of the factor in an individual case.

I.58   On the other hand, Schiedt's table was successfully applied to different groups by Maywerk and Schwaab:

I.59   Maywerk,[70] as head of the Crimino-biological Service at Hamburg, applied it in 1938 to a sample of 200 prisoners examined by that Service between 1929 and 1933.   He found that the favourable prognoses made by the Service had been wrong in $61 \cdot 6\%$ and the unfavourable prognoses in $46 \cdot 7\%$ of the cases.   According to the point system, however, only $11 \cdot 4\%$

of the favourable and 6·1% of the unfavourable prognoses were wrong. In the case of both techniques, the point system and the "intuitive" technique applied by the Service, the percentage of "doubtful" prognoses was unduly high, namely 65·4% and 62% respectively. He showed, however, that Scheidt's category of doubtful cases, which included all those with from 4 to 9 bad points, was unnecessarily wide and could be reduced to a category including only those with from 5 to 7 bad points. He was also critical of some of Scheidt's 15 factors.

I.60 Schwaab[71] applied Scheidt's table to a sample of 400 recidivist offenders guilty of offences against property. Omitting Scheidt's factor 2 (serious criminality of ascendants), for which no adequate information was available, he found that none of the offenders possessing no bad points had become failures, whereas all those with 14 bad points had failed.

I.61 Kohnle,[72] examined in 1938 the files of 203 boys discharged from German Reformatories (*Fürsorge-Erziehung*) between 1926 and 1932, of whom 67% had subsequently been convicted. His object was also to apply and, if possible, validate Scheidt's table. In view of the lower ages of his cases and of gaps in the files, however, he had to modify or to omit some of Scheidt's factors, but a number of the remaining factors proved to be of predictive value.

I.62 In the third part of his recent book "*Der Frühkriminelle Rückfalls-verbrecher*"[73] or "*Criminalité Précoce et Récidivisme*", the Swiss criminologist and former Juvenile Court judge, Dr. Erwin Frey, has produced what probably amounts to the most determined criticism of the American prediction studies. At the same time, he has presented an elaborate prognostic scheme of his own. All American studies so far published suffer in his view from the following weaknessess: their data are inadequate for the vital period of early childhood and in particular with regard to biological and hereditary factors. As psychiatric reports are likewise missing for the majority of cases, there is inevitably, he thinks, an undue emphasis on social factors, and all this together has produced a distorted picture. Overcomplicated statistical techniques take the place of comprehensive and reliable information about the all-round development and structure of the human personality as a whole. Dr. Frey rejects the idea that a correct prognosis can be made by using, instead of a logically and criminologically coherent and integrated picture of the development of the total personality, a small number of isolated and in no way interrelated factors. In view of the attempts made by the Gluecks in "Unraveling Juvenile Delinquency" to establish prediction tables for very young children, he stresses that no reliable prognosis is possible before the age of 16. The German studies referred to above are regarded by Dr. Frey as superior to their American models in view of the more thorough examination of individual offenders carried out by the German Criminological Service; they, too, are inadequate, however, with regard to early childhood. He favours the suggestion made by Gerecke (above) to differentiate the various factors by attaching to them different point values and to multiply the point values according to the intensity of the factor concerned in an individual case.

I.63 Dr. Frey's own scheme is essentially a combination of an assessment of the personality as a whole (*Ganzheitsbewertung*), on the lines of intuitive prognosis, and of the usual point system modified by differentiations and multiplications similar to Gerecke's suggestions. Two different forms of prediction are worked out: the one, of a preliminary nature (*Vorprognose*), to be prepared during the preliminary proceedings for offenders between 16 and 18; and the second, more definitive prognosis (*Nachprognose*), adding to it information concerning the institutional and post-institutional periods of the offender's life and prepared not before the age of 24 has been reached and at least 3 years have elapsed after discharge. Dr. Frey's prognostic table contains concise extracts of the contents of the files, arranged in 8, for the *Nachprognose* in 10, main sections, most of which are divided into several subsections or factors. To these extracts a statistical assessment is given according to a point system. The factors, or groups of factors, are of a fairly general nature (e.g. "personality type", "home milieu", "educational difficulties"), and their weight is assessed by the author in accordance with his views on their criminogenic significance, e.g. the factor "leisure milieu" receives a value (*Basispunktwert*) of only 5, early criminality, however, one of 35. The intensity which each factor shows in an individual case is measured by coefficients ranging from 1 to 5, a highly criminogenic form of psychopathy, for example, receiving the coefficient of 4·5, a simple case of mental deficiency, however, only one of 1 or 2. By applying this table to a group of 75 cases correct results were obtained in 84% of the cases, whereas an intuitive prognosis made by the author without using the table achieved only 74·6% of accuracy. On the other hand, the author admits the presence of strong intuitive elements in his application of the table.

I.64 In a monograph entitled "*Pahantapaisuus Yksilon Sopeutumatto-muuden Oireena*" (Delinquency as a Symptom of Later Social Maladjustment),[74] Dr. Erkki Saari, the Director of the Observation and Classification Centre at the Jarvilinna State Reformatory in Finland, presents the results of a follow-up study of 465 boys referred to the Centre in the years between 1921 and 1927. From the English summary the following data may be quoted: The average follow-up period was 15 years and 5 months, and the average age of the sample was 16 years and 10 months on leaving the Reformatory and 34 years and 2 months at the end of the follow-up period.

The information given in the official records was supplemented by personal interview with each boy, his relatives, neighbours and local officials. It was found that within the follow-up period 51·3% of the ex-Reformatory boys had had no further convictions, 17·6% had become habitual criminals and the rest occasional offenders. About 80% had attained a fairly independent economic status. For purposes of research, the whole group was divided into those who had become recidivists, once-convicted and non-delinquents, and the correlations were worked out (Pearson's coefficient of contingency) between 21 background factors and subsequent criminal history. No marked correlations were found between any single of these factors and success or failure; in fact the highest correlation was ·21 (for a factor called "Number of abnormalities in environmental conditions"). Special care, he says, was taken "to eliminate spurious correlations". The correlations obtained were further checked by subdividing the recidivist group into two sub-groups, according to the frequency of recon-victions, in order to ascertain whether this would make the originally observed trends even more definite. Eventually, only 3 factors were regarded as showing clear correlations with the criterion, i.e. intelligence level, length of time in Reformatory and elementary schooling in the Institution. For a few other factors correlations were obtained similar to those given by the Gluecks in "One Thousand Juvenile Delinquents".

I.65 In a study of juvenile delinquency at Cambridge, England, one of the present authors presented some figures to show that there was "a fairly close correlation between the pre-probation history of the boys as expressed in bad points and their subsequent conduct", and that "from the case histories available to the Cambridge Juvenile Court an approximate fore-cast was possible as to the likely outcome of probation".[75] Using a scheme of bad and good points, it was found that of a group of boys who had been successful on probation 65·9% had either no bad points or not more than 10 out of a possible maximum of 86 bad points. On the other hand, of boys who became recidivists only 40%, and of boys who became persistent offenders only 18·2%, were in these two categories. It was stressed in that study, however, that in view of the small numbers of cases and for other reasons the construction of prediction tables had not been feasible.

I.66 In spite of the great variety of predictive techniques employed by different workers, this survey has also shown a considerable degree of uniformity of results. It cannot reasonably be expected, of course, that the same factors will invariably have the same predictive value regardless of time and place, of the age and other characteristics of the case material concerned. Moreover, even slight variations in the definition of an item may produce important differences in the results. To give but a few illustrations. Whereas according to Burgess and Tibbitts "emotional instability" is a favourable predictive category, other investigators, in particular the Gluecks, report a very high positive correlation between "mental distortion" or "marked adolescent instability" and recidivism. The "lone wolf" has a high violation rate in the Burgess and Tibbitts studies, whereas the Gluecks have found a significant positive correlation between gang membership and failure. On the other hand, there is a fair amount of agreement with regard to such factors as work record, frequency of previous convictions, disciplinary record in penal and reformatory institutions. The seriousness of the offence for which the offender had been committed to the institution is generally regarded as of little predictive value; for Burgess, greater seriousness even indicates likelihood of success; and sex offences have, ever since Warner, persistently shown the lowest rates of failure.

In view of the fact that a number of prediction tables (or, better, "experience tables") are already available, in particular in the United States, it may be pertinent to enquire whether any practical use has been made of them. The answer is disappointing. The Illinois Division of Correction which, for the past 20 years, has been using the tables described by Ohlin (see above I.39) seems to have found no successor as yet. There is not only in the various Glueck studies no indication of any official acceptance of their tables, but the same is also true of more recent American publications.[76]

It can hardly be maintained that this lack of success in the field of the practical administration of criminal justice has been due to any exaggerated claims made by the theorists. On the contrary, in nearly every piece of prediction research so far published it has been stressed, firstly, that the applicability of experience tables to actual cases was dependent on their previous validation; and, secondly, that these tables were intended merely to supplement, but in no way to replace, the individual discretion and judgment of Courts, Parole Boards and penal administrators.

Interpreted in this limited sense, as a servant rather than as the master, the use of experience tables has been suggested mainly for the following purposes: to assist

    (a) Criminal Courts in their choice between the various methods of disposal, which, of course, presupposes the existence of tables capable of adequately discriminating between the latter;

    (b) Prison and probation officers in adapting their treatment to the specific needs of the individual offender as indicated by the tables;

    (c) Parole Boards and corresponding agencies in fixing the length of indeterminate sentences and in selecting the most effective form of after-care.

How far experience tables are capable of giving such assistance cannot be judged unless they are actually applied to suitably selected experimental groups of offenders.

SUMMARY OF CHAPTER I

[From *Prediction Methods in Relation to Borstal Training* by H. Mannheim and L. T. Wilkins.]

S.I.1   A survey has been made of the principal prediction studies published in the past 30 years in the United States and Europe. Most of them are concerned with male parolees, only a few with ex-probationers and with women. Considerable progress has been made in the development of prediction techniques, due mainly to growing experience and further refinements in statistical method. Two techniques, each of them with numerous variants, dominate the field, the Burgess technique, using a large number of predictive factors without any weighting, and the Glueck technique, employing only a small number of factors and a weighting system. Special attention has been devoted by various research workers to the following problems: how to avoid the use of overlapping factors and of subjective factors; how to reduce the size of the middle category of "doubtful" cases on which no statistical prognosis can be made; the need for individual interviews to supplement the information obtained from official files; and the length of the follow-up period required.

S.I.2   Although the work of the past 30 years has brought some of these problems nearer to their solution and has narrowed the area of controversy it cannot be claimed that unanimity has everywhere been reached. The now prevailing view favours, for example, prediction tables based on a few factors only (the Gluecks, Ohlin, Reiss and others), but there are still dissentients such as Burgess and Frey; it favours the avoidance of subjective factors, but they have been used by Burgess, Tibbitts, Ohlin, Reiss and Frey; it accepts the desirability of supplementary individual interviews, but important practical schemes such as the prediction procedure adopted by the State of Illinois have had to omit them as too expensive. Even from the almost universally shared experience that most relapses occur during the first months after discharge there is one exception reported by Vold. No effective way has been shown in previous studies of how to reduce the excessive size of the "doubtful" middle group and of how, without impairing the reliability of the tables, to make use of subjective factors so as to avoid the recent criticism by Burgess and Sellin that statistical prediction has so far been dealing only with the "external aspects of behaviour".   Nor has the controversy between statistical and intuitive individual prediction been completely silenced, especially as the latter has occasionally produced results not greatly inferior to those of statistical prediction (e.g. in the Cambridge-Somerville Study).

S.I.3 Although validation studies, very rare in the initial stages of prediction research, are, in particular through the persistent efforts of the Gluecks, becoming more frequent, it cannot be said that a perfect validation of any of the existing tables has so far been achieved.

REFERENCES TO CHAPTER I

[From *Prediction Methods in Relation to Borstal Training* by
H. Mannheim and L. T. Wilkins.]

Historical Survey of Prediction Studies in the Field of Criminology

(1) Many such follow-up studies are conveniently summarised in Walter C. Reckless, "Criminal Behavior" (1940), Chapter XX. Jan Rumney and Joseph P. Murphy, Probation and Social Adjustment (1952, New Brunswick, New Jersey, Rutgers University Press) is an important follow-up study of probationers with a special chapter on prognosis (Chapter XIV), but without prediction tables.

(2) A useful account of American prediction studies is given by Elio D. Monachesi in 41 Journal of Criminal Law and Criminology, September–October, 1950.

(3) S. B. Warner, "Factors determining Parole from the Massachusetts Reformatory", 14 Journal of Criminal Law and Criminology (1923), 172–207.

(4) Hornell Hart, "Predicting Parole Success", 14 Journal Criminal Law and Criminology (1923), 405–413.

(5) Bruce, Burgess and Harno, "The Working of the Indeterminate Sentence Law and the Parole System in Illinois" (1928), Chapters XXVIII and XXX.

(6) op. cit., p. 246.

(7) op. cit., p. 248.

(8) See the list given by George B. Vold, "Prediction Methods and Parole" (1931), p. 16.

(9) Sheldon Glueck and Eleanor T. Glueck, "500 Criminal Careers" (1930, New York, Alfred A. Knopf).

(10) Monachesi in the paper quoted above under (2) on p. 274.

(11) "500 Criminal Careers", p. 7.

(11a) In "Later Criminal Careers", p. 1, the beginning of the investigation is dated 1925.

(12) op. cit., p. 166.

(13) op. cit., p. 150.

(14) op. cit., pp. 175–6.

(15) pp. 8 et seq.

(16) pp. 7 and 85, 93 et seq.

(17) pp. 101 et seq.

(18) For the exact definitions see pp. 187 et seq.

(19) pp. 256 et seq.

(20) pp. 281 et seq.

(21) Sheldon and Eleanor Glueck, "Later Criminal Careers" (1937, New York, The Commonwealth Fund; London, Humphrey Milford, Oxford University Press).

(22) See in particular Chapter XI.

(23) Chapter IX.

(24) Sheldon and Eleanor Glueck, "Criminal Careers in Retrospect" (1943, New York, The Commonwealth Fund).

(25) op. cit., pp. 227 et seq.
(26) Sheldon and Eleanor Glueck, "One Thousand Juvenile Delinquents" (1934, Cambridge, Mass., Harvard University Press).
(27) Sheldon and Eleanor Glueck, "Juvenile Delinquents Grown Up" (1940, New York, The Commonwealth Fund).
(28) See Chapter XXI.
(29) Chapters XIII–XVIII.
(30) Sheldon and Eleanor Glueck, "Five Hundred Delinquent Women" (1934, New York, Alfred A. Knopf).
(31) See Appendices A and B.
(32) See pp. 341, 344, 345 et seq.
(33) See p. 306.
(34) pp. 286 et seq.
(35) p. 285.
(36) Sheldon and Eleanor Glueck, "After-conduct of Discharged Offenders" (1945, London, Macmillan and Company, Limited.)
(37) Sheldon and Eleanor Glueck, "Unraveling Juvenile Delinquency" (1950, New York, The Commonwealth Fund).   Chapter XX deals with prediction.   See also the simplified version, "Delinquents in the Making" (1952, New York, Harper and Brothers) and Mrs. Eleanor Glueck's article, "Predicting Juvenile Delinquency" in 2 British Journal of Delinquency, April, 1952.
(37a) See the definitions in "500 Criminal Careers", pp. 135, fn. 25 and 200; "Later Criminal Careers", pp. 135, 238 and 257.
(38) "After-conduct of Discharged Offenders", pp. 66, fn. 1.
(39) "Criminal Careers in Retrospect", p. 221, fn. 15.
(40) "Criminal Careers in Retrospect", p. 221.   See also "Five Hundred Delinquent Women", p. 288.
(41) George B. Vold, "Prediction Methods and Parole" (1931, Hanover N. H., Minneapolis, Liverpool, The Sociological Press).
(42) op. cit., pp. 53 and 57.
(43) pp. 84–5.
(44) In "Criminal Careers in Retrospect", p. 219, fn. 10, the Gluecks point out that this criticism refers only to the original construction of the tables, whereas their application, in view of the smaller number of items, involves less work than the Burgess method.
(45) ibid., pp. 98 and 105.
(46) George B. Vold, "Prediction Methods Applied to Problems of Classification within Institutions", 26 Journal of Criminal Law and Criminology, July 1935, pp. 202–9.
(47) Elio D. Monachesi, "Prediction Factors in Probation" (1932, Hanover N.H., Minneapolis, Liverpool, The Sociological Press).
(48) Clark Tibbitts, "Success and Failure in Parole can be predicted", 22 Journal of Criminal Law and Criminology, May, 1931; "The Reliability of Factors used in predicting Success or Failure on Parole", ibidem, March, 1932.
(49) Walter Webster Argow, "A Criminal-Liability Index for Predicting Possibility of Rehabilitation", 26 Journal of Criminal Law and Criminology, November, 1935.
(50) Norman Fenton, "The Delinquent Boy and the Correctional School" (1935, Claremont Colleges Guidance Center, Claremont Colleges Library).   See in particular Chapter X.
(51) op. cit., pp. 150 and 155.
(52) Ferris F. Laune, "Predicting Criminality" (1936, Chicago, North Western University Studies in Social Sciences, No. 1).
(53) H. Ashley Weeks, "Predicting Juvenile Delinquency", 8 American Sociological Review, 1943.

(53a) "Attorney-General's Survey of Release Procedures. Volume IV: Parole." (Department of Justice, Washington, 1939). Chapter XI and Appendix A.

(54) Lloyd E. Ohlin, "Selection for Parole, A Manual of Parole Prediction" (1951, New York, Russell Sage Foundation).

(55) According to Ohlin, p. 46, Illinois is still the only State of the U.S.A. which possesses such a routine prediction system.

(56) Definitions of these factors are given in Appendix F of Ohlin's book.

(57) Morris G. Caldwell, "Preview of a new type of Probation Study made in Alabama" (15 Federal Probation, June, 1951).

(58) Albert J. Reiss, "The Accuracy, Efficiency and Validity of a Prediction Instrument", 61 American Journal of Sociology, May, 1951, pp. 552–561.

(59) Albert J. Reiss, "Delinquency as the Failure of Personal and Social Controls", 16 American Sociological Review, April, 1951, pp. 196–207.

(60) Edwin Powers and Helen Witmer, "An Experiment in the Prevention of Delinquency". The Cambridge-Somerville Youth Study (1951, New York, Columbia University Press).

(61) See Powers-Witmer: Chapter XVIII "Can Delinquency be predicted?"

(62) "The Prediction of Personal Adjustment" by Paul Horst et al., Social Science Research Council Bulletin 48 (1941, New York).

(63) Schneider and La Grone, "Prediction of Behaviour of Civilian Delinquents in the Armed Forces", 28 Mental Hygiene (1944), 456–475.

(64) "Recidivism at the Hawthorne-Cedar Knolls School. Predicted vs. actual outcome for delinquent boys". By Bertram J. Black and Selma J. Glick. Research Monograph No. 2, Jewish Board of Guardians. New York, 3, N.Y. (1952).

(65) Richard E. Thompson, 43 Journal of Criminal Law, Criminology and Police Science (1952), pp. 451–70. See also 3 British Journal of Delinquency (April 1953).

(66) Franz Exner, "Kriminalistischer Bericht über eine Reise nach Amerika" (Berlin, 1935). On German prediction studies in general see Franz Exner, "Kriminologie", (Springer-Verlag, Berlin-Göttingen-Heidelberg, 1949). Chapter 32.

(67) Robert Schiedt, "Ein Beitrag zum Problem der Rückfallsprognose" (München, 1936). This book was not available, and the account given above is based on information derived from Nos. 66, 68, 69, 70, 72.

(68) Hans Trunk, "Soziale Prognosen an Strafgefangenen, 28 Monatsschrift für Kriminal-biologie und Strafrechtsreform" (1937), pp. 209–27; with commentary by Exner, pp. 227–30.

(69) Gerecke, "Zur Frage der Rückfallsprognose, 30 Monatsschrift für Kriminal-biologie und Strafrechtsreform" (1939), pp. 35–38.

(70) Wilhelm Meywerk, "Beitrag zur Bestimmung der sozialen Prognose an Rückfallsverbrechern, 29 Monatsschrift" (1938), pp. 422–5.

(71) F. Schwaab, "Die soziale Prognose bei rückfälligen Vermögensverbrechern". This book was not available, and the references are taken from Exner, "Kriminologie" (above No. 66).

(72) E. F. Kohnle, "Die Kriminalität entlassener Fürsorgezöglinge und die Möglichkeit einer Erfolgsprognose". Kriminalistische Abhandlungen No. 33 (1938), Leipzig.

(73) Erwin Frey, "Der Frühkriminelle Rückfallsverbrecher. Criminalité précoce et Récidivisme". Schweizerische Criminalistische Studien, Vol. 4, Basel, Verlag für Recht und Gesellschaft (1951). See on this book the "Critical Notice" in 3 British Journal of Delinquency (October 1952), pp. 132.

(74) Erkki Saari, "Pahantapaisuus Yksilön Sopeutumattomuuden Oireena, Jyväskyla" (1951).

(75) Hermann Mannheim, "Juvenile Delinquency in an English Middle-town" (International Library of Sociology and Social Reconstruction. 1948. Routledge and Kegan Paul, London).

(76) See the authoritative survey of recent developments in the American parole system by Dr. George G. Killinger in "Contemporary Correction", edited by Paul W. Tappan (McGraw-Hill Book Company, Inc., New York-Toronto-London, 1951), p. 379, where the need for the construction and application of prediction tables is stressed, but no reference is made to any present use.   Charles H. Z. Meyer, in "A Half Century of Probation and Parole" (The Journal of Criminal Law, Criminology and Police Science, Vol. 42, No. 6, March–April, 1952, p. 727) complains that probation and parole officers do not use such tables wisely, but gives no indication of where and how much they are actually being used.   In "Correctional Research", Bulletin No. 1, January 1953 (published by the United Prison Association of Massachusetts): "What is new in Parole", Ohlin's claim that "Illinois has the distinction of being the only state in this country in which a routine system of parole prediction has been established" is reproduced without contradiction.   Moreover, Ohlin's own discussion of the possibility of a "master experience table" for use by the Parole Boards of the other states of U.S.A. (pp. 64 et seq.) also seems to confirm that no experience tables have so far been employed outside Illinois.

After this had gone to Press, we have been informed by Professor Norman S. Hayner of the University of Washington, Seattle, that the State of Washington Board of Prison Terms and Paroles, of which he is a member, has for the past few years been using prediction techniques in an experimental way and that it is hoped to use them in the near future as a matter of routine.

*   *   *

As the references to prediction studies presented in Mannheim's and Wilkins' Chapter I extend only to 1954, we deemed it advisable to include additional references to later publications in the field of prediction.   The supplementary bibliography of American prediction studies which follows was provided by Richard E. Thompson and the German bibliography by Judge Wolf Middendorf of Freiburg, Germany.   We append also reference to two prediction studies made in Japan.

SUPPLEMENTARY BIBLIOGRAPHY OF AMERICAN PREDICTION STUDIES: 1955–1958

Balogh, Joseph K., and Charles J. Rumage, 'Juvenile Delinquency Proneness; A Study of the Kvaraceus Scale," Washington, D.C., Public Affairs Press, 1956.

Beall, Herbert S., and James H. Panton, "Use of the Minnesota Multiphasic Personality Inventory as an Index to 'Escapism'," 12 *Journal of Clinical Psychology* (1956), pp. 392–394.

Glueck, Eleanor T., "Identifying Juvenile Delinquents and Neurotics," 40 *Mental Hygiene* (1956), pp. 24–43.

———— "Predictive Techniques in the Prevention and Treatment of Delinquency. Part II: The Workability of Predictive Techniques," *Salute to Youth*, Boston Conference of National Juvenile Court Foundation, Inc., 1956, pp. 57–66.

———— "Status of Glueck Prediction Studies," 47 *Journal of Criminal Law, Criminology and Police Science* (1956), pp. 18–32.

———— "Spotting Potential Delinquents: Can It Be Done?" 20 *Federal Probation Quarterly* (1956), pp. 7–13.

———— "Body Build and the Prediction of Delinquency," 48 *Journal of Criminal Law, Criminology and Police Science* (1958), pp. 577–579.

Glueck, Sheldon, "Predictive Techniques in the Prevention and Treatment of Delinquency. Part I: The Nature of Predictive Techniques," *Salute to Youth*, Boston Conference of National Juvenile Court Foundation, Inc., 1956, pp. 47–56.

Glueck, Sheldon, and Eleanor T. Glueck, "Early Detection of Future Delinquents," 47 *Journal of Criminal Law, Criminology and Police Science* (1956), pp. 174–182.

Hathaway, Starke R., and Elio D. Monachesi, "The Personalities of Predelinquent Boys," 48 *Journal of Criminal Law, Criminology and Police Science* (1957), pp. 149–163.

Kvaraceus, William C., "A Partial Validation of the KD Proneness Check List Via Case Records of Institutionalized Delinquents," 14 *Forum of Education* (1955), pp. 28–30.

——— "Prediction Studies of Delinquent Behavior," 34 *Personnel and Guidance Journal* (1955), pp. 146–149.

——— "Preventing and Treating Juvenile Delinquency: Some Basic Approaches," 63 *School Review* (1955), pp. 477–479.

——— "Forecasting Juvenile Delinquency," 138 (4) *Journal of Education* (1956), pp. 1–43.

Monachesi, Elio D., "The Prognosis of Recidivism: American Studies," 20 (1) *Midwest Sociologist* (1957), 7 pp.

New York City Youth Board, Research Department, *An Experiment in the Validation of the Glueck Prediction Scale*, July 1957. (Progress Report from November 1952 to December 1956.)

Quay, Herbert, and Donald R. Peterson, "A Brief Scale for Juvenile Delinquency," 14 *Journal of Clinical Psychology* (1958), pp. 139–142.

Rexford, Eveoleen N., Maxwell Schleifer, and Suzanne Taets von Amerongen, "A Follow-up of a Psychiatric Study of. 57 Antisocial Young Children," 40 *Mental Hygiene* (1956), pp. 196–214.

State Department of Institutions and Agencies, Trenton, N.J., "Predicting Juvenile Delinquency," 124 *Research Bulletin* (April 1955).

Thompson, Richard E., "Further Validation of the Glueck Social Prediction Table for Identifying Potential Delinquents," 48 *Journal of Criminal Law, Criminology and Police Science* (1957), pp. 175–184.

SUPPLEMENTARY BIBLIOGRAPHY OF FOREIGN PREDICTION STUDIES: 1956–1958

Abe, Harno, and Kokichi Higuchi, *An Introduction to the Glueck Prediction Method*, Tokyo, Ichiryusha Publishing Co., Ltd., 1959. (In Japanese.)

Brückner, Günther, "Untersuchungen über die Rückfallsprognose bei chronischen Vermögensverbrechern," *Monatsschrift für Kriminologie und Strafrechtsreform*, 1958.

Emmerig, Ernst, *Kriminalprognose auf staitistischer Grundlage*, dissertation, München, 1948.

Leferenz, Heinz, "Zur Problematik der kriminologischen Prognose," *Zeitschrift für die gesamte Strafrechtswissenschaft* (ZStW), 1956.

Leferenz, Heinz, *Die Kriminalität der Kinder*, Tübingen, 1957.

Meyer, Fritz, *Rückfallsprognose bei unbestimmt verurteilten Jugendlichen*, Bonn, 1956.

Meyer, Fritz, "Ein Beitrag zum Problem der Rückfallsprognose," *Deutsche Richterzeitung*, 1957.

Middendorff, Wolf, *Die Möglichkeiten der sozialen Prognose, Ein kriminologischer Bericht über den internationalen Stand der Forschung*, Freiburg/Br., 1958.

Middendorff, Wolf, "Bemerkungen zur Sozialen Prognose, insbesondere in bezug auf Jugendliche," in: *Soziologie der Jugendkriminalität*, hrsg. von Peter Heintz und René König, Kölner Zeitschrift für Soziologie und Sozialpsychologie, Sonderheft 2, 1958.

Müggenburg, Willi, *Statistische Untersuchungen zum Problem der Rückfallsprognose von Strafgefangenen*, dissertation, Heidelburg, 1956.

Schumann, Werner and Werner Hopmann, "Über Voraussagemöglichkeiten hinsichtlich der Jugendkriminalität und Jugendverwahrlosung nach Sheldon und Eleanor Glueck," *Praxis der Kinderpsychologie und Kinderpsychiatrie*, 1956.

Stutte, Hermann, "Die soziale Individualprognose bei verwahrlosten und kriminellen Jugendlichen," in: *Handbuch der Heimerziehung*, 6. Lieferung, Frankfurt/M., 1956.

Stutte, Hermann, *Grenzen der Sozialpädagogik*, Marburg, 1958.

Tatezawa, Tokuhiro, *A Study of Prediction of Juvenile Delinquency*, Japan, Ministry of Justice, 1958. (Multilithed.)

Appendix B

*Glueck Prediction Tables, Predictive Factors, Scores,
and Definitions*

Note of Explanation

The prediction tables are keyed to the chapters in which they are discussed (III, V, VII, IX, XI) so that, for example, tables (summaries of which are presented in Chapters III, V, etc.,) are here identified as Tables III–1, V–5, and so on, in the order of their textual discussion.

Immediately following each table below are listed the predictive factors which entered into its construction (see Chapter II for the method of selecting the factors and constructing the table) together with the violation, maladaptation, recidivism, delinquency, or neuroticism scores which are to be assigned to an offender in a particular subcategory of a factor. It is to be noted that the actual number of cases from which the scores were derived is generally larger than the number of cases that make up the prediction table itself since in the latter it was only possible to include those cases for which *all* the five factors entering into the construction of the table were known.

At the end of the appendix of tables are presented, in alphabetical order, all relevant definitions of factors.

Violation of conditions of striaght probation, probation with suspended sentence, or parole refers to the commission of serious offenses such as larceny, burglary, robbery, assault with intent to murder, rape, rob; pathological sex crimes; stealing automobiles; going away after accident. It refers also to the persistent commission of minor offenses such as running away, drunkenness, malicious mischief, disturbing the peace. Violations of the conditions of supervision are also included, except for an isolated minor infringement (such as neglect to report to probation or parole officer in time, or changing jobs without permission, or arrest for a traffic violation).

Included also as violations are desertion and dishonorable discharge from the Armed Forces.

Maladaptation in an institution refers to behavior that reflects rebellion against authority (insolence, defiance, disobedience, refusal to work, malicious mischief, attempting to escape, "crookedness"); violence against the person (fighting, quarreling, assault); offenses against property, or stealing; sex offenses; persistent commission of offenses reflecting a lack of self-control (inattention, idleness, laziness, shirking, "fooling," carelessness about appearance, care of room, and so on). The isolated commission of an offense reflecting lack of self-control is not included as maladapted behavior.

Recidivism during the years following completion of first sentence imposed by a juvenile or adult court refers to the commission of offenses such as larceny, burglary, robbery, assault with intent to murder, rape, rob; pathological sex crimes; stealing automobiles; going away after accident. It refers also to the persistent commission of minor offenses such as running away, drunkenness, malicious mischief, disturbing the peace. Violations of the conditions of probation or parole are also included, except for occasional minor infringements (such as neglect to report to probation or parole officer in time, or changing jobs without permission, or arrest for a traffic violation).

Included also are desertion and dishonorable discharge from the Armed Forces.

Delinquency refers to repeated acts of a kind which, if committed beyond the statutory juvenile court age of sixteen, are punishable as crimes (either felonies or misdemeanors), except for persistent stubbornness, or truancy, or running away, or associating with immoral persons. Children who once or twice steal a toy or sneak into a subway or motion picture theater, or play hooky, and soon outgrow such peccadilloes, are not true delinquents, even though they violate the law.

Neuroticism is a condition in which the individual suffers from more than average insecurity and anxiety (conscious or unconscious) against which he develops protective devices differing quantitatively or qualitatively from the culturally accepted ones and leading to conflicts which are, as a rule, not solvable by him for the time being. If the neurosis interferes with efficient adaptation, the boy is classified as a marked neurotic. When the neurosis does not prevent the individual from efficient adaptation, he is classified as a mild neurotic. However, neuroticism, whether marked or mild, is encompassed here.

Table III–I. Prediction of Behavior of Male Juvenile Offenders
during Straight Probation

Score Class	Violation Rate	Non-Violation Rate	Total Number of Cases
Less than 240	36.0%	64.0%	25
240–270	66.7	33.3	48
270 or Over	85.6	14.4	291

Predictive Factors	Violation Scores
BIRTHPLACE OF FATHER	
Poland, Russia, Lithuania	45.4
Italy, Ireland	53.7
United States or Foreign Countries other than Poland, Russia, Lithuania, Italy, Ireland	65.5
DISCIPLINE BY FATHER	
Firm but Kindly	16.7
Erratic	45.5
Overstrict or Lax	62.9
DISCIPLINE BY MOTHER	
Firm but Kindly	15.4
Erratic	48.6
Overstrict or Lax	65.2
SCHOOL RETARDATION	
None	43.5
One Year	54.9
Two or More Years	62.7
SCHOOL MISCONDUCT	
None	41.7
Misconduct other than Truancy	51.5
Truancy	62.1

Source: *Juvenile Delinquents Grown Up*, Tables 69 and 70, pp. 202 and 203.

Table III–2.   Prediction of Behavior of Male Juvenile Offenders
during Probation with Suspended Sentence

Score Class	Violation Rate	Non-Violation Rate	Total Number of Cases
Less than 300	50.0%	50.0%	16
300–330	62.2	37.8	45
330 or Over	86.7	13.3	173

Predictive Factors	Violation Scores
BIRTHPLACE OF FATHER	
Foreign Countries other than Italy, Ireland	58.6
Italy	66.2
United States, Ireland	78.4
DISCIPLINE BY FATHER	
Firm but Kindly	37.5
Erratic	55.8
Overstrict or Lax	76.4
DISCIPLINE BY MOTHER	
Firm but Kindly	33.3
Erratic	58.8
Overstrict or Lax	75.0
AFFECTION OF FATHER FOR OFFENDER	
Warm	64.1
Indifferent or Hostile	79.4
SCHOOL MISCONDUCT	
None	51.1
Some	73.9

Source: *Juvenile Delinquents Grown Up*, Tables 71 and 72, pp. 204 and 205.

Table III–3. Prediction of Behavior of Male Juvenile Offenders
in Correctional Schools

Score Class	Maladaptation Rate	Adaptation Rate	Total Number of Cases
Less than 210	45.0%	55.0%	20
210 or Over	65.5	34.5	142

Predictive Factors	Maladaptation Scores
MORAL STANDARDS OF HOME	
Fair or Poor	42.3
Good	57.7
NUMBER OF CHILDREN IN FAMILY OF OFFENDER	
Two or More	41.9
One	57.1
CONJUGAL RELATIONS OF PARENTS	
Good	36.9
Fair	48.1
Poor	54.3
BAD HABITS IN CHILDHOOD	
None	31.5
Some	45.7
TIME BETWEEN ONSET OF ANTISOCIAL BEHAVIOR AND FIRST ARREST	
None	23.1
Some	43.2

Source: *Juvenile Delinquents Grown Up*, Tables 75 and 76, pp. 208 and 209.

Appendix B

Table III–4. Prediction of Behavior of Male Juvenile Offenders
in Correctional Schools under Seventeen Years of Age

Score Class	Maladaptation Rate	Adaptation Rate	Total Number of Cases
Less than 290	20.0%	80.0%	20
290 or Over	72.2	27.8	54

Predictive Factors	Maladaptation Scores
FAMILY RELATIONSHIPS	
Socially Acceptable	27.8
Socially Unacceptable	64.9
AGE AT ONSET OF ANTISOCIAL BEHAVIOR	
Eleven or Older	57.3
Under Eleven	80.0
SCHOOL RETARDATION	
None	33.3
One or More Years	64.2
AGE FIRST LEFT HOME	
Fourteen or Older	42.1
Under Fourteen	69.9
AGE BEGAN WORK	
Under Fifteen	37.8
Fifteen or Older	72.5

Source: *Criminal Careers in Retrospect*, Tables A and 33, pp. 258 and 259.

Table III–5. Prediction of Behavior of Male Juvenile Offenders in
Correctional Schools at Seventeen through Twenty-one Years of Age

Score Class	Maladaptation Rate	Adaptation Rate	Total Number of Cases
Less than 380	61.5%	38.5%	13
380 or Over	100.0	0.0	11

Predictive Factors	Maladaptation Scores
NATIVITY OF PARENTS AND OFFENDER	
One or Both Parents Foreign-Born; Offender Native-Born	68.0
All Native-Born	90.9
All Foreign-Born	100.0
ECONOMIC STATUS OF CHILDHOOD HOME	
Dependent	60.0
Marginal	79.2
Comfortable	87.5
FAMILY RELATIONSHIPS	
Socially Acceptable	69.2
Socially Unacceptable	90.0
ECONOMIC RESPONSIBILITY OF OFFENDER	
Responsible	50.0
Irresponsible	78.6
SCHOOL RETARDATION	
None	50.0
One or More Years	77.4

Source: *Criminal Careers in Retrospect*, Tables D and 34, p. 259.

Appendix B

Table III–6.   Prediction of Behavior of Male Juvenile
Offenders during Parole

Score Class	Violation Rate	Non-Violation Rate	Total Number of Cases
Less than 290	0.0%	100.0%	1
290 or Over	89.8	10.2	215

Predictive Factors	Violation Scores
BIRTHPLACE OF FATHER	
Foreign Countries other than Ireland	64.3
United States	77.9
Ireland	89.7
BIRTHPLACE OF MOTHER	
United States, Poland, Russia, Lithuania, Italy	66.9
Foreign Countries other than Poland, Russia,	
Lithuania, Italy, Ireland	72.7
Ireland	86.7
DISCIPLINE BY FATHER	
Firm but Kindly	40.3
Erratic	63.9
Overstrict or Lax	74.1
DISCIPLINE BY MOTHER	
Firm but Kindly	50.0
Erratic	61.7
Overstrict or Lax	73.8
SCHOOL MISCONDUCT	
None	55.2
Some	72.2

Source: *Juvenile Delinquents Grown Up*, Tables 73 and 74, pp. 206 and 207.

Table III–7.   Prediction of Behavior of Male Juvenile Offenders
during Five Years after Completion of First Sentence
Imposed by Juvenile Court

Score Class	Recidivism Rate	Non-Recidivism Rate	Total Number of Cases
Less than 476	50.0%	50.0%	*
476–501	67.0	33.0	*
501–526	83.1	16.9	*
526 or Over	91.3	8.7	*

Predictive Factors	Recidivism Scores
DISCIPLINE BY FATHER	
Firm but Kindly	54.2
Erratic	83.6
Overstrict or Lax	91.1
DISCIPLINE BY MOTHER	
Firm but Kindly	68.4
Erratic	80.9
Overstrict or Lax	90.8
SCHOOL RETARDATION	
None	78.4
One or Two Years	88.1
Three or More Years	93.5
SCHOOL MISCONDUCT	
None	72.4
Some	91.3
AGE AT ONSET OF ANTISOCIAL BEHAVIOR	
Fifteen or Sixteen	61.1
Thirteen or Fourteen	84.3
Eleven or Twelve	84.8
Under Eleven	92.0
TIME BETWEEN ONSET OF ANTISOCIAL BEHAVIOR AND FIRST ARREST	
Less than One Year	72.1
One or Two Years	82.4
Three or More Years	90.8

* Not available.
Source: *One Thousand Juvenile Delinquents*, Tables 38 and 39, pp. 187 and 188.

Appendix B

Table III–8.   Prediction of Behavior of Male Juvenile Offenders
during Fifteen Years after Completion of First Sentence
Imposed by Juvenile Court

Score Class	Recidivism Rate	Non-Recidivism Rate	Total Number of Cases
Less than 180	27.2%	72.8%	385
180 or Over	56.6	43.4	30

Predictive Factors	Recidivism Scores
BIRTHPLACE OF FATHER	
Poland, Russia, Lithuania	19.0
Italy, Ireland	25.2
Foreign Countries other than Poland, Russia, Lithuania, Italy, Ireland	30.2
United States	45.0
BIRTHPLACE OF MOTHER	
Poland, Russia, Lithuania	16.0
Italy, Ireland	25.8
United States or Foreign Countries other than Poland, Russia, Lithuania, Italy, Ireland	36.1
TIME PARENTS WERE IN UNITED STATES	
Not for Life	22.9
For Life	36.8
RELIGION OF PARENTS	
Both Hebrew	11.5
Both Catholic or Both Protestant	30.0
Mixed	37.5
AGE AT ONSET OF ANTISOCIAL BEHAVIOR	
Thirteen to Seventeen	16.1
Nine to Thirteen	28.9
Under Nine	35.3

Source: *Juvenile Delinquents Grown Up*, Tables 30 and 32, pp. 139 and 142.

Table III–9. Prediction of Behavior of Former Male Juvenile
Offenders in Reformatories

Score Class	Maladaptation Rate	Adaptation Rate	Total Number of Cases
Less than 200	33.3%	66.7%	18
200–210	44.2	55.8	43
210–220	59.1	40.9	22
220–230	72.4	27.6	29
230 or Over	100.0	0.0	4

Predictive Factors	Maladaptation Scores
BIRTHPLACE OF FATHER	
Foreign Countries other than Poland, Russia, Lithuania, Italy	32.6
United States, Poland, Russia, Lithuania, Italy	45.7
CONJUGAL RELATIONS OF PARENTS	
Fair or Poor	39.2
Good	48.1
INTELLIGENCE OF OFFENDER	
I.Q. 70 or Over	40.0
I.Q. Less than 70	55.0
SCHOOL MISCONDUCT	
None	25.0
Some	40.6
MEMBER OF GANG OR CROWD	
Yes	34.5
No	48.0

Source: *Juvenile Delinquents Grown Up*, Tables 77 and 78, pp. 209 and 210.

Table III–10.   Prediction of Behavior of Former Male Juvenile
Offenders in Prisons

Score Class	Maladaptation Rate	Adaptation Rate	Total Number of Cases
Less than 120	66.7%	33.3%	9
120 or Over	34.3	65.7	35

Predictive Factors	Maladaptation Scores
AGE OF YOUNGER PARENT AT MARRIAGE	
Twenty-one or Older	7.7
Under Twenty-one	41.9
CONJUGAL RELATIONS OF PARENTS	
Good or Fair	25.8
Poor	61.5
DISCIPLINE BY FATHER	
Overstrict or Lax	24.0
Firm but Kindly or Erratic	40.0
AFFECTION OF FATHER FOR OFFENDER	
Indifferent or Hostile	16.0
Warm	34.2
AGE OF OFFENDER AT FIRST ARREST	
Eleven or Older	21.0
Under Eleven	36.4

Source: *Juvenile Delinquents Grown Up*, Tables 79 and 80, p. 211.

Table V–1. Prediction of Behavior of Adult Male Offenders
during Straight Probation

Score Class	Violation Rate	Non-Violation Rate	Total Number of Cases
Less than 440	0.0%	100.0%	4
440 or Over	98.0	2.0	197

Predictive Factors	Violation Scores*
FAMILY RELATIONSHIPS	
Socially Acceptable	86.3
Socially Unacceptable	94.5
EDUCATION OF PARENTS	
One or Both Common School	85.7
No Formal Schooling	93.0
CHURCH ATTENDANCE	
Regular	84.2
Irregular	93.1
AGE AT ONSET OF ANTISOCIAL BEHAVIOR	
Under Eleven	86.2
Eleven to Seventeen	91.9
Seventeen or Older	97.7
NUMBER OF CHILDREN IN FAMILY OF OFFENDER	
Seven or More	84.6
Less than Seven	95.0

* The high scores in each subcategory of the factors suggest that this may not prove to be a competent predictive instrument.
Source: *Criminal Careers in Retrospect*, Tables B and 22, p. 237.

Table V–2.   Prediction of Behavior of Male Offenders during
Straight Probation under Twenty-seven Years of Age

Score Class	Violation Rate	Non-Violation Rate	Total Number of Cases
Less than 460	0.0%	100.0%	1
460 or Over	95.7	4.3	164

Predictive Factors	Violation Scores*
AGE AT ONSET OF ANTISOCIAL BEHAVIOR	
Under Eleven	92.0
Eleven to Seventeen	96.0
Seventeen or Older	100.0
BAD HABITS IN CHILDHOOD	
None	85.7
Some	96.4
CHURCH ATTENDANCE	
Regular	88.2
Irregular	96.6
FAMILY RELATIONSHIPS	
Socially Acceptable	89.8
Socially Unacceptable	98.3
INDUSTRIAL SKILL OF OFFENDER	
Skilled	90.9
Semiskilled or Unskilled	96.3

* The high scores in each subcategory of the factors suggest that this may not prove to be a
competent predictive instrument.
Source: *Criminal Careers in Retrospect*, Tables C and 23, pp. 238 and 239.

Table V–3. Prediction of Behavior of Male Offenders during
Straight Probation at Ages Twenty-seven or Older

Score Class	Violation Rate	Non-Violation Rate	Total Number of Cases
Less than 410	25.0%	75.0%	4
410–420	76.9	23.1	13
420 or Over	96.0	4.0	50

Predictive Factors	Violation Scores
NUMBER OF CHILDREN IN FAMILY OF OFFENDER	
Seven or More	78.3
Four, Five, or Six	84.2
Two or Three	95.8
One	100.0
ECONOMIC STATUS OF CHILDHOOD HOME	
Comfortable or Marginal	80.0
Dependent	100.0
ADEQUACY OF CHILDHOOD HOME	
Adequate	78.6
Broken or Inadequate	88.1
AGE AT ONSET OF ANTISOCIAL BEHAVIOR	
Under Eleven	69.2
Eleven or Older	86.2
MENTAL DISEASE OR DISTORTION	
Not Psychotic or Psychopathic	81.3
Psychotic or Psychopathic Personality	92.5

Source: *Criminal Careers in Retrospect*, Tables D and 24, p. 239.

Appendix B

Table V–4.   Prediction of Behavior of Adult Male Offenders during
Probation with Suspended Sentence

It was unfortunately not possible to construct an over-all table for behavior on probation under suspended sentence because in none of the cases of offenders who succeeded under this form of treatment were all the five factors known. As the predictive factors themselves have been determined, however, it should be possible at some later time to construct the prediction table from another series of cases.

Predictive Factors	Violation Scores
NATIVITY OF OFFENDER	
Foreign-Born	78.7
Native-Born	92.9
INTELLIGENCE OF OFFENDER	
I.Q. Less than 70	84.0
I.Q. 70 or Over	94.0
GRADE ATTAINED IN SCHOOL	
Less than Sixth Grade	87.8
Sixth, Seventh, or Eighth Grades	94.0
Ninth Grade or Higher	100.0
AGE AT ONSET OF ANTISOCIAL BEHAVIOR	
Eleven or Older	89.5
Under Eleven	100.0
INDUSTRIAL SKILL OF OFFENDER	
Skilled	61.1
Semiskilled or Unskilled	95.9

Source: *Criminal Careers in Retrospect*, Table E, p. 240.

Table V–5. Prediction of Behavior of Male Offenders during
Probation with Suspended Sentence under Thirty-two
Years of Age

Score Class	Violation Rate	Non-Violation Rate	Total Number of Cases
Less than 440	0.0%	100.0%	1
440 or Over	99.0	1.0	101

Predictive Factors	Violation Scores*
NATIVITY OF OFFENDER	
Foreign-Born	90.0
Native-Born	99.0
AGE AT ONSET OF ANTISOCIAL BEHAVIOR	
Seventeen or Older	92.9
Fourteen to Seventeen	97.9
Under Fourteen	100.0
INTELLIGENCE OF OFFENDER	
I.Q. Less than 70	89.5
I.Q. 70 or Over	100.0
MOBILITY	
Excessive	93.5
Not Excessive	100.0
USE OF LEISURE	
Negative	50.0
Harmful	99.1

* The high scores in each subcategory of the factors suggest that this may not prove to be a competent predictive instrument.
Source: *Criminal Careers in Retrospect*, Tables F and 25, pp. 241 and 242.

Table V–6.   Prediction of Behavior of Male Offenders during
Probation with Suspended Sentence at Ages Thirty-two or Older

Score Class	Violation Rate	Non-Violation Rate	Total Number of Cases
Less than 410	61.5%	38.5%	13
410 or Over	92.0	8.0	50

Predictive Factors	Violation Scores
NUMBER OF CHILDREN IN FAMILY OF OFFENDER	
Seven or More	76.5
Four, Five, or Six	82.1
Two or Three	94.4
One	100.0
ECONOMIC STATUS OF CHILDHOOD HOME	
Dependent	76.9
Marginal	83.3
Comfortable	90.5
INTELLIGENCE OF OFFENDER	
I.Q. Less than 90	81.8
I.Q. 90 or Over	94.4
AGE AT ONSET OF ANTISOCIAL BEHAVIOR	
Eleven or Older	83.3
Under Eleven	100.0
INDUSTRIAL SKILL OF OFFENDER	
Semiskilled or Unskilled	83.6
Skilled	100.0

Source: *Criminal Careers in Retrospect*, Tables G and 26, p. 242.

Table V–7.   Prediction of Behavior of Adult Male Offenders in
Reformatories

Score Class	Maladaptation Rate	Adaptation Rate	Total Number of Cases
Less than 270	29.2%	70.8%	24
270–290	51.5	48.5	97
290–310	70.0	30.0	170
310 or Over	86.0	14.0	157

Predictive Factors	Maladaptation Scores
NATIVITY OF PARENTS AND OFFENDER	
All Native-Born	53.5
One or Both Parents Foreign-Born; Offender Native-Born	62.8
EDUCATION OF PARENTS	
One or Both Common School	49.4
No Formal Schooling	62.3
ADEQUACY OF CHILDHOOD HOME	
Adequate	51.5
Broken or Inadequate	62.5
AGE AT ONSET OF ANTISOCIAL BEHAVIOR	
Seventeen or Older	38.9
Fourteen to Seventeen	61.5
Under Fourteen	72.1
INDUSTRIAL SKILL OF OFFENDER	
Skilled	42.9
Semiskilled	59.4
Unskilled	63.1

Source: *Criminal Careers in Retrospect*, Tables E and 35, p. 260.

Table V–8. Prediction of Behavior of Male Offenders in
Reformatories at Seventeen through Twenty-one Years of Age

Score Class	Maladaptation Rate	Adaptation Rate	Total Number of Cases
Less than 330	0.0%	100.0%	7
330–350	42.9	57.1	28
350–370	67.9	32.1	84
370 or Over	84.6	15.4	143

Predictive Factors	Maladaptation Scores
INTELLIGENCE OF OFFENDER	
I.Q. 90 or Over	66.7
I.Q. Less than 90	77.9
AGE AT ONSET OF ANTISOCIAL BEHAVIOR	
Seventeen or Older	52.8
Fourteen to Seventeen	71.7
Under Fourteen	84.6
GRADE ATTAINED IN SCHOOL	
Ninth Grade or Higher	53.4
Less than Ninth Grade	77.5
FAMILY RELATIONSHIPS	
Socially Acceptable	63.3
Socially Unacceptable	77.1
INDUSTRIAL SKILL OF OFFENDER	
Skilled	47.4
Semiskilled or Unskilled	76.6

Source: *Criminal Careers in Retrospect*, Tables F and 36, p. 264.

Table V–9.   Prediction of Behavior of Male Offenders in
Reformatories at Twenty-two through Twenty-six Years of Age

Score Class	Maladaptation Rate	Adaptation Rate	Total Number of Cases
Less than 280	11.1%	88.9%	9
280–300	47.8	52.2	23
300–330	65.6	34.4	61
330 or Over	73.1	26.9	52

Predictive Factors	Maladaptation Scores
DELINQUENCY IN FAMILY	
Absent	50.0
Present	66.1
ADEQUACY OF CHILDHOOD HOME	
Adequate	46.7
Broken or Inadequate	66.2
OCCUPATION OF MOTHER	
Housewife	62.6
Gainfully Employed	80.5
AGE AT ONSET OF ANTISOCIAL BEHAVIOR	
Seventeen or Older	44.4
Fourteen to Seventeen	60.5
Under Fourteen	76.0
INTELLIGENCE OF OFFENDER	
I.Q. 90 or Over	46.2
I.Q. Less than 90	69.6

Source: *Criminal Careers in Retrospect*, Tables G and 37, pp. 264 and 265.

Table V–10. Prediction of Behavior of Male Offenders in
Reformatories at Ages Twenty-seven or Older

Score Class	Maladaptation Rate	Adaptation Rate	Total Number of Cases
Less than 160	0.0%	100.0%	4
160 or Over	40.7	59.3	54

Predictive Factors	Maladaptation Scores
EDUCATION OF PARENTS	
One or Both Common School	15.4
No Formal Schooling	42.5
ECONOMIC STATUS OF CHILDHOOD HOME	
Comfortable	30.0
Dependent or Marginal	46.9
WORK HABITS OF OFFENDER	
Good	25.0
Fair or Poor	44.2
ECONOMIC RESPONSIBILITY OF OFFENDER	
Responsible	26.7
Irresponsible	46.4
USE OF LEISURE	
Negative	0.0
Harmful	41.5

Source: *Criminal Careers in Retrospect*, Tables H and 38, p. 266.

Table V–11. Prediction of Behavior of Adult Male Offenders in Prisons

Score Class	Maladaptation Rate	Adaptation Rate	Total Number of Cases
Less than 110	15.4%	84.6%	13
110–130	38.8	61.2	49
130–150	56.4	43.6	39
150 or Over	100.0	0.0	7

Predictive Factors	Maladaptation Scores
NATIVITY OF PARENTS AND OFFENDER	
All Native-Born	19.5
One or Both Parents Foreign-Born; Offender Native-Born	25.4
All Foreign-Born	35.3
EDUCATION OF PARENTS	
One or Both Common School	11.1
No Formal Schooling	26.7
ADEQUACY OF CHILDHOOD HOME	
Broken or Inadequate	23.2
Adequate	34.8
INTELLIGENCE OF OFFENDER	
I.Q. 80 or Over	18.8
I.Q. Less than 80	36.7
AGE AT ONSET OF ANTISOCIAL BEHAVIOR	
Seventeen or Older	9.1
Under Seventeen	27.6

Source: *Criminal Careers in Retrospect*, Tables I and 39, pp. 266 and 267.

Table V–12.   Prediction of Behavior of Male Offenders in Prisons
under Twenty-seven Years of Age

Score Class	Maladaptation Rate	Adaptation Rate	Total Number of Cases
Less than 220	0.0%	100.0%	4
220–230	20.0	80.0	5
230–270	52.5	47.5	40
270–290	83.3	16.7	6
290 or Over	100.0	0.0	2

Predictive Factors	Maladaptation Scores
EDUCATION OF PARENTS	
One or Both Common School	25.0
No Formal Schooling	56.3
INTELLIGENCE OF OFFENDER	
I.Q. 80 or Over	44.1
I.Q. Less than 80	58.3
ADEQUACY OF CHILDHOOD HOME	
Broken or Inadequate	44.0
Adequate	72.7
AGE AT ONSET OF ANTISOCIAL BEHAVIOR	
Eleven or Older	46.4
Under Eleven	66.7
INDUSTRIAL SKILL OF OFFENDER	
Skilled	0.0
Semiskilled or Unskilled	46.6

Source: *Criminal Careers in Retrospect*, Tables J and 40, p. 268.

Table V–13.   Prediction of Behavior of Male Offenders in
Prisons at Twenty-seven through Thirty-one Years of Age

Score Class	Maladaptation Rate	Adaptation Rate	Total Number of Cases
Less than 200	16.7%	83.3%	12
200 or Over	56.2	43.8	32

Predictive Factors	Maladaptation Scores
NATIVITY OF PARENTS AND OFFENDER	
All Native-Born	33.3
One or Both Parents Foreign-Born; Offender Native-Born	42.3
All Foreign-Born	57.1
EDUCATION OF PARENTS	
One or Both Common School	11.1
No Formal Schooling	46.5
CONJUGAL RELATIONS OF PARENTS	
Poor	20.0
Good or Fair	46.1
NUMBER OF CHILDREN IN FAMILY OF OFFENDER	
One	16.7
Two or More	42.5
INTELLIGENCE OF OFFENDER	
I.Q. 80 or Over	32.2
I.Q. Less than 80	55.0

Source: *Criminal Careers in Retrospect*, Tables K and 41, pp. 268 and 269.

Table V–14.   Prediction of Behavior of Male Offenders in
Prisons at Thirty-Two through Thirty-six Years of Age

Score Class	Maladaptation Rate	Adaptation Rate	Total Number of Cases
Less than 180	10.0%	90.0%	22
180–210	55.5	44.5	9
210 or Over	100.0	0.0	4

Predictive Factors	Maladaptation Scores
NUMBER OF CHILDREN IN FAMILY OF OFFENDER	
One	0.0
Two or More	33.3
INTELLIGENCE OF OFFENDER	
I.Q. 80 or Over	12.0
I.Q. Less than 80	58.0
GRADE ATTAINED IN SCHOOL	
Ninth Grade or Higher	0.0
Sixth, Seventh, or Eighth Grades	31.6
Less than Sixth Grade	50.0
CONJUGAL RELATIONS OF PARENTS	
Poor	0.0
Good or Fair	40.6
ADEQUACY OF CHILDHOOD HOME	
Broken or Inadequate	22.5
Adequate	50.0

Source: *Criminal Careers in Retrospect*, Tables L and 42, pp. 269 and 270.

Table V–15.   Prediction of Behavior of Male Offenders in Prisons
at Ages Thirty-seven or Older

Score Class	Maladaptation Rate	Adaptation Rate	Total Number of Cases
Less than 120	7.4%	92.6%	27
120–140	45.5	54.5	11
140 or Over	100.0	0.0	1

Predictive Factors	Maladaptation Scores
RANK OF OFFENDER AMONG SIBLINGS	
Only Child	0.0
First Child	12.5
Second or Later Child	27.6
INTELLIGENCE OF OFFENDER	
I.Q. 80 or Over	12.0
I.Q. Less than 80	40.0
GRADE ATTAINED IN SCHOOL	
Ninth Grade or Higher	0.0
Less than Ninth Grade	24.2
AGE AT ONSET OF ANTISOCIAL BEHAVIOR	
Seventeen or Older	0.0
Under Seventeen	25.7
INDUSTRIAL SKILL OF OFFENDER	
Semiskilled or Unskilled	18.9
Skilled	66.7

Source: *Criminal Careers in Retrospect*, Tables M and 43, p. 270.

Table V–16. Prediction of Behavior of Adult Male Offenders
in Jails and Houses of Correction

Score Class	Maladaptation Rate	Adaptation Rate	Total Number of Cases
Less than 120	25.0%	75.0%	56
120–140	34.0	66.0	53
140 or Over	64.0	36.0	25

Predictive Factors	Maladaptation Scores
NATIVITY OF PARENTS AND OFFENDER	
All Foreign-Born	18.5
All Native-Born	22.5
One or Both Parents Foreign-Born; Offender Native-Born	30.8
ECONOMIC STATUS OF CHILDHOOD HOME	
Dependent or Marginal	19.4
Comfortable	35.6
RANK OF OFFENDER AMONG SIBLINGS	
Second or Later Child	20.2
Only Child or First Child	33.3
GRADE ATTAINED IN SCHOOL	
Less than Ninth Grade	23.5
Ninth Grade or Higher	50.0
AGE BEGAN WORK	
Under Fifteen	15.6
Fifteen or Older	29.9

Source: *Criminal Careers in Retrospect*, Tables N and 44, p. 271.

Table V–17. Prediction of Behavior of Male Offenders in Jails and Houses of Correction under Twenty-two Years of Age

Score Class	Maladaptation Rate	Adaptation Rate	Total Number of Cases
Less than 240	40.0%	60.0%	10
240–270	53.8	46.2	13
270 or Over	100.0	0.0	3

Predictive Factors	Maladaptation Scores
NUMBER OF CHILDREN IN FAMILY OF OFFENDER	
Four or More	42.8
Two or Three	57.1
One	100.0
ADEQUACY OF CHILDHOOD HOME	
Adequate	40.0
Broken or Inadequate	54.1
GRADE ATTAINED IN SCHOOL	
Less than Sixth Grade	36.3
Sixth, Seventh, or Eighth Grades	53.8
Ninth Grade or Higher	66.6
AGE AT ONSET OF ANTISOCIAL BEHAVIOR	
Under Fourteen	40.0
Fourteen or Older	60.0
AGE FIRST LEFT HOME	
Fourteen or Older	44.4
Under Fourteen	63.3

Source: *Criminal Careers in Retrospect*, Tables O and 45, pp. 272 and 273.

Appendix B

Table V–18.   Prediction of Behavior of Male Offenders in Jails
and Houses of Correction at Twenty-two through Twenty-six
Years of Age

Score Class	Maladaptation Rate	Adaptation Rate	Total Number of Cases
Less than 180	4.2%	95.8%	24
180 or Over	53.6	46.4	28

Predictive Factors	Maladaptation Scores
NUMBER OF CHILDREN IN FAMILY OF OFFENDER	
One	0.0
Two or More	35.7
ECONOMIC STATUS OF CHILDHOOD HOME	
Dependent	21.0
Marginal	31.0
Comfortable	50.0
MOBILITY	
Not Excessive	31.6
Excessive	55.0
AGE BEGAN WORK	
Under Fifteen	17.4
Fifteen or Older	47.2
INDUSTRIAL SKILL OF OFFENDER	
Skilled	0.0
Semiskilled	26.3
Unskilled	45.0

Source: *Criminal Careers in Retrospect*, Tables P and 46, pp. 273 and 274.

Table V–19. Prediction of Behavior of Male Offenders in Jails
and Houses of Correction at Twenty-seven through Thirty-one
Years of Age

Score Class	Maladaptation Rate	Adaptation Rate	Total Number of Cases
Less than 200	0.0%	100.0%	10
200–230	45.8	54.2	24
230 or Over	66.7	33.3	14

Predictive Factors	Maladaptation Scores
NUMBER OF CHILDREN IN FAMILY OF OFFENDER	
One	0.0
Two or More	45.7
INTELLIGENCE OF OFFENDER	
I.Q. 90 or Over	23.5
I.Q. Less than 90	54.4
ECONOMIC STATUS OF CHILDHOOD HOME	
Dependent or Marginal	40.8
Comfortable	58.8
AGE BEGAN WORK	
Under Fifteen	33.3
Fifteen or Older	58.1
INDUSTRIAL SKILL OF OFFENDER	
Skilled	0.0
Semiskilled	33.3
Unskilled	55.6

Source: *Criminal Careers in Retrospect*, Tables Q and 47, p. 274.

Table V–20.   Prediction of Behavior of Male Offenders in Jails and Houses of Correction at Thirty-two through Thirty-six Years of Age

Score Class	Maladaptation Rate	Adaptation Rate	Total Number of Cases
Less than 130	0.0%	100.0%	9
130–150	66.7	33.3	3
150 or Over	75.0	25.0	4

Predictive Factors	Maladaptation Scores
CONJUGAL RELATIONS OF PARENTS	
Fair or Poor	0.0
Good	39.3
ADEQUACY OF CHILDHOOD HOME	
Broken	15.4
Inadequate	25.0
Adequate	44.4
SCHOOL MISCONDUCT	
Some	26.3
None	66.7
INDUSTRIAL SKILL OF OFFENDER	
Skilled	0.0
Semiskilled	11.8
Unskilled	29.4
MENTAL DISEASE OR DISTORTION	
Not Psychotic or Psychopathic	13.3
Psychotic or Psychopathic Personality	33.3

Source: *Criminal Careers in Retrospect*, Tables R and 48, pp. 275 and 276.

Table V–21. Prediction of Behavior of Adult Male Offenders
during Parole

Score Class	Violation Rate	Non-Violation Rate	Total Number of Cases
Less than 290	50.0%	50.0%	2
290–330	74.2	25.8	264
330 or Over	89.5	10.5	124

Predictive Factors	Violation Scores
EDUCATION OF PARENTS	
One or Both Common School	52.9
No Formal Schooling	65.5
NUMBER OF CHILDREN IN FAMILY OF OFFENDER	
Two or More	62.5
One	80.0
ADEQUACY OF CHILDHOOD HOME	
Adequate	50.0
Broken or Inadequate	67.1
INTELLIGENCE OF OFFENDER	
I.Q. 90 or Over	55.9
I.Q. 80–90	61.3
I.Q. Less than 80	72.0
GRADE ATTAINED IN SCHOOL	
Ninth Grade or Higher	56.3
Less than Ninth Grade	65.2
No Schooling	75.0

Source: *Criminal Careers in Retrospect*, Tables H and 27, pp. 243 and 244.

Table V–22.   Prediction of Behavior of Male Offenders during
Parole under Twenty-two Years of Age

Score Class	Violation Rate	Non-Violation Rate	Total Number of Cases
Less than 390	45.2%	54.8%	31
390–400	61.5	38.5	13
400–410	82.9	17.1	35
410 or Over	92.7	7.3	151

Predictive Factors	Violation Scores
DELINQUENCY IN FAMILY	
Absent	67.9
Present	87.0
AGE AT ONSET OF ANTISOCIAL BEHAVIOR	
Seventeen or Older	65.4
Fourteen to Seventeen	74.1
Under Fourteen	91.8
BAD HABITS IN CHILDHOOD	
None	52.6
Some	84.6
INDUSTRIAL SKILL OF OFFENDER	
Semiskilled or Skilled	77.8
Unskilled	86.7
PHYSICAL CONDITION	
Good or Fair	81.0
Poor	100.0

Source: *Criminal Careers in Retrospect*, Tables I and 28, pp. 247 and 248.

Table V–23. Prediction of Behavior of Male Offenders during Parole at Twenty-two through Twenty-six Years of Age

Score Class	Violation Rate	Non-Violation Rate	Total Number of Cases
Less than 300	28.6%	71.4%	14
300–340	54.2	45.8	24
340–360	60.9	39.1	23
360–370	76.3	23.7	59
370 or Over	96.7	3.3	30

Predictive Factors	Violation Scores
DELINQUENCY IN FAMILY	
Absent	54.2
Present	75.7
ECONOMIC STATUS OF CHILDHOOD HOME	
Marginal or Comfortable	65.2
Dependent	92.3
ADEQUACY OF CHILDHOOD HOME	
Adequate	52.8
Broken or Inadequate	73.3
WORK HABITS OF OFFENDER	
Good	47.2
Fair or Poor	75.6
ECONOMIC RESPONSIBILITY OF OFFENDER	
Responsible	47.5
Irresponsible	74.8

Source: *Criminal Careers in Retrospect*, Tables J and 29, pp. 248 and 249.

Appendix B

Table V–24. Prediction of Behavior of Male Offenders during
Parole at Ages Twenty-seven or Older

Score Class	Violation Rate	Non-Violation Rate	Total Number of Cases
Less than 340	53.8%	46.2%	13
340–360	60.4	39.6	48
360 or Over	75.0	25.0	100

Predictive Factors	Violation Scores
NATIVITY OF OFFENDER	
Foreign-Born	59.4
Native-Born	75.2
RANK OF OFFENDER AMONG SIBLINGS	
Second or Later Child	69.0
First Child	75.6
Only Child	84.6
AGE AT ONSET OF ANTISOCIAL BEHAVIOR	
Seventeen or Older	63.6
Under Seventeen	75.1
USE OF LEISURE	
Negative	50.0
Harmful	73.1
PHYSICAL CONDITION	
Good	69.7
Fair	78.9
Poor	87.5

Source: *Criminal Careers in Retrospect*, Tables K and 30, p. 249.

Table V–25.   Prediction of Behavior of Male Offenders during
Five Years after Completion of First Reformatory Sentence

Score Class	Recidivism Rate	Non-Recidivism Rate	Total Number of Cases
Less than 296	5.0%	95.0%	*
296–396	54.3	45.7	*
396 or Over	80.6	19.4	*

Predictive Factors	Recidivism Scores
WORK HABITS PRECEDING SENTENCE	
Good	43
Fair	59
Poor	68
SERIOUSNESS AND FREQUENCY OF PREREFORMATORY CRIMES	
Non-Offender	21
Occasional Minor Offender	35
Frequent Minor Offender	53
Serious Offender	67
ARRESTS PRECEDING OFFENSE FOR WHICH SENTENCED	
None	32
Some	69
PENAL EXPERIENCES PRIOR TO REFORMATORY SENTENCE	
None	47
Some	74
ECONOMIC RESPONSIBILITY PRECEDING SENTENCE	
Responsible	41
Irresponsible	64
MENTAL DISEASE OR DISTORTION ON ENTRANCE TO REFORMATORY	
Not Psychotic or Psychopathic	60
Psychopathic Personality	75
Psychotic	87

* Not available.
   Source: *500 Criminal Careers*, Table 112, pp. 281, 282, and 285. This table was derived from behavior of male offenders over a five-year span following completion of a reformatory sentence. As the average age at commitment was 20.2 years (see *500 Criminal Careers*, p. 153) and the average sentence was five years, the table presented should be useful in determining the probable behavior of male offenders in age span twenty-five through twenty-nine years.

Table V–26.   Prediction of Behavior of Male Offenders during
Ten Years after Completion of First Reformatory Sentence

Score Class	Recidivism Rate	Non-Recidivism Rate	Total Number of Cases
Less than 325	20.0%	80.0%	10
325–350	30.8	69.2	13
350 or Over	72.4	27.6	165

Predictive Factors	Recidivism Scores
WORK HABITS PRECEDING SENTENCE	
Good	50.9
Fair	80.8
Poor	88.6
ECONOMIC RESPONSIBILITY PRECEDING SENTENCE	
Responsible	53.8
Irresponsible	84.3
AGE AT ONSET OF ANTISOCIAL BEHAVIOR	
Fourteen or Older	72.0
Under Fourteen	87.9
ARRESTS PRECEDING OFFENSE FOR WHICH SENTENCED	
None	51.4
Some	82.7
MENTAL DISEASE OR DISTORTION ON ENTRANCE TO REFORMATORY	
Not Psychotic or Psychopathic	65.7
Psychotic	96.8
Psychopathic Personality	100.0

Source: *Later Criminal Careers*, Table 32, pp. 137 and 141. This table was derived from behavior of male offenders over a ten-year span following completion of a reformatory sentence. As the average age at commitment was 20.2 years (see *500 Criminal Careers*, p. 153) and the average sentence was five years, the table presented should be useful in determining the probable behavior of male offenders in age span thirty through thirty-four years. Their behavior in age span twenty-five through twenty-nine years is presented in Table V–25.

The score classes and failure scores in this table differ from those presented in Table 32 of *Later Criminal Careers*, where non-delinquency rather than delinquency scores were presented.

Table V–27.   Prediction of Behavior of Male Offenders during Fifteen Years
after Completion of First Reformatory Sentence

Score Class	Recidivism Rate	Non-Recidivism Rate	Total Number of Cases
Less than 150	22.1%	77.9%	77
150–160	28.0	72.0	100
160–170	36.0	64.0	100
170–180	45.0	55.0	40
180 or Over	66.7	33.3	6

Predictive Factors	Recidivism Scores
NUMBER OF CHILDREN IN FAMILY OF OFFENDER	
Seven or More	26.7
Two to Seven	33.2
One	48.1
ECONOMIC STATUS OF CHILDHOOD HOME	
Dependent or Marginal	27.5
Comfortable	39.8
INDUSTRIAL SKILL OF FATHER	
Unskilled	23.3
Semiskilled or Skilled	36.1
INTELLIGENCE OF OFFENDER	
I.Q. 70 or Over	30.5
I.Q. Less than 70	40.8
AGE AT ONSET OF ANTISOCIAL BEHAVIOR	
Fourteen or Older	24.7
Under Fourteen	36.3

Source: *Criminal Careers in Retrospect*, Table 18, p. 224. This table was derived from behavior of male offenders over a fifteen-year span following completion of a reformatory sentence. As the average age at commitment was 20.2 years (see *500 Criminal Careers*, p. 153) and the average sentence was five years, the table presented should be useful in determining the probable behavior of male offenders in age span thirty-five through thirty-nine years. Behavior in age span twenty-five through twenty-nine years and thirty through thirty-four years are presented in Tables V–25 and V–26, respectively.

Appendix B

Table V–28. Prediction of Behavior of Civilian Delinquents in
Armed Forces

Score Class	Maladaptation Rate	Adaptation Rate	Total Number of Cases
Less than 180	17.4%	82.6%	23
180–190	42.3	57.7	26
190–220	62.9	37.1	62
220 or Over	70.0	30.0	20

Predictive Factors	Maladaptation Scores
EDUCATION OF PARENTS	
No Formal Schooling	37.1
One or Both Common School	66.7
INTELLIGENCE OF OFFENDER	
I.Q. 90 or Over	29.3
I.Q. Less than 90	44.0
AGE AT ONSET OF ANTISOCIAL BEHAVIOR	
Seventeen or Older	21.4
Eleven to Seventeen	41.3
Under Eleven	66.7
AGE BEGAN WORK	
Under Fifteen	31.1
Fifteen or Older	47.3
INDUSTRIAL SKILL OF OFFENDER	
Skilled	0.0
Semiskilled	34.0
Unskilled	49.4

Source: *Criminal Careers in Retrospect*, Tables T and 50. p. 277.

Table V–29.   Prediction of Behavior of Civilian Delinquents in
Armed Forces under Twenty-two Years of Age

Score Class	Maladaptation Rate	Adaptation Rate	Total Number of Cases
Less than 270	18.2%	81.8%	11
270–280	36.4	63.6	11
280 or Over	78.6	21.4	28

Predictive Factors	Maladaptation Scores
ECONOMIC STATUS OF CHILDHOOD HOME	
Dependent or Marginal	52.3
Comfortable	77.8
CONJUGAL RELATIONS OF PARENTS	
Good	48.4
Fair or Poor	66.6
NUMBER OF CHILDREN IN FAMILY OF OFFENDER	
Two or More	52.2
One	90.0
GRADE ATTAINED IN SCHOOL	
Less than Ninth Grade	56.8
Ninth Grade or Higher	100.0
INDUSTRIAL SKILL OF OFFENDER	
Skilled	0.0
Semiskilled	50.0
Unskilled	69.4

Source: *Criminal Careers in Retrospect*, Tables X and 51, pp. 278 and 279.

Table V–30.   Prediction of Behavior of Civilian Delinquents in
Armed Forces at Ages Twenty-two or Older

Score Class	Maladaptation Rate	Adaptation Rate	Total Number of Cases
Less than 170	0.0%	100.0%	2
170–200	25.9	74.1	27
200–230	51.4	48.6	25
230 or Over	77.8	22.2	9

Predictive Factors	Maladaptation Scores
NATIVITY OF OFFENDER	
Foreign-Born	18.2
Native-Born	44.6
ECONOMIC STATUS OF CHILDHOOD HOME	
Dependent	33.3
Marginal or Comfortable	43.5
CONJUGAL RELATIONS OF PARENTS	
Poor	24.0
Good or Fair	50.9
ADEQUACY OF CHILDHOOD HOME	
Broken	36.5
Inadequate	43.8
Adequate	60.0
INDUSTRIAL SKILL OF OFFENDER	
Skilled	16.7
Semiskilled	38.7
Unskilled	45.8

Source: *Criminal Careers in Retrospect*, Tables Y and 52, p. 279.

Table VII–I.   Prediction of Behavior of Female Offenders in
Reformatories

Score Class	Maladaptation Rate	Adaptation Rate	Total Number of Cases
Less than 325	0.0%	100.0%	2
325–350	50.0	50.0	14
350–375	68.7	31.3	61
375 or Over	85.7	14.3	140

Predictive Factors	Maladaptation Scores
MENTAL DISEASE OR DISTORTION	
None	70.8
Psychopathic, Psychoneurotic, Neurasthenic	77.2
Epileptic, Congenital Syphilis, Drug Addict	80.8
Alcoholic Deteriotera	91.0
Psychotic or Question of Psychosis	100.0
SCHOOL RETARDATION	
None	57.6
One or More Years	79.7
No Schooling	86.7
NEIGHBORHOOD INFLUENCES	
Good	54.5
Fair or Poor	72.6
STEADINESS OF EMPLOYMENT	
Regular	53.6
Fairly Regular	70.8
Irregular or No Work	81.8
ECONOMIC RESPONSIBILITY OF OFFENDER	
Responsible	72.4
Irresponsible	91.2
Self-support Not Necessary	95.0

Source: *Five Hundred Delinquent Women*, Table 9, p. 290. This table does not resemble the one presented in *Five Hundred Delinquent Women;* it has been revised to conform to the other prediction tables in which the score classes are based on *delinquency* rather than on *non-delinquency* scores. The maladaptation scores listed above have also been revised and delinquency scores substituted for non-delinquency scores.

Appendix B

Table VII–2. Prediction of Behavior of Female Offenders during Parole

Score Class	Violation Rate	Non-Violation Rate	Total Number of Cases
Less than 400	0.0%	100.0%	4
400–425	52.4	47.6	21
425 or Over	81.1	18.9	180

Predictive Factors	Violation Scores
MENTAL DISEASE OR DISTORTION	
None	70.8
Psychopathic, Psychoneurotic, Neurasthenic	77.2
Epileptic, Congenital Syphilis, Drug Addict	80.8
Alcoholic Deteriorate	91.0
Psychotic or Question of Psychosis	100.0
SCHOOL RETARDATION	
None	57.6
One or More Years	79.7
No Schooling	86.7
NEIGHBORHOOD INFLUENCES	
Good	54.5
Fair or Poor	72.6
STEADINESS OF EMPLOYMENT	
Regular	53.6
Fairly Regular	70.8
Irregular or No Work	81.8
ECONOMIC RESPONSIBILITY OF OFFENDER	
Responsible	72.4
Irresponsible	91.2
Self-support Not Necessary	95.0
KIND OF WORKER IN REFORMATORY	
Good	67.3
Fair or Poor	82.0

Source: *Five Hundred Delinquent Women*, Table 10, p. 292. This table does not resemble the one presented in *Five Hundred Delinquent Women*; it has been revised to conform to the other prediction tables in which the score classes are based on *delinquency* rather than on *non-delinquency* scores. The violation scores listed above have also been revised and delinquency scores substituted for non-delinquency scores.

231

Table VII–3.   Prediction of Behavior of Female Offenders Five
Years after Completion of First Reformatory Sentence

Score Class	Recidivism Rate	Non-Recidivism Rate	Total Number of Cases
Less than 475	0.0%	100.0%	9
475–525	64.1	35.9	37
525 or Over	87.7	12.3	130

Predictive Factors	Recidivism Scores
MENTAL DISEASE OR DISTORTION	
None	70.8
Psychopathic, Psychoneurotic, Neurasthenic	77.2
Epileptic, Congenital Syphilis, Drug Addict	80.8
Alcoholic Deteriorate	91.0
Psychotic or Question of Psychosis	100.0
SCHOOL RETARDATION	
None	57.6
One or More Years	79.7
No Schooling	86.7
NEIGHBORHOOD INFLUENCES	
Good	54.5
Fair or Poor	72.6
STEADINESS OF EMPLOYMENT	
Regular	53.6
Fairly Regular	70.8
Irregular or No Work	81.8
ECONOMIC RESPONSIBILITY OF OFFENDER	
Responsible	72.4
Irresponsible	91.2
Self-support Not Necessary	95.0
KIND OF WORKER IN REFORMATORY	
Good	67.3
Fair or Poor	82.0
RECREATIONS AND INTERESTS DURING PAROLE*	
Constructive	34.8
Not Constructive	80.3
Not Paroled	88.2

* A failure score of 88.2 is assigned to those offenders who were not paroled.

Source: *Five Hundred Delinquent Women*, Table 11, p. 293. This table does not resemble the one presented in *Five Hundred Delinquent Women;* it has been revised to conform to the other prediction tables in which the score classes are based on *delinquency* rather than on *non-delinquency* scores. The recidivism scores listed above have also been revised and delinquency scores substituted for non-delinquency scores.

This table was derived from behavior of female offenders over a five-year span following completion of a reformatory sentence. As the average age at commitment was 27.6 years and the average sentence was five years, the table presented should be useful in determining the probable behavior of female offenders in age span twenty-eight through thirty-two years.

Appendix B

Table IX–I. Identification of Potential Juvenile Delinquents
Based on Five Social Factors *

Score Class	Delinquency Rate	Non-Delinquency Rate	Total Number of Cases
Less than 200	8.2%	91.8%	293
200–250	37.0	63.0	108
250–300	63.5	36.5	192
300 or Over	89.2	10.8	297

Predictive Factors	Delinquency Scores
DISCIPLINE OF BOY BY FATHER	
Firm but Kindly	9.3
Lax	59.8
Overstrict or Erratic	72.5
SUPERVISION OF BOY BY MOTHER	
Suitable	9.9
Fair	57.5
Unsuitable	83.2
AFFECTION OF FATHER FOR BOY	
Warm (including overprotective)	33.8
Indifferent or Hostile	75.9
AFFECTION OF MOTHER FOR BOY	
Warm (including overprotective)	43.1
Indifferent or Hostile	86.2
COHESIVENESS OF FAMILY	
Marked	20.6
Some	61.3
None	96.9

* See Tables IX–1a through IX–1e for four-, three-, and two-factor tables.

Note: The particular subcategory into which a case falls is based on the situation typically prevailing up to the time the prediction is made. In instances in which the child lives with both parents, but their affection for him is difficult to judge, the three-factor table (IX–1b) should be used. Where the father has not been part of the family group, at least since the child was three years of age, and there is no father substitute, the two-factor table (IX–1e) has to be utilized. It is evident that the shortened tables make it possible to categorize every case, even in the absence of certain data.

Source: *Unraveling Juvenile Delinquency*, Table XX–3, pp. 261 and 262.

Table IX–Ia. Identification of Potential Juvenile Delinquents
Based on Four Social Factors[1]

Score Class	Delinquency Rate	Non-Delinquency Rate	Total Number of Cases
Less than 150	8.6%	91.4%	291
150–200	36.3	63.7	113
200–250	58.8	41.2	148
250 or Over	88.2	11.8	338

[1] Predictive Factors: Discipline of Boy by Father; Supervision of Boy by Mother; Affection of Father for Boy; Cohesiveness of Family.

Coefficient of Correlation of Four-Factor Total Scores
with Total Scores for Five Factors = .987

Table IX–Ib. Identification of Potential Juvenile Delinquents
Based on Three Social Factors[2]

Score Class	Delinquency Rate	Non-Delinquency Rate	Total Number of Cases
Less than 125	9.3%	90.7%	302
125–175	38.8	61.2	147
175–225	79.1	20.9	339
225 or Over	96.1	3.9	102

[2] Predictive Factors: Discipline of Boy by Father; Supervision of Boy by Mother; Cohesiveness of Family.

Coefficient of Correlation of Three-Factor Total Scores
with Total Scores for Five Factors = .966

Table IX–Ic. Identification of Potential Juvenile Delinquents
Based on Three Social Factors[3]

Score Class	Delinquency Rate	Non-Delinquency Rate	Total Number of Cases
Less than 100	6.1%	93.9%	228
100–150	34.7	65.3	202
150–200	69.2	30.8	240
200 or Over	91.4	8.6	220

[3] Predictive Factors: Supervision of Boy by Mother; Affection of Father for Boy; Cohesiveness of Family.

Coefficient of Correlation of Three-Factor Total Scores
with Total Scores for Five Factors = .961

Table IX–1d.   Identification of Potential Juvenile Delinquents
Based on Three Social Factors[4]

Score Class	Delinquency Rate	Non-Delinquency Rate	Total Number of Cases
Less than 125	9.5%	90.5%	294
125–175	57.9	42.1	280
175–225	76.7	23.3	227
225 or Over	97.8	2.2	89

[4] Predictive Factors: Discipline of Boy by Father; Affection of Father for Boy; Cohesiveness of Family.

Coefficient of Correlation of Three-Factor Total Scores
with Total Scores for Five Factors = .942

Table IX–1e.   Identification of Potential Juvenile Delinquents
Based on Two Social Factors[5]

Score Class	Delinquency Rate	Non-Delinquency Rate	Total Number of Cases
Less than 75	9.5%	90.5%	315
75–100	45.8	54.2	83
100–125	62.6	37.4	187
125 or Over	87.2	12.8	305

[5] Predictive Factors: Supervision of Boy by Mother; Cohesiveness of Family.

Coefficient of Correlation of Two-Factor Total Scores
with Total Scores for Five Factors = .932

Table IX–2. Identification of Potential Juvenile Delinquents
Based on Five Traits of Character Structure

Score Class	Delinquency Rate	Non-Delinquency Rate	Total Number of Cases
Less than 205	14.7%	85.3%	143
205–255	38.9	61.1	203
255–280	64.0	36.0	50
280 or Over	87.9	12.1	140

Predictive Traits	Delinquency Scores
SOCIAL ASSERTIVENESS	
Absent	39.7
Slight	63.8
Present	75.9
DEFIANCE	
Absent	34.9
Slight	76.7
Present	91.0
SUSPICIOUSNESS	
Absent	37.5
Slight	47.3
Present	67.3
DESTRUCTIVENESS	
Absent	35.7
Slight	69.9
Present	77.7
EMOTIONAL LABILITY	
Absent	40.0
Slight	65.0
Present	75.2

Note: In the predictive traits above, *absent* means that the trait does not play a relevant or significant role in the character structure; *slight* indicates that the trait, although it may be present, is
not clearly so; *present* indicates that the trait is clearly evident in the character structure.
Source: *Unraveling Juvenile Delinquency*, Table XX–7, pp. 263 and 264.

Appendix B

Table IX–2a. Identification of Potential Juvenile Delinquents
Based on Four Traits of Character Structure[1]

Score Class	Delinquency Rate	Non-Delinquency Rate	Total Number of Cases
Less than 175	21.3%	78.7%	249
175–225	54.3	45.7	151
225–275	88.0	12.0	83
275 or Over	88.7	11.3	53

[1] Predictive Traits: Social Assertion; Defiance; Destructiveness; Emotional Lability.

Coefficient of Correlation of Four-Trait Total Scores
with Total Scores for Five Traits = .978

Table IX–2b. Identification of Potential Juvenile Delinquents
Based on Three Traits of Character Structure[2]

Score Class	Delinquency Rate	Non-Delinquency Rate	Total Number of Cases
Less than 125	25.9%	74.1%	243
125–175	45.4	54.6	152
175–225	83.5	16.5	103
225 or Over	97.4	2.6	38

[2] Predictive Traits: Social Assertion; Defiance; Destructiveness.

Coefficient of Correlation of Three-Trait Total Scores
with Total Scores for Five Traits = .947

Table IX–2c. Identification of Potential Juvenile Delinquents
Based on Three Traits of Character Structure[3]

Score Class	Delinquency Rate	Non-Delinquency Rate	Total Number of Cases
Less than 125	22.3%	77.7%	256
125–175	55.0	45.0	140
175–225	86.0	14.0	107
225 or Over	87.9	12.1	33

[3] Predictive Traits: Defiance; Destructiveness; Emotional Lability.

Coefficient of Correlation of Three-Trait Total Scores
with Total Scores for Five Traits = .962

Table IX–2d.   Identification of Potential Juvenile Delinquents
Based on Two Traits of Character Structure[4]

Score Class	Delinquency Rate	Non-Delinquency Rate	Total Number of Cases
Less than 100	30.1%	69.3%	326
100–125	58.9	41.1	95
125–150	80.6	19.4	31
150 or Over	90.5	9.5	84

[4] Predictive Traits: Defiance; Destructiveness.

Coefficient of Correlation of Two-Trait Total Scores
with Total Scores for Five Traits = .919

Table IX–3.   Identification of Potential Juvenile Delinquents
Based on Five Personality Traits

Score Class	Delinquency Rate	Non-Delinquency Rate	Total Number of Cases
Less than 220	10.4%	89.6%	328
220–245	43.0	57.0	172
245–270	63.0	37.0	81
270 or Over	87.4	12.6	356

Predictive Traits	Delinquency Scores
ADVENTUROUSNESS	
Absent	35.4
Present	75.3
EXTROVERSION IN ACTION	
Absent	37.8
Present	66.5
SUGGESTIBILITY	
Absent	35.5
Present	69.4
STUBBORNNESS	
Absent	39.0
Present	83.4
EMOTIONAL INSTABILITY	
Absent	26.5
Present	62.0

Note: In the predictive traits above, *present* means that the trait is so clear that the psychiatrist cannot question its presence; *absent* means that the trait is either not prominent or that it is probably absent.

Source: *Unraveling Juvenile Delinquency*, Table XX–11, pp. 264 and 266.

Table IX–4.   Identification of Potential Juvenile Delinquents
Based on Five Psychological Test Factors

Score Class	Delinquency Rate	Non-Delinquency Rate	Total Number of Cases
Less than 230	36.1%	63.9%	413
230–290	53.9	46.1	315
290 or Over	73.3	26.7	228

Predictive Factors	Delinquency Scores
Information Weighted Score (Derived from	
Wechsler-Bellevue Test)	
6 or Above	42.5
Below 6	69.4
Deviation of Digit Symbol Weighted Score from	
Mean Performance Weighted Score	
(Derived from Wechsler-Bellevue Test)	
1.2 or Above	41.0
Below 1.2	60.8
Reading Quotient (Derived from Stanford Test, Form D)	
80 or Above	41.1
Below 80	59.3
Arithmetic Quotient (Derived from Stanford Test, Form D)	
66 or Above	42.8
Below 66	74.4
Arithmetic Computation Age Score in Months	
(Derived from Stanford Test, Form D)	
120 or Above	37.9
Below 120	67.4

Table IX–4a. Identification of Potential Juvenile Delinquents
Based on Four Psychological Test Factors[1]

Score Class	Delinquency Rate	Non-Delinquency Rate	Total Number of Cases
Less than 175	35.2%	64.8%	369
175–200	40.9	59.1	237
200–225	59.8	40.2	122
225 or Over	74.6	25.4	228

[1] Predictive Factors: Information Weighted Score (Derived from Wechsler-Bellevue' Test); Arithmetic Computation Age Score in Months (Derived from Stanford Test, Form D); Arithmetic Quotient (Derived from Stanford Test, Form D); Reading Quotient (Derived from Stanford Test, Form D).

Coefficient of Correlation of Four-Factor Total Scores
with Total Scores for Five Factors = .961

Table IX–4b. Identification of Potential Juvenile Delinquents
Based on Three Psychological Test Factors[2]

Score Class	Delinquency Rate	Non-Delinquency Rate	Total Number of Cases
Less than 150	34.8%	65.2%	497
150–175	54.5	45.5	200
175–200	67.7	32.3	167
200 or Over	81.5	18.5	92

[2] Predictive Factors: Information Weighted Score (Derived from Wechsler-Bellevue Test); Arithmetic Computation Age Score in Months (Derived from Stanford Test, Form D); Arithmetic Quotient (Derived from Stanford Test, Form D).

Coefficient of Correlation of Three-Factor Total Scores
with Total Scores for Five Factors = .932

Appendix B

Table XI–I.   Identification of Neurotics among Juvenile
Delinquents

Score Class	Neuroticism Rate	Non-Neuroticism Rate	Total Number of Cases
400 or Over	0.0%	100.0%	69
300–400	23.3	76.7	120
200–300	78.9	21.1	38
Less than 200	100.0	0.0	15

Predictive Traits	Neuroticism Scores
COMMON SENSE	
Absent	28.8
Present	73.9
ENHANCED FEELING OF INSECURITY AND/OR ANXIETY	
Present	21.4
Absent	81.7
FEELING OF HELPLESSNESS AND POWERLESSNESS	
Present	46.1
Absent	85.6
FEAR OF FAILURE AND DEFEAT	
Present	50.0
Absent	86.4
DEFENSIVE ATTITUDE	
Present	51.4
Absent	86.4

Note: In the predictive traits above, *present* indicates that the trait is clearly evident in the character structure; *absent*, that although there may be some suggestion of it, this is not clear.
Source: E. T. Glueck, "Identifying Juvenile Delinquents and Neurotics," 40 *Mental Hygiene*, January, 1956, pp. 24–43; Table 1, pp. 35 and 36.

Table XI–2.   Identification of Potential Delinquents among
Neurotic Juveniles

Score Class	Delinquency Rate	Non-Delinquency Rate	Total Number of Cases
Less than 200	20.7%	79.3%	77
200–250	70.9	29.1	79
250 or Over	92.3	7.7	13

Predictive Traits	Delinquency Scores
ENHANCED FEELING OF INSECURITY AND/OR ANXIETY	
Present	34.0
Absent	54.4
SUSPICIOUSNESS	
Absent	31.3
Present	51.2
MASOCHISTIC TRENDS	
Present	28.3
Absent	61.9
SELF-CONTROL	
Present	32.4
Absent	49.3
COMPULSORY TRENDS	
Present	30.2
Absent	52.8

Note: In the predictive traits above, *present* indicates that the trait is clearly evident in the character structure; *absent*, that although there may be some suggestion of it, it is not clear.
Source: E. T. Glueck, "Identifying Juvenile Delinquents and Neurotics," 40 *Mental Hygiene*, January, 1956, pp. 24–43; Table 2, pp. 38 and 39.

Table XI–3.   Identification of Neurotics among Juvenile
Non-Delinquents

Score Class	Neuroticism Rate	Non-Neuroticism Rate	Total Number of Cases
Less than 200	10.8%	89.2%	130
200–250	41.7	58.3	24
250–300	76.9	23.1	26
300 or Over	94.1	5.9	34

Predictive Traits	Neuroticism Scores
ENHANCED FEELING OF INSECURITY AND/OR ANXIETY	
Absent	14.0
Present	89.2
FEAR OF FAILURE AND DEFEAT	
Absent	12.0
Present	54.9
FEELING OF RESENTMENT	
Absent	13.8
Present	58.9
DEFENSIVE ATTITUDE	
Absent	15.9
Present	66.9
COMPULSORY TRENDS	
Absent	23.3
Present	68.2

Note: In the predictive traits above, *present* indicates that the trait is clearly evident in the character structure; *absent*, that although there may be some suggestion of it, it is not clear.
Source: E. T. Glueck, "Identifying Juvenile Delinquents and Neurotics," 40 *Mental Hygiene*, January, 1956, pp. 24–43; Table 3, pp. 41 and 42.

Table XI–4. Identification of Treatable Juvenile Delinquents*

Score Class	Treatability Rate	Untreatability Rate	Total Number of Cases
Less than 300	95.8%	4.2%	48
300–350	49.4	50.6	81
350–400	17.5	82.5	246
400 or Over	6.3	93.7	79

Predictive Factors	Failure Scores
DISCIPLINE OF BOY BY FATHER	
Firm but Kindly	0.0
Erratic	56.0
Overstrict	88.3
Lax	91.8
DISCIPLINE OF BOY BY MOTHER	
Firm but Kindly	0.0
Erratic	61.6
Overstrict	81.8
Lax	83.3
SUPERVISION OF BOY BY MOTHER	
Suitable	51.4
Fair	64.1
Unsuitable	78.3
AFFECTION OF FATHER FOR BOY	
Warm (including overprotective)	59.6
Indifferent	79.1
Hostile	84.3
COHESIVENESS OF FAMILY	
Marked	42.5
Some	77.0
None	80.5

* See text, pp. 109–111, for discussion of this table.

Appendix B

Definitions of Predictive Factors
(*Arranged in Alphabetical Order*)

Adequacy of Childhood Home

Broken Home: A home from which one or both parents were absent by reason of death, desertion, separation, or divorce, or absent for a year or longer as a result of imprisonment, illness, or emigration.

Inadequate Home: A home which, though not broken, was unsuited to the wholesome rearing of children because of intemperance, immorality, delinquency of parents, neglect or improper oversight by parents, constant quarreling between parents, and so on.

Adventurousness

Has impulse for change, excitement, or risk.

Affection of Father for Boy
Affection of Mother for Boy

Warm (including overprotective): Father (or mother) is sympathetic, kind, attached, even overprotective.

Indifferent: Father (or mother) does not pay much attention to child; relationship is neither warm, overprotective, or hostile.

Hostile: Father (or mother) rejects child.

Age Began Work

Includes full-time and part-time work but does not include helping a father or other relative after school. The emphasis is on paid work, either part- or full-time, which marks the beginning of a wage-earning career. Occasional Saturday work or occasional work after school would not be considered. In other words, the age of first employment represents the point at which the boy began to contribute consistently toward his own or his family's support.

Age First Left Home

Here are excluded temporary departures such as brief hospitalization or visits to relatives. Refers only to departures from home that represent a real break with home ties.

Age of Offender at First Arrest

Self-explanatory.

245

Age at Onset of Antisocial Behavior

Not confined to age at first arrest but refers to age at first persistent signs of a developing criminal career, including any misbehavior for which a youth might have been arrested. The fact that he did not come to the attention of the police means only that the police are not active or that the offender knows how to protect himself from detection. The stealing of candy or fruit or small articles from the "five and ten" would certainly be included if this were the beginning of a pattern of misbehavior; if one or two isolated events of this nature had occurred, they would be disregarded.

Age of Younger Parent at Marriage

Self-explanatory.

Arrests Preceding Offense for Which Sentenced

Self-explanatory.

Bad Habits in Childhood

This refers to any persistent habits which might lead to conflict with the law, as drinking, use of narcotics, gambling, stealing, pathological lying, sexual perversion.

Birthplace of Father
Birthplace of Mother

Self-explanatory.

Church Attendance

Regular: Every Sunday.
Irregular: Occasionally.

Cohesiveness of Family

Marked: There is a strong "we" feeling among members of the immediate family as evidenced by cooperativeness, group interests, pride in the home, affection for each other.

Some: Even if the family group may not be entirely intact (because of absence of one or more members), the remaining group has at least some of the characteristics of the cohesive family.

None: Home is just a place to "hang your hat;" self-interest of the members exceeds group interest.

246

Common Sense

The faculty of thinking and acting in the ways of the community; it may be present even if some acts of the individual run counter to accepted mores; there may be, for instance, a conflict between common sense and a fantastic thirst for adventure.

Compulsory Trends

Includes both the classical neurotic compulsions as well as the less dramatic and less manifest cases of a rigidity that does not permit of flexible adaptation to changing situations, and usually originates from anxiety. It is an attempt to overcome anxiety and to defend oneself against it. The anxiety may be conscious, or more often, unconscious.

Conjugal Relations of Parents

Refers to own parents unless offender has had a substitute parent since he was at least three years old.

Good: Parents living together compatibly without undue quarreling.

Fair: Parents living together but grossly incompatible; indifferent or hostile to each other but no open breach has occurred.

Poor: Separation, desertion, divorce, or occasional desertion or separation.

Defensive Attitude

Unwarranted defensiveness, either exaggerated in proportion to the attack, or against an entirely imagined attack. The means of defending oneself are varied: they consist sometimes of a "shell-like" attitude of warding off every approach and erecting a wall around oneself; they sometimes take a more agressive form, as, for instance, in persons who are very sensitive to any criticism and are provoked by it to defiant or obstinate or opinionated behavior; and so on.

Defiance

Aggressive self-assertion borne out of deep insecurity or weakness and therefore often indiscriminate in its aims and means.

Delinquency in Family

Refers to family in which reared and includes unofficial as well as official misconduct that did or might have resulted in arrest. Excludes technical automobile violations.

Destructiveness

The tendency to destroy, to hurt, to be negativistic. This tendency may be directed against others or against oneself; usually both trends run parallel, often one being more manifest and the other more suppressed.

Discipline by Father
Discipline by Mother

Refers to usual discipline of the boy on the part of the parent or of a parent surrogate, if he has lived with the latter at least since he was three years old.

Firm but Kindly: Discipline based on sound reason which the child understands and accepts as fair.

Erratic: Parent vacillates between strictness and laxity; is not consistent in control.

Overstrict: Parent is harsh, unreasoning, demands obedience through fear.

Lax: Parent is negligent, indifferent, lets boy do what he likes. In cases in which one or another parent has left or has been removed from the home before a child was three years old, and there is no parent surrogate (step-parent, foster-parent), discipline of the missing parent is graded as lax.

Economic Responsibility of Offender

Responsible: If single, separated, widowed, or divorced, and is without legal dependents (wife, children, or parents), supports self even if by illegitimate employment and at least in marginal circumstances with only occasional public or private aid or sporadic assistance from relatives; if he has dependents (wife, children, or parents), makes every reasonable effort to support them at least in marginal circumstances. See *Economic Status of Childhood Home* for definition.

Irresponsible: Does not meet the above standard through his own fault, or contracts avoidable debts or receives frequent aid from social agencies or relatives when should be self-supporting.

Economic Status of Childhood Home

Refers to the usual economic condition of the home in which offender was reared.

Comfortable: Having accumulated resources sufficient to maintain self and family for at least four months.

Marginal: Living on daily earnings and accumulating little or nothing;

being on the border between self-support and dependency. Here are included instances in which temporary aid is resorted to occasionally in order to tide over a critical period; for example, in case of illness or seasonal unemployment, aid may have been given for a few days or even a month, and with this little assistance the family was able to manage its own support.

Dependent: Receiving aid continuously from public funds or from persons outside the immediate family. Aid may have been given in the form of money, clothing, food, fuel, or medical assistance.

Education of Parents

Self-explanatory.

Emotional Instability

Unharmonious and inappropriate feeling reaction, conflict of feeling tendencies; not to be confused with lability of emotion.

Emotional Lability

Qualities in the affective reactions of a person which permit inner drives, urges, feelings to take their course, allow tensions to explode, and which thus lead to certain actions and moods more or less regardless of consequences and of the objective requirements of the situation. The term "emotional lability" refers to the way in which affectivity is discharged, and not to the general "lability" or "stableness" of a person.

Enhanced Feeling of Insecurity and/or Anxiety

While insecurity and anxiety play a considerable role not only in pathological cases but also in many normal persons, enhanced insecurity and/or anxiety designates a state in which these feelings play a decidedly stronger role in the personality, either quantitatively or qualitatively, than is usual in the average person. They may, however, remain largely unconscious.

Extroverted in Action

Gives free expression to feelings in activity.

Family Relationships

If offender is married, his relation to his wife and children is judged. If offender is separated, divorced, or widowed, his relation to his children is judged. If offender has no children, his relation to his parents and siblings is judged. If offender is single, separated, divorced, or widowed before beginning of period studied and has no children, his relation to his parents and siblings is judged. If offender has a common-law wife, his relation to her is judged as though she were his legal wife.

The standard of *socially acceptable* conduct in regard to family relationships adopted for our purposes is the following: The offender must not be harming his family in any way deemed injurious to the institution of the family; that is, if married, he must not neglect or desert his wife or children during the period judged, or be separated or divorced from his wife during the period judged, or have illicit relations with other women, or be abusive to his wife or children, or be continually away evenings if this is not necessary to his business. If single, separated, widowed, or divorced before beginning of period and living away from home, he must be in touch with his parents or nearest relatives. If single, separated, widowed, or divorced, and living at home, he must give evidence that he considers it more than merely a convenient place to sleep and eat; for example, he must not be continually out in the evening if this is not necessary to his work, or live at home only when he is in need of funds.

A man is a failure in his family relationships if he does not meet the above standard; i.e., his conduct is *socially unacceptable*.

Fear of Failure and Defeat

A frequent consequence of anxiety, especially in persons with an over-competitive attitude. Fear of failure may concern every sphere of life, not only work or play, but all human relations. It may lead either to greater effort or to inhibitions, aloofness, and to recoiling from competition.

Feeling of Helplessness and Powerlessness

Particularly frequent and important, and very often unconscious kind of insecurity feeling, in which the individual feels he cannot do or change or influence anything, especially with regard to the course of his own life.

Feeling of Resentment

The feeling of frustration, envy, or dissatisfaction, with particular emphasis not on the positive attempt or hope to better one's own situation, but on the negative wish that others should be denied the satisfaction or enjoyment that one feels is lacking or withheld from oneself.

Grade Attained in School

Self-explanatory.

Industrial Skill of Father or Father Substitute
Industrial Skill of Offender

Refers to skill in usual occupation, or if this is difficult to determine, the highest degree of skill of the individual in any of the occupations he has held. The *unskilled* laborer does any kind of rough work to which he can be sent without any training whatever. Mere strength of hand or keenness of eye, untutored through any course of apprenticeship or training, serves for him. The *semiskilled* worker uses tools and processes requiring learning. He cannot take up the kind of work unless he has had a period of experience under guidance or study. The processes, however, are not greatly complicated and the period of training is likely to be short (three days to three months, perhaps). The *skilled* worker uses tools and processes which are usable only by one who has given a long period of time, perhaps at least a year, to the acquiring of the skill.

Intelligence of Offender

Self-explanatory.

Kind of Worker in Reformatory

Good: Reliable, industrious, capable, efficient.
Fair: Effort and willingness are great, but ineffective unless under some supervision.
Poor: Unreliable, lazy, dishonest, and needs constant supervision.

Member of Gang or Crowd

A *gang* is organized for a specific antisocial purpose and has specific leadership; a *crowd* is an aggregation of individuals with no purpose and no leadership.

Mental Disease or Distortion

Refers to mental condition as determined by psychiatric examination. Includes psychoses, psychoneuroses, psychopathies, epilepsies, sex perversions, delirium tremens, marked emotional instability; also marked liabilities of personality such as unusually strong emotional or conative traits (impulsiveness, lack of self-control, self-indulgence, egocentricity, fault finding, hypochondria, introspectiveness, jealousy, melodramaty, obscenity, opinionation, profanity, seclusiveness, self-pity, self-justification, vanity, unsociality, lack of foresight, irresponsibility).

251

Mobility

Changes in environment which indicate that the individual does not take root and establish close associations in any one community. This is indicated by excessive moving within a city (more than once a year); or from city to city on the average of once in two years; or by coming from or going to a foreign country.

Moral Standards of Home

Refers to the parental home unless offender has lived with a foster-family since he was at least three years old.

Good: Wholesome ideals, and no delinquency among members of the family other than the offender, except for slight automobile violations or violation of license laws.

Fair: Homes in which, though there are no delinquent members, no immorality or alcoholism, there is nevertheless an absence of wholesome ideals.

Poor: Homes in which there is immorality, alcoholism, or other delinquency.

Nativity of Offender

Nativity of Parents and Offender

Self-explanatory.

Neighborhood Influences

Good: No street gangs, no centers of vice or crime within a radius of two square blocks of offender's home if living in city or a mile in country; opportunity for constructive recreation within easy walking distance, as public playgrounds, school or community centers, parks, and so on.

Fair: No street gangs, no centers of vice or crime within a radius of two square blocks if living in city or a mile in country, but no opportunities for constructive recreation within walking distance.

Poor: Corner gangs, centers of vice or crime within a radius of two square blocks if in city or a mile in country, regardless of whether facilities for constructive recreation exist within walking distance.

Number of Children in Family of Offender

Includes the offender himself; refers only to *living* siblings and includes half- and step-siblings.

Occupation of Mother

Refers to own mother, step- or foster-mother.

Appendix B

Penal Experiences Prior to Reformatory Sentence

Self-explanatory.

Physical Condition

Good: Free from disease, well-nourished and strong, very minor defects may be present such as slightly carious teeth.

Fair: Some minor ailment but not sufficient to interfere with efficiency. General development not good, however.

Poor: Presence of serious disease such as epilepsy, well-advanced pulmonary tuberculosis, congenital syphilis, heart disorder, or disabling handicaps, such as blindness, partial paralysis, or atrophy of arm or leg.

Rank of Offender among Siblings

Refers only to living siblings and includes half- and step-siblings.

Recreations and Interests during Parole

Constructive: Member of well-supervised recreational groups or is utilizing leisure time to further self educationally or vocationally; has no bad habits.

Not Constructive: Pronounced bad habits, associations, recreations, which may lead to criminal conduct; such as immoral companions, gangs, drug addiction, excessive drinking, gambling. The presence of any one or combination of these factors places the offender in this group. Included among those whose recreations and interests are not constructive are offenders who, though not having bad habits, associates, and recreations during parole, do not make constructive use of their leisure time.

Religion of Parents

Self-explanatory.

School Misconduct

Refers to truancy and other serious or persistent minor misbehavior in school such as stealing, cheating, or persistent evidence of minor misconduct such as tantrums, attracting attention, and otherwise causing interference with school routine.

School Retardation

Determined by most recent grade attained in school in relation to his age, according to the following scale:

Age:	6	7	8	9	10	11	12	13	14	15
Grade:	I	II	III	IV	V	VI	VII	VIII	IX	X

If, for example, a child is thirteen years old at time of court appearance and is in Grade VI, he is two years behind the expected grade for his age.

Seriousness and Frequency of Prereformatory Crimes

Serious Offenses: Property crimes, i.e., burglary, larceny, robbery, assault with intent to rob, arson, embezzlement; violent sex offenses; homicide, being fugitive from justice, escaping, serious automobile offenses; dishonorable discharge from Armed Forces.

Minor Offenses: Use of habit-forming drugs, drunkenness, vagrancy; adultery, fornication; non-support, simple assaults, disturbing the peace, malicious mischief; technical automobile violations, peddling without license.

Social Assertiveness

Refers to the more superficial quality of expressing will and ambition in relation to the environment (unlike self-assertion, which is usually based on the development of a genuine and spontaneous self).

Steadiness of Employment

Refers to employment from beginning of work history until arrest for offense for which committed.

Regular: Continual employment with not more than an average of two months unemployment a year.

Fairly Regular: Periods of unemployment in excess of two months a year, interspersed with periods of sustained work.

Irregular: Frequent or long periods of unemployment, and none of sustained employment.

Stubbornness

Resistive or persistent, but not in a freely expressed drive; probably the result of thwarted dynamic qualities.

Suggestibility

Easily swayed by appeal to feelings even though against better judgment.

Supervision of Boy by Mother

Suitable: If mother does not work outside the home and is not ill, she personally keeps close watch on the child or provides for his leisure hours in clubs and playgrounds; if she is ill or out of the home a great deal, there is a responsible adult in charge.

Fair: Mother, though home, gives only partial supervision to child.

Unsuitable: Mother is careless in her supervision, leaving the child to his own devices without guidance, or in the care of an irresponsible person.

Suspiciousness

Indiscriminate or exaggerated mistrust of others, not warranted by the objective situation. The individual is generally unaware of being unduly suspicious, believing that he is merely cautious, or realistic, or being persecuted, and so on. Suspicion often accompanies hostility and fear of hostility.

Time Between Onset of Antisocial Behavior and First Arrest

See *Age at Onset of Antisocial Behavior.*

Time Parents Were in United States

Self-explanatory.

Use of Leisure

Negative: At least not engaging in harmful activities, even though not utilizing time constructively.

Harmful: Indulging in forms of recreation which might lead to criminal conduct (such as membership in gangs, association with bootleggers, prostitutes, loafers, drug addicts, drunkards, gamblers).

Work Habits of Offender

Good: Reliable, industrious, commended by employers; is an asset to them.

Fair: Has qualifications of good worker but permits work to be interrupted by periodic drinking, drug addiction, occasional vagabondage; deliberate choice of irregular occupations such as longshoring, for the chief purpose of having leisure time.

Poor: Unreliable, loafs, is lazy, dishonest, unstable, a vagabond and floater, ambitionless, wayward, or is engaged in illicit work.

Appendix C

Tables Concerning Agreement Between Predicted and Actual Behavior of Juvenile Offenders during Peno-Correctional Treatments on Which Prediction Validation Is Based from Onset of Delinquency to Twenty-third Birthday

Note: Final preparation of the data and editing of the results were carried out in close cooperation with Rose W. Kneznek, Executive Secretary of the Bureau of Business Research, Harvard Business School.

Table I. Distribution of Offenders According to Number of Peno-Correctional Treatments

Number of Treatments	Number of Offenders	Per Cent of Total	Accumulative	
			Number of Offenders	Per Cent
Less than Four	78	15.7%	78	15.7%
Four	66	13.3	144	29.0
Five	63	12.7	207	41.7
Six	52	10.4	259	52.1
Seven	51	10.3	310	62.4
Eight	49	9.9	359	72.3
Nine	31	6.2	390	78.5
Ten	29	5.8	419	84.3
Eleven	30	6.0	449	90.3
Twelve or Over	48	9.7	497	100.0

Mean = Six Treatments.

Table 2. Distribution of Offenders According to Number of Types of Peno-Correctional Treatments

Number of Types of Treatments	Number of Offenders	Per Cent of Total
One	10	2.0%
Two	53	10.7
Three	156	31.4
Four	191	38.4
Five	76	15.3
Six	11	2.2
Total	497	100.0%

256

Appendix C

Table 3. Summary of Types of Peno-Correctional Treatments on Which Prediction Validation Based

Type of Treatment	Number of Offenders	Number of Each Type of Treatment
Straight Probation	297	380
Probation with Suspended Sentence	356	548
Correctional School	488	1,055
Parole	461	1,053
Reformatory	157	320
Prison	35	41
Total		3,397

Table 4. Comparison of Predicted Distributions for Total Group of Juvenile Offenders vs. Offenders Actually Experiencing Particular Peno-Correctional Treatment

Type of Treatment*		Score Class	Predicted Distributions: More than or Even Chance of Violation			
			Total Group of Offenders		Offenders Actually Experiencing Treatment	
			Number of Offenders	Per Cent of Total	Number of Offenders	Per Cent of Total
Straight Probation	(III–1)	240 or Over	470	96.3%	286	96.6%
Probation with Suspended Sentence	(III–2)	300 or Over	477	97.3	344	96.9
Correctional School	(III–3)	210 or Over	475	95.6	465	95.5
Parole	(III–6)	290 or Over	485	99.4	458	99.4
Reformatory	(III–9)	210 or Over	102	20.9	10	6.4
Prison	(III–10)	Less than 120	96	19.5	4	11.4

* See Summary Tables III–A through III–E.

Table 5. Behavior of Juvenile Offenders during Peno-Correctional Treatments

Type of Treatment	Total Number of Offenders	Serious or Persistent Minor Offender		Occasional Minor Offender or Non-Offender	
		Number	Per Cent	Number	Per Cent
Straight Probation	297	277	93.3%	20	6.7%
Probation with Suspended Sentence	356	349	98.0	7	2.0
Correctional School	488	376	77.0	112	23.0
Parole	461	418	90.7	43	9.3
Reformatory	157	59	37.6	98	62.4
Prison	35	9	25.7	26	74.3

Table 6. Comparison of Predicted vs. Actual Behavior by Type of Treatment

Predicted Behavior	Total Number of Offenders	Actual Behavior Serious or Persistent Minor Offender	
		Number	Per Cent
More than Even Chance of "Failure"			
Straight Probation	286	270	94.4%
Probation with Suspended Sentence	344	337	98.0
Correctional School	465	366	78.7
Parole	458	417	91.0
Reformatory	39	21	53.8
Prison	4	3	75.0

		Occasional Minor Offender or Non-Offender	
Less than Even Chance of "Failure"			
Straight Probation	10	4	40.0
Probation with Suspended Sentence	11	0	0.0
Correctional School	22	12	54.5
Parole	3	2	66.7
Reformatory	118	80	67.8
Prison	31	25	80.6

Note: The small number of cases in certain categories is due to the nature of the sample which is made up of true juvenile offenders (serious or persistent minor).

Table 7.   Peno-Correctional Treatments Classified by Agreement
Between Predicted and Actual Behavior and Type of Treatment *

Type of Treatment	Total Number of Treatments	Agreement		Disagreement	
		Number	Per Cent	Number	Per Cent
Straight Probation	380	350	92.1%	30	7.9%
Probation with Suspended Sentence	545	510	93.6	35	6.4
Correctional School	1,054	831	78.8	223	21.2
Parole	1,053	968	91.9	85	8.1
Reformatory	320	234	73.1	86	26.9
Prison	41	31	75.6	10	24.4

* *Agreement between predicted and actual behavior* is judged as follows: (1) an offender is predicted as having more than an even chance of delinquency during a particular form of treatment and he actually commits serious or persistent minor offenses; (2) an offender is predicted as having more than an even chance of non-delinquency and he actually is a non-offender or commits only a very occasional minor offense.

Note: It was not possible to determine agreement between predicted and actual behavior for one offender experiencing three probations with suspended sentence and one correctional school commitment.

Table 8.   Peno-Correctional Treatments Classified by Agreement
Between Predicted and Actual Behavior and Age of Offender

Age of Offender	Total Number of Treatments	Agreement		Disagreement	
		Number	Per Cent	Number	Per Cent
7–10 Years	122	118	96.7%	4	3.3%
11–12 Years	393	355	90.3	38	9.7
13–14 Years	791	712	90.0	79	10.0
15–16 Years	1,101	937	85.1	164	14.9
17–18 Years	534	446	83.5	88	16.5
19–20 Years	257	206	80.2	51	19.8
21–22 Years	195	150	76.9	45	23.1

Table 9.   Peno-Correctional Treatments Classified by Behavior
and Age of Offender

Age of Offender	Total Number of Treatments	Serious or Persistent Minor Offenses		Occasional Minor Offenses or No Offense	
		Number	Per Cent	Number	Per Cent
7–10 Years	122	117	95.9%	5	4.1%
11–12 Years	393	353	89.8	40	10.2
13–14 Years	791	699	88.4	92	11.6
15–16 Years	1,104	893	80.9	211	19.1
17–18 Years	534	398	74.5	136	25.5
19–20 Years	257	158	61.5	99	38.5
21–22 Years	196	111	56.6	85	43.4

Table 10.   Straight Probations Classified by Behavior
and Age of Offender

Age of Offender	Total Number of Probations	Serious or Persistent Minor Offenses		Occasional Minor Offenses or No Offense	
		Number	Per Cent	Number	Per Cent
7–10 Years	57	53	93.0%	4	7.0%
11–12 Years	115	109	94.8	6	5.2
13–14 Years	111	103	92.8	8	7.2
15–16 Years	53	50	94.3	3	5.7
17–18 Years	18	16	88.9	2	11.1
19–20 Years	15	13	86.7	2	13.3
21–22 Years	11	10	90.9	1	9.1
Total	380	354	93.2%	26	6.8%

Table 11.   Probations with Suspended Sentence Classified by
Behavior and Age of Offender

Age of Offender	Total Number of Probations with Suspended Sentence	Serious or Persistent Minor Offenses		Occasional Minor Offenses or No Offense	
		Number	Per Cent	Number	Per Cent
7–10 Years	29	29	100.0%	0	0.0%
11–12 Years	75	72	96.0	3	4.0
13–14 Years	147	145	98.6	2	1.4
15–16 Years	138	137	99.3	1	0.7
17–18 Years	54	48	88.9	6	11.1
19–20 Years	45	42	93.3	3	6.7
21–22 Years	60	51	85.0	9	15.0
Total	548	524	95.6%	24	4.4%

Table 12.   Paroles Classified by Behavior and Age of Offender

Age of Offender	Total Number of Paroles	Serious or Persistent Minor Offenses		Occasional Minor Offenses or No Offense	
		Number	Per Cent	Number	Per Cent
Under 12 Years	80	79	98.7%	1	1.3%
13–14 Years	226	219	96.9	7	3.1
15–16 Years	390	355	91.0	35	9.0
17–18 Years	236	217	91.9	19	8.1
19–20 Years	71	62	87.3	9	12.7
21–22 Years	50	35	70.0	15	30.0
Total	1,053	967	91.8%	86	8.2%

Table 13. Correctional School Commitments Classified by
Behavior and Age of Offender

Age of Offender	Total Number of Correctional School Commitments	Serious or Persistent Minor Offenses		Occasional Minor Offenses or No Offense	
		Number	Per Cent	Number	Per Cent
7–10 Years	30	29	96.7%	1	3.3%
11–12 Years	129	99	76.7	30	23.3
13–14 Years	305	232	76.1	73	23.9
15–16 Years	478	342	71.5	136	28.5
17–18 Years	107	80	74.8	27	25.2
19–20 Years	6	3	50.0	3	50.0
Total	1,055	785	74.4%	270	25.6%

Table 14. Reformatory Commitments Classified by Behavior
and Age of Offender

Age of Offender	Total Number of Reformatory Commitments	Serious or Persistent Minor Offenses		Occasional Minor Offenses or No Offense	
		Number	Per Cent	Number	Per Cent
13–18 Years	157	44	28.0%	113	72.0%
19–20 Years	106	35	33.0	71	67.0
21–22 Years	57	9	15.8	48	84.2
Total	320	88	27.5%	232	72.5%

Table 15. Prison Commitments Classified by Behavior and Age
of Offender

Age of Offender	Total Number of Prison Commitments	Serious or Persistent Minor Offenses		Occasional Minor Offenses or No Offense	
		Number	Per Cent	Number	Per Cent
17–18 Years	9	2	22.2%	7	77.8%
19–20 Years	14	3	21.4	11	78.6
21–22 Years	18	6	33.3	12	66.7
Total	41	11	26.8%	30	73.2%

261

Table 16. Peno-Correctional Treatments Classified by
Behavior and Length of Treatment

Length of Treatment	Total Number of Treatments	Serious or Persistent Minor Offenses		Occasional Minor Offenses or No Offense	
		Number	Per Cent	Number	Per Cent
Less than 7 Months	1,375	1,143	83.1%	232	16.9%
7–12 Months	1,167	928	79.5	239	20.5
13–18 Months	392	310	79.1	82	20.9
19–24 Months	179	139	77.7	40	22.3
25 Months or Over	284	209	73.6	75	26.4
Total	3,397	2,729	80.3%	668	19.7%

Table 17. Comparison of Predicted vs. Actual Behavior of
Offenders during Five Years after Completion of First
Treatment Imposed by Juvenile Court

Score Class	Probability of Delinquency	Predicted Distribution of Total Group of Offenders		Actual Behavior of Offenders	
		Number	Per Cent	Number	Per Cent
406.6–476	Even Chance	6	1.4%	16	3.7%
476 or Over	More than Even Chance	435	98.6	419	96.3
Total		441	100.0%	435	100.0%

Table 18. Treatability Profiles of 479 Juvenile Offenders

	Profile A	Profile B	Profile C	Profile D	Profile E	Profile F	Profile G
Number of Offenders	362	28	29	28	18	8	6
Type of Treatment	*Chances of Good Behavior*						
Probation	$1\frac{1}{2}$	$1\frac{1}{2}$	$3\frac{1}{2}$	$3\frac{1}{2}$	$1\frac{1}{2}$	$6\frac{1}{2}$	$6\frac{1}{2}$
Probation with Suspended Sentence	$1\frac{1}{2}$	4	4	$1\frac{1}{2}$	$1\frac{1}{2}$	5	4
Correctional School	$3\frac{1}{2}$	$3\frac{1}{2}$	$3\frac{1}{2}$	$3\frac{1}{2}$	$5\frac{1}{2}$	$3\frac{1}{2}$	$3\frac{1}{2}$
Parole	1	1	1	1	1	1	1

Note: Only profile "A" represents the juvenile offenders probably untreatable by one or other of the above methods. See text, Chapter VIII, pp. 109–111.

Appendix D

From Prediction to Etiology: A Table Summarizing
Significant Differences Between Typical and Atypical
Delinquents as Derived from Social, Rorschach, and
Psychiatric Prediction Tables for Identifying
Potential Delinquents

Note of Explanation

The tabulation which follows comprises a listing of the factors and traits in *Unraveling* which have been related to:

(a) The cluster of social prediction factors, broken down into two groups: (1) atypical delinquents, i.e., those with failure scores of less than 250 vs. typical delinquents, i.e., those with failure scores of 250 or over; (2) atypical non-delinquents with failure scores of 250 or over vs. typical non-delinquents with failure scores of less than 250.

(b) The cluster of Rorschach prediction traits, broken down into two groups: (1) atypical delinquents (failure scores of less than 255) vs. typical delinquents (failure scores of 255 or over); (2) atypical non-delinquents (failure scores of 255 or over) vs. typical non-delinquents (failure scores of less than 255).

(c) The cluster of psychiatric prediction traits, broken down into two groups: (1) atypical delinquents (failure scores of less than 245) vs. typical delinquents (failure scores of 245 or over); (2) atypical non-delinquents (failure scores of 245 or over) vs. typical non-delinquents (failure scores of less than 245).

As it is not possible, for reasons of space, to reproduce the large number of tables that resulted from relating each cluster of prediction factors or traits (social, Rorschach, psychiatric) to certain factors in *Unraveling Juvenile Delinquency*, a listing of the factors with special indication (L = Lower; H = Higher) of those in which a statistically significant difference[1] was found between the atypical and the typical delinquents, or between the atypical and the typical non-delinquents, as distinguished

[1] The reader interested in the nature of this computation is asked to consult Appendix A of *Physique and Delinquency*, New York, Harper, 1956.

by each of the three clusters of five predictive factors or traits, had to be resorted to. The factors constituting the Social Prediction Table are identified by an S; the traits constituting the Rorschach Prediction Table are identified by an R; and those comprising the Psychiatric Prediction Table are identified by a P.

The numbers in parentheses immediately to the left of the factors or traits are the table numbers in *Unraveling Juvenile Delinquency*, provided in order to make reference to the original tables easier.

The purpose of presenting these data is to furnish at least a partial basis for arriving at the reasons why the prediction tables do not correctly identify all the cases. (In the text of Chapter IX, note 8, it was pointed out that only 2.4% of the cases were incorrectly identified as delinquents or non-delinquents by all the tables.) Examination of the results presented in Column 1 reveals that all the boys incorrectly predicted by the Social Prediction Table as non-delinquents, but who were nevertheless true delinquents, would have been identified by the cluster of Rorschach predictive traits, for they are not found to differ from the group correctly predicted as delinquents in so far as the five predictive Rorschach traits are concerned. Likewise, as we examine the traits which are the basis for the psychiatric prediction table, we see that the group of boys incorrectly predicted as non-delinquents on the basis of the social predictive factors are nevertheless not found to differ from the correctly predicted delinquents by the cluster of five psychiatric traits.

Turning now to the Rorschach Prediction Table (Columns 3 and 4), and focusing our attention on those boys who would not have been properly identified as delinquents had the predictive cluster of Rorschach traits been applied in their early years, we again see that in these cases the boys would, nevertheless, have been correctly identified by the cluster of social factors in which they resemble the typical delinquents, and thus would have been properly identified as potential delinquents; and they would have been identified as delinquents by the cluster of the five psychiatric traits because in these it will be seen that they do not differ from the typical delinquents.

We turn now to the boys who would not have been correctly identified as potential delinquents in their early years on the basis of the cluster of psychiatric factors. Once again, examination of the differences between those incorrectly predicted as non-delinquents and those correctly predicted as delinquents indicates that these two groups do not differ from each other as regards the cluster of Rorschach traits and would therefore be properly identified as delinquents by the Rorschach Prediction Table and likewise by the cluster of social predictive factors.

264

We can reason, therefore, that boys of wholesome family background (as reflected in a prediction score of less than 250 on the five social prediction factors) may nevertheless be potential delinquents if they have certain traits of character structure and/or temperament; that those who do not have an unwholesome character structure may nevertheless become delinquent if their interpersonal family relations and/or their temperament impel them to antisocial conduct; and that those whose temperament would not place them in the potential delinquent group may nevertheless be potential delinquents if their interpersonal family relationships are unwholesome and/or they have a delinquent character structure. Further research into the etiology of delinquency is obviously necessary because influences other than the ones included in *Unraveling* may account for the results.

Appendix D
From Prediction to Etiology

(A Table Summarizing Significant Differences Between Typical and Atypical Delinquents as Derived from Social, Rorschach, and Psychiatric Prediction Tables for Identifying Potential Delinquents)

Factors or Traits		Cluster of Social Prediction Factors		Cluster of Rorschach Prediction Traits		Cluster of Psychiatric Prediction Traits	
		Atypical vs. Typical		Atypical vs. Typical		Atypical vs. Typical	
		Delin-quents (1)	Non-Delin-quents (2)	Delin-quents (3)	Non-Delin-quents (4)	Delin-quents (5)	Non-Delin-quents (6)
INTELLIGENCE							
(IV–7)	High Intelligence Quotient						
PHYSICAL CONDITION							
(XIV–1)	Poor Health in Infancy						
(XIV–2)	Extreme Restlessness in Early Childhood	L					
(XIV–2)	Enuresis in Early Childhood	L					
(XIV–3)	Immunity to Contagion						
(XIV–4)	Strength of Hand Grip	L				H	
(XIV–6)	Irregular Reflexes						
(XIV–6)	Functional Deviations	L					
(XIV–9)	Genital Under-Development						
(XIV–13)	Dermographia				L		
(XIV–13)	Cyanosis						
(XIV–13)	Tremors						
(XIV–16)	Good General Health Status						
(XV–1)	Physique Types						
CHARACTER STRUCTURE							
(XVII–1)	Originality				H		
(XVII–3)	Banality						
(XVII–4)	Marked Power of Observation						
(XVII–6)	Common Sense	H		H			
(XVII–7)	Intuition						

Note: Numbers in parentheses are from *Unraveling Juvenile Delinquency*.
H = Higher; L = Lower.

From Prediction to Etiology (Continued)

Factors or Traits		Cluster of Social Prediction Factors		Cluster of Rorschach Prediction Traits		Cluster of Psychiatric Prediction Traits	
		Atypical vs. Typical		Atypical vs. Typical		Atypical vs. Typical	
		Delinquents	Non-Delinquents	Delinquents	Non-Delinquents	Delinquents	Non-Delinquents
		(1)	(2)	(3)	(4)	(5)	(6)
	CHARACTER STRUCTURE (Continued)						
(XVII–8)	Tendency to Phantasy						
(XVII–10)	Methodical Approach to Problems						
(XVII–11)	Potential Capacity for Objective Interests			H			
(XVIII–2)	Social Assertiveness (R)			L	H	L	
(XVIII–3)	Defiance (R)			L	H		
(XVIII–4)	Marked Submissiveness			H		H	
(XVIII–5)	Ambivalence to Authority			L	H		
(XVIII–7)	Enhanced Feelings of Insecurity					H	
(XVIII–8)	Marked Feeling of Not Being Wanted or Loved				H		
(XVIII–9)	Feeling of Not Being Taken Care of		H				H
(XVIII–10)	Marked Feeling of Not Being Taken Seriously						
(XVIII–11)	Feeling of Not Being Appreciated						
(XVIII–12)	Feeling of Helplessness						
(XVIII–13)	Fear of Failure and Defeat					H	
(XVIII–14)	Feeling of Resentment			L	H		
(XVIII–17)	Good Surface Contacts with Others			H			
(XVIII–22)	Hostility			L	H		
(XVIII–23)	Marked Suspiciousness (R)			L	H		
(XVIII–24)	Destructiveness (R)			L	H		
(XVIII–25)	Feeling of Isolation						
(XVIII–26)	Defensive Attitude			L	H		
(XVIII–27)	Marked Dependence on Others			H			

Note: Numbers in parentheses are from *Unraveling Juvenile Delinquency.*
   H = Higher; L = Lower.

Predicting Delinquency and Crime

From Prediction to Etiology (Continued)

Factors or Traits	Cluster of Social Prediction Factors		Cluster of Rorschach Prediction Traits		Cluster of Psychiatric Prediction Traits	
	Atypical vs. Typical		Atypical vs. Typical		Atypical vs. Typical	
	Delin-quents (1)	Non-Delin-quents (2)	Delin-quents (3)	Non-Delin-quents (4)	Delin-quents (5)	Non-Delin-quents (6)
CHARACTER STRUCTURE (Continued)						
(XVIII–29) Conventionality in Ideas, Feelings, Behavior			H			
(XVIII–32) Feeling of Being Able to Manage Own Life						
(XVIII–33) Narcissistic Trends						
(XVIII–34) Masochistic Trends						
(XVIII–35) Receptive Trends						
(XVIII–36) Destructive-Sadistic Trends			L	H	L	
(XVIII–37) Emotional Lability (R)			L	H		
(XVIII–38) Self-Control			H			
(XVIII–39) Vivacity			L			
(XVIII–40) Compulsory Trends						
(XVIII–41) Preponderance of Extroversive Trends			L			
(XVIII–42) Preponderance of Introversive Trends						
MENTAL CONDITION						
(XVIII–43) No Mental Pathology			H	L		
(XVIII–43) Neuroticism					H	
(XVIII–43) Psychopathy			L		L	L
(XIX–4) Emotional Conflicts						H
(XIX–5) Conflict in Relationship of Boy and Father	L	H				
(XIX–5) Conflict in Sexual Identification						
(XIX–10) Resolution of Conflicts			H			

Note: Numbers in parentheses are from *Unraveling Juvenile Delinquency*.
H = Higher; L = Lower.

From Prediction to Etiology (Continued)

Factors or Traits	Cluster of Social Prediction Factors		Cluster of Rorschach Prediction Traits		Cluster of Psychiatric Prediction Traits	
	Atypical vs. Typical		Atypical vs. Typical		Atypical vs. Typical	
	Delinquents	Non-Delinquents	Delinquents	Non-Delinquents	Delinquents	Non-Delinquents
	(1)	(2)	(3)	(4)	(5)	(6)
TEMPERAMENT						
(XIX–1) Sensitivity						
(XIX–1) Suggestibility (P)						
(XIX–1) Adequacy						L
(XIX–1) Stubbornness (P)					L	H
(XIX–1) Adventurousness (P)					L	H
(XIX–1) Uninhibited Motor Responses to Stimuli (P)					L	H
(XIX–1) Emotional Stability (P)					H	L
(XIX–2) Aestheticism		L				L
(XIX–2) Sensuousness				L		
(XIX–2) Acquisitiveness					L	L
(XIX–3) Conventionality	H				H	L
(XIX–3) Lack of Self-Criticism					L	H
(XIX–3) Conscientiousness					H	L
(XIX–3) Practicality		L				L
FAMILY AND HOME BACKGROUND						
(IV–6) Ethnic Origin: a. English						
b. Italian						
c. Irish						
(VIII–7) Crowded Home						
(VIII–8) Clean and Orderly Home	H	L				
(IX–2) One or Both Parents Foreign-Born						
(IX–7) No Formal Schooling of Parents						
(IX–10) Delinquency of Father	L	H				
(IX–10) Alcoholism of Father	L	H				

Note: Numbers in parentheses are from *Unraveling Juvenile Delinquency*.
H = Higher; L = Lower.

From Prediction to Etiology (Continued)

Factors or Traits		Cluster of Social Prediction Factors		Cluster of Rorschach Prediction Traits		Cluster of Psychiatric Prediction Traits	
		Atypical vs. Typical		Atypical vs. Typical		Atypical vs. Typical	
		Delin-quents (1)	Non-Delin-quents (2)	Delin-quents (3)	Non-Delin-quents (4)	Delin-quents (5)	Non-Delin-quents (6)
	FAMILY AND HOME BACKGROUND (Continued)						
(IX–10)	Emotional Disturbance in Father	L	H				
(IX–10)	Serious Physical Ailment in Father						
(IX–10)	Delinquency of Mother	L	H				
(IX–10)	Alcoholism of Mother	L					
(IX–10)	Emotional Disturbance in Mother	L	H				
(IX–10)	Serious Physical Ailment in Mother		H			H	
(IX–14)	Financial Dependence of Family	L	H				
(IX–18)	Unsatisfactory Work Habits of Father	L	H				
(X–1)	Poor Management of Family Income	L	H				
(X–2)	Careless Household Routine	L	H				
(X–3)	Lack of Cultural Refinement in Home	L	H				
(X–4)	Self-Respect of Parents Lacking	L	H				
(X–5)	Ambition of Parents Lacking	L	H				
(X–6)	Low Conduct Standards of Family	L	H				
(X–7)	Incompatibility of Parents	L	H				
(X–8)	Dominance of Mother in Family Affairs	L	H				
(X–9)	Gainful Employment of Mother	L	H				
(X–10)	Unsuitable Supervision by Mother (S)	L	H				
(X–11)	Family Group Recreations Lacking	L	H				
(X–12)	Parents Uninterested in Children's Friends	L	H				
(X–13)	Meager Recreational Facilities in Home	L	H				
(X–14)	Lack of Family Cohesiveness (S)	L	H				

Note: Numbers in parentheses are from *Unraveling Juvenile Delinquency*.
H = Higher; L = Lower.

From Prediction to Etiology (Continued)

Factors or Traits		Cluster of Social Prediction Factors		Cluster of Rorschach Prediction Traits		Cluster of Psychiatric Prediction Traits	
		Atypical vs. Typical		Atypical vs. Typical		Atypical vs. Typical	
		Delinquents (1)	Non-Delinquents (2)	Delinquents (3)	Non-Delinquents (4)	Delinquents (5)	Non-Delinquents (6)
	FAMILY AND HOME BACKGROUND (Continued)						
(XI–5)	Rank of Boy among Siblings						H
(XI–8)	Broken Home	L	H				
(XI–12)	Rearing by Parent Substitute	L					
(X1–13)	Father Not attached to Boy (S)	L	H	L			
(XI–14)	Mother Not Attached to Boy (S)	L	H		L		
(XI–15)	Boy Not Attached to Father	L	H				H
(XI–16)	Father Unacceptable to Boy for Emulation	L	H				
(XI–17)	Boy Not Attached to Mother						
(XI–18)	Siblings Not Attached to Boy	L	H				
(XI–19)	Boy Feels Mother Not Concerned for His Welfare	L	H		L		H
(XI–19)	Boy Feels Father Not Concerned for His Welfare	L	H				H
(XI–22)	Unsuitable Discipline by Father (S)	L	H				
(XI–22)	Unsuitable Discipline by Mother	L	H			L	
(XI–23)	Physical Punishment by Father		H				
(XI–23)	Scolding or Threatening by Father		H				
(XI–23)	Physical Punishment by Mother						
(XI–23)	Scolding or Threatening by Mother						
(XIII–2)	Frequent Moves	L	H				
	SCHOOL BEHAVIOR						
(IV–1)	Less than 8 Years of Age at Onset of Misbehavior	L					
(XII–5)	Not Retarded in School	H					L
(XII–10)	Poor Scholarship						

Note: Numbers in parentheses are from *Unraveling Juvenile Delinquency.*
 H = Higher; L = Lower.

From Prediction to Etiology (Continued)

Factors or Traits	Cluster of Social Prediction Factors		Cluster of Rorschach Prediction Traits		Cluster of Psychiatric Prediction Traits	
	Atypical vs. Typical		Atypical vs. Typical		Atypical vs. Typical	
	Delinquents (1)	Non-Delinquents (2)	Delinquents (3)	Non-Delinquents (4)	Delinquents (5)	Non-Delinquents (6)
SCHOOL BEHAVIOR (Continued)						
(XII–11) Low Reading Quotient						
(XII–13) Low Arithmetic Quotient						
(XII–17) Marked Dislike of School	H					
(XII–19) Lacking Academic Ambition	H					H
(XII–21) Poor Adjustment to Schoolmates						
(XII–26) Truanted	H		L			H
(XII–27) Truancy Started at Less than 11 Years of Age	L	H		L		
BACKGROUND OF BOY						
(XIII–10) No Household Duties	H				H	'
(XIII–11) Preference for Adventurous Recreation					L	H
(XIII–12) Frequent Movie Attendance	H		L			
(XIII–13) Stole Rides/Hopped Trucks	H	H				H
(XIII–13) Kept Late Hours			L			
(XIII–13) Began Smoking at Early Age	H					H
(XIII–13) Sneaked Admissions						
(XIII–13) Destroyed Property						
(XIII–13) Ran Away from Home	L					
(XIII–13) Bunked Out						
(XIII–13) Gambled	H					H
(XIII–13) Began Drinking at Early Age					L	
(XIII–14) Hung Around Street Corners						
(XIII–14) Sought Recreation in Distant Places	H					H

Note: Numbers in parentheses are from *Unraveling Juvenile Delinquency.*
H = Higher; L = Lower.

From Prediction to Etiology (Concluded)

Factors or Traits	Cluster of Social Prediction Factors		Cluster of Rorschach Prediction Traits		Cluster of Psychiatric Prediction Traits	
	Atypical vs. Typical		Atypical vs. Typical		Atypical vs. Typical	
	Delin-quents (1)	Non-Delin-quents (2)	Delin-quents (3)	Non-Delin-quents (4)	Delin-quents (5)	Non-Delin-quents (6)
BACKGROUND OF BOY (Continued)						
(XIII–14) Spent Some Leisure Hours at Home	H					
(XIII–14) Used Playgrounds						
(XIII–16) Member of Gang						
(XIII–16) Preferred Older Companions						
(XIII–20) Welcomed Supervised Recreation						
(XIII–21) Irregular Church Attendance	L					

Note: Numbers in parentheses are from *Unraveling Juvenile Delinquency.*
H = Higher; L = Lower.

Index

Family: delinquency of, 249; relationships and prediction, 16–17, 43, 45, 45n, 79, 193–194, 200–201, 207, 249–250

Father's birthplace, 190, 191, 192–194, 195, 197–198, 246

Father's discipline of boy, 190–196, 199

Fear of failure and defeat, 241, 243, 250

Federal Parole Board, 169

Feeling: of helplessness and powerlessness, 241; of resentment, 243, 250

Fenton, N., 168, 184

Ferri, E., 10, 11, 11n

Fishman, J., 70n

Follow-up investigations, 20–22

Frankfurter, F., xix

Freedom of will and prediction, 144

French use of Glueck Social Prediction Table, 132

Frey, E., 178, 182, 185

Gang membership of offender and prediction, 44, 198, 251

Gardiner, G., xix

Garrett, P. W., 88n

Gaudet, F. J., 5n

Gerecke, 177, 179, 185

Ghostlaw, E., ix, 51n

Glick, S. J., 127, 130, 185

Glueck, E. T., 23n, 31n, 51, 137n, 140n, 176, 186, 187

Glueck, S., 1n, 3n, 5n, 24n, 75n, 124n, 144n, 146n, 186

Glueck, S. and E. T., 2n, 4n, 18n, 36n, 47n, 56n, 61n, 62n, 83n, 91n, 100n, 105n, 106n, 111n, 112n, 113n, 114n, 117n, 127n, 137n, 158, 161, 165, 166, 174, 181, 183, 186

Glueck Prediction Tables: 12n, 18–31; adequacy of childhood home as factor in, 79–80; age offender began work as factor in, 78, 81, 85; age at onset of delinquency as factor in, 44, 81, 86; and age, 44, 81, 86, 129, *see also* age-spans *below*; and ethnic derivation, 59, 133; and "mechanical jurisprudence," 31; and parole, 27, 129, 170; and religious affiliation, 78; and screening of potential delinquents, 114–136; and sex, 130; application of, to adult offenders, 111–112, to armed forces, 31, 75–76, to juvenile delinquents, 100–111, to

predelinquents, 114–136, to neurotics and non-neurotics, 137–142; arrests preceding present offense as factor in, 82; as experience tables, 24, 61, 76, 127; by-product of follow-up and causal researches, 19; checkup of, for juvenile offenders, 47–60; checkup of, for effectiveness, 24, 127–136; childhood habits as factor in, 81; choice of factors for, 26; church attendance as factor in, 78, 81; class categories of, 23, 24, 26–28; comparison of factors in, for male and female offenders, 95–96; construction of, method of, 24–31; definitions used in, 188–189; delinquency in family as factor in, 79; disagreement between actual and predicted behavior in, 57–58; economic factor in, 77, 84; economic irresponsibility as factor in, 78, 91, 93; economic status of childhood home as factor in, 77, 87; educational achievement of parents as factor in, 79; evolution of, 20–23; for adult male offenders, 61–76; for age spans, 35–38, 63, 67, 69, 71, 73, 75, 77–82; for Armed Forces, 75–76; for behavior after juvenile court treatment, 51–57; factors in, 16–17, 27, 28, 43–44, 77–85; family relationships as factor in, 79; for correctional schools, 192; for distinguishing delinquents and neurotics, 137–142; for early detection of potential delinquents, 133–136; for female offenders, 88–98, 230–232; frequency and seriousness of prereformatory crimes as factor in, 82; French application of, 132; for fifteen year postsentence (or reformatory) period, 197, 226; for five year postsentence (or reformatory) period, 196, 224; for identification of neurotics among delinquents, 241; for identification of neurotics among non-delinquents 243; for identification of potential delinquents, 236–240; for identification of treatable delinquents, 71–72, 215–219, 244; for jails and houses of correction, 62–65, 190, 191; for male adult probationers, 62–65, 190, 191; for male juvenile delinquents,

277

33–60; for male adult prisoners of twenty-seven to thirty-two, 212, thirty-two to thirty-seven, 213, thirty-seven or older, 214; for offenders under twenty-seven, 211; for parole, 28, 38, 72–73, 91, 92–95, 195, 214, 220–223; for prisons, 40–42, 68–69, 210–214; for probation, 33–34, 62–64, 190–191; for reformatories and correctional schools, 35–38, 41, 67, 192, 193, 230; for reformatories, 40–41, 65–67, 91–92, 206–209, 230; for ten year postreformatory period, 225; generalizations regarding, 86–87; grade offender attained in school as factor in, 67, 81, 250; illustrations of applications of, 99–113; incidence of various factors in, 42–46; industrial capacity as factor in, 78, 87; industrial skill of father as factor in, 79; industrial skill of offender as factor in, 78, 87, 201; intelligence as factor in, 80, 86; interpretation of, 31; Japanese application of, 131–132; kind of worker in reformatory as factor in, 91; leisure, use of, by offenders as factor in, 81; maternal occupation as factor in, 79; mental disease or distortion as factor in, 80, 85, 91; method of construction of, 23–31, 90–91; mobility of family as factor in, 80; nativity as factor in, 77; neighborhood influences as factor in, 96; network of, 20; number of factors in, 167; of civilian delinquents in Armed Forces, 227–228; offender's rank among siblings as factor in, 79; overlapping of factors in, 165; parental conjugal relations as factor in, 79; parental education as factor in, 79; penal experiences prior to reformatory sentence as factor in, 82; predictive efficiency of, 150n, 167; profiles of juvenile offenders derived from, 90–111; raw materials entering into construction of, 24; relationship of various predictive-factor clusters in, 264; school children, test of on young, 133; school misconduct as factor in, 81; school retardation as factor in, 95; seriousness and frequency of prereformatory crimes as

factor in, 82; size of family as factor in, 78, 87; status of, 23; steadiness of employment as factor in, 96; studies involved in, 157–166; test of, on young school children, 133; use of varied, to place offender in proper category, 123–125; validations of, 20–21, 127–139, 174; verification of data used in, 24; versus intuitive prognoses, 182; why they do not correctly identify all cases, 265; wide applicability of, 58–60; work habits of offender as factor in, 78

Glueck Social Prediction Table, 176

Grades attained in school, 81, 86, 203, 207, 213, 214, 215, 216, 220, 228, 250

Griswold, E. N., viii

Guides for Sentencing, of National Probation and Parole Association, 3, 3n, 7n, 11n

Habits, childhood, 246

Haggerty-Olsen-Wickman Scale, 174

Hall, L., 8n

Harno, Dean A. J., 155, 183

Harris, G. S., 7n

Harris, R., 8n

Hart, H., 154, 155, 183

Harvard Business School, 51n

Harvard Law School, 2

Hathaway, S. R., 187

Hawkins, H., 8, 8n

Hawthorne-Cedar Knolls School, New York State, 128, 175

Hayner, N. S., 181, 186

Healy, W., 19n

Helplessness and powerlessness, feeling of, 250

Hodder, J. D., 89, 97n

Holmes, O. W., xix

Holton, K., 30n

Home, childhood, 245

Home, moral standards of, 43, 192, 251–253

Hooten, E. A., 25n

Hopmann, W., 187

Horst, P., 174, 185

Hunch method of sentencing, 2, 7

Identification of potential delinquents, 16–17, 115–126, 127–136

Illinois, Cook County Juvenile Court of, 172